Mystery Classics
on Film

Mystery Classics on Film

The Adaptation of 65 Novels and Stories

Ron Miller

McFarland & Company, Inc., Publishers
Jefferson, North Carolina

ISBN (print) 978-1-4766-6685-3 ∞
ISBN (ebook) 978-1-4766-2671-0

LIBRARY OF CONGRESS CATALOGUING DATA ARE AVAILABLE

BRITISH LIBRARY CATALOGUING DATA ARE AVAILABLE

© 2017 Ron Miller. All rights reserved

No part of this book may be reproduced or transmitted in any form or by any means, electronic or mechanical, including photocopying or recording, or by any information storage and retrieval system, without permission in writing from the publisher.

On the cover: shown from left: Martha Vickers as Carmen Sternwood, John Ridgely as Eddie Mars, Humphrey Bogart as Philip Marlowe in *The Big Sleep*, 1946 (Warner Bros./Photofest)

Printed in the United States of America

McFarland & Company, Inc., Publishers
Box 611, Jefferson, North Carolina 28640
www.mcfarlandpub.com

To my most loyal supporter, my wife Darla,
who loves mysteries and movies as much as I do.

But I'd also like to share this dedication
with the finest producer of television mysteries
I've met in my 40 years of involvement with that medium:
Rebecca Eaton of WGBH-TV in Boston,
the executive producer of PBS's *Masterpiece Mystery!*,
the most enduring showcase for high-quality
mysteries in television history.

Spoiler Alert!

This book contains plot details of novels and stories and the films and TV programs made from them. If you have not yet read the mysteries involved nor seen the filmed versions discussed, you may want to avoid reading those chapters until after you do.

Table of Contents

(Titles in parentheses are of the film versions)

Acknowledgments	x
Preface	1
Introduction: Why Can't the Movie Be Just Like the Book?	3
Charlotte Armstrong: *The Case of the Weird Sisters*	11
The Unsuspected	13
Mischief (*Don't Bother to Knock*)	15
John Ball: *In the Heat of the Night*	18
Earl Derr Biggers: *The Black Camel*	21
John Buchan: *The Thirty-Nine Steps*	23
W.R. Burnett: *The Asphalt Jungle*	27
James M. Cain: *Love's Lovely Counterfeit* (*Slightly Scarlet*)	29
Vera Caspary: *Laura*	32
Raymond Chandler: *The Big Sleep*	34
The Lady in the Lake (*Lady in the Lake*)	40
Lee Child: *One Shot* (*Jack Reacher*)	42
Agatha Christie: *4:50 from Paddington* (*Murder, She Said; What Mrs. McGillicuddy Saw*)	44
Mary Higgins Clark: *The Cradle Will Fall*	48
Wilkie Collins: *The Woman in White*	50
Sir Arthur Conan Doyle: *A Study in Scarlet*	54
The Hound of the Baskervilles	56
Michael Connelly: *Blood Work*	61
Daphne du Maurier: *Rebecca*	63
Dick Francis: *Dead Cert*	68
Blood Sport	70
Erle Stanley Gardner: *The Case of the Velvet Claws*	72

David Goodis: *Down There* (*Shoot the Piano Player*; *Tirez sur le Pianiste*)	74
Graham Greene: *A Gun for Sale* (*This Gun for Hire*; *Short Cut to Hell*)	77
Patrick Hamilton: *Hangover Square*	80
Dashiell Hammett: *The Maltese Falcon* (*Satan Met a Lady*)	84
The Thin Man	89
A.P. Herbert: *The House by the River*	93
Patricia Highsmith: *Strangers on a Train* (*Once You Kiss [Meet] a Stranger...*)	96
The Talented Mr. Ripley (*Purple Noon*; *Plain Soleil*)	103
Tony Hillerman: *The Dark Wind*	106
A Thief of Time	108
Dorothy B. Hughes: *In a Lonely Place*	111
Francis Iles: *Before the Fact* (*Suspicion*)	113
Carolyn Keene: *The Hidden Staircase* (*Nancy Drew and the Hidden Staircase*)	116
Gypsy Rose Lee: *The G-String Murders* (*Lady of Burlesque*)	118
Jeff Lindsay: *Darkly Dreaming Dexter* (*Dexter*)	120
John D. MacDonald: *The Executioners* (*Cape Fear*)	123
Ross Macdonald: *The Moving Target* (*Harper*)	128
John P. Marquand: *Think Fast, Mr. Moto*	132
Ed McBain: *Cop Hater*	135
Fuzz	138
King's Ransom (*High and Low*; *Tengoku to jigoku*)	140
Walter Mosley: *Devil in a Blue Dress*	142
Stuart Palmer: *The Penguin Pool Murder*	145
Robert B. Parker: *Ceremony*	149
Edgar Allan Poe: "Murders in the Rue Morgue" (*Phantom of the Rue Morgue*)	153
"The Mystery of Marie Roget"	160
Ellery Queen: *The Chinese Orange Mystery* (*The Mandarin Mystery*)	163
Patrick Quentin: *Black Widow*	165
Ruth Rendell: *A Judgment in Stone* (*La Cérémonie*)	169
Craig Rice: *Home Sweet Homicide*	171
Dorothy L. Sayers: *Busman's Honeymoon* (*Haunted Honeymoon*)	173
Maj Sjöwall and Per Wahlöö: *The Laughing Policeman*	176
Mickey Spillane: *My Gun Is Quick*	179
Josephine Tey: *A Shilling for Candles* (*Young and Innocent*)	181

Table of Contents

Jim Thompson: *Pop. 1280* (*Coup de Torchon*) 184
    After Dark, My Sweet 187
S.S. Van Dine: *The Kennel Murder Case* 189
    The Gracie Allen Murder Case 192
Ethel Lina White: *Some Must Watch* (*The Spiral Staircase*) 194
Cornell Woolrich: *Black Alibi* (*The Leopard Man*) 198
    Rear Window 200
    The Black Path of Fear (*The Chase*) 203
    I Married a Dead Man (*No Man of Her Own*; *I Married a Shadow*;
      Mrs. Winterbourne) 206

Bibliography 211
Index 213

Acknowledgments

Earlier versions of some of this book's chapters appeared on the Dark Corridors pages of the website thecolumnistswww under the copyright notice of the author. They have been revised, updated and expanded for book publication.

The chapter on Dashiell Hammett's *The Maltese Falcon* was previously published in *Mystery Scene Magazine* and is used with the permission of *Mystery Scene*.

The author wishes to thank all the motion picture companies, television networks and television stations who originally provided the publicity and promotional photographs used to illustrate this book. Whenever possible, the author has attempted to acknowledge the source for each photo and include it with the caption. Special thanks also go to Dollie Banner at Jerry Ohlinger's Movie Material Store in New York City for her help in rounding up 34 of the photos in the book. More special thanks to my friend and frequent co-author James Bawden of Toronto, Canada, for providing me with other valuable stills from his private collection.

The author also wants to thank the many mystery authors who so warmly granted me time for interviews about their work. The late Robert B. Parker twice granted me interviews about his great detective, Spenser. Ed McBain (a.k.a. Salvatore Lombino and Evan Hunter) talked with me about his 87th Precinct novels; Mary Higgins Clark and the late Dick Francis talked with me about their work discussed in this book. I also spoke with several authors whose experiences with screen adaptations are mentioned in this book's introduction. The late P.D. James not only talked with me twice about her detectives, Adam Dalgliesh and Cordelia Gray (and kindly wrote the introduction to my 1996 book *Mystery! A Celebration*). Elizabeth George talked with me about the TV versions of her Inspector Lynley novels and Colin Dexter talked with me about the TV versions of his Inspector Morse novels while I was writing *Mystery! A Celebration*.

While researching the authors whose stories are discussed in this book, I did extensive reading of biographical and autobiographical volumes about them. By the same token, I also read many books by filmmakers, screenwriters and actors whose memoirs provided insight into the making of the screen versions of classic mysteries.

Preface

This book is not intended as a crusade by a disgruntled mystery fan who wants to vent his anger at those wicked filmmakers who so often seem to mess up our favorite books and stories while trying to turn them into movies or TV shows. Nor is it intended to be a spirited defense by a passionate movie fan of the standard—and frequently troublesome—process of putting a literary work on the screen.

To be sure, I am both a rabid mystery reader and a passionate movie fan and so I'm often torn between my feelings about how the two media discharge their responsibilities to their respective audiences.

In this book, I call attention to some really dreadful decisions made by filmmakers in the process of adapting written stories to the screen. But I also point out some very astute decisions made by other filmmakers that helped make a moviegoing experience better by *not* hewing to the original storyline.

In fact, there are some amazing examples of great books that were radically overhauled by filmmakers, but turned out to be great films, too. Take the very important novel *Strangers on a Train* by Patricia Highsmith. Filmmaker Alfred Hitchcock turned the plot inside out, adding a great many scenes that never take place in the book, giving the protagonist a different occupation and completely changing the way the story ends. His film is taut and suspenseful and has thrilled and excited millions for many decades.

As mystery author Robert B. Parker often said, the book is still the book. Highsmith's *Strangers on a Train* is as good as it ever was and Hitchcock didn't change that at all. A book is a book and it's not meant to be performed as a visual drama. When a book is turned into a visual drama, sometimes changes need to be made to make it compelling entertainment for large groups of people who sit in the darkness together and watch it unfold for two hours or so.

On the other hand, there's no way to excuse what RKO did to Raymond Chandler's well-crafted mystery novel *Farewell, My Lovely* in 1942 when it threw out Chandler's hard-boiled detective, the immortal sleuth Philip Marlowe, and gave the storyline instead to the urbane gentleman detective known as the Falcon for an undistinguished "programmer" called *The Falcon Takes Over*.

As often as possible, I've tried to cite some reasons why moviemakers made changes to mystery stories. It's not always easy to figure out. A book or short story is generally the creative work of a single individual, laboring alone until his editors begin to exert their influence on the final product. However, a movie or TV show is a much more collective endeavor with lots of individuals wanting to express themselves in its production.

If you cast the wrong person, for instance, you can affect the entire impact of the movie. The slick "Latin lover"–type actor Ricardo Cortez was nobody's idea of tough guy shamus Sam Spade in the 1931 *The Maltese Falcon* and it probably ruined the movie for anyone who had read Dashiell Hammett's classic novel. A decade later, Hollywood remade the movie with Humphrey Bogart as Sam Spade and got it right.

It's also very likely that no mystery fan was seriously put off by the changes Hitchcock and producer David O. Selznick made in Daphne du Maurier's *Rebecca* in 1940. The film was so beautifully photographed, had such a haunting musical score and boasted so many truly brilliant performances that it was a seductive viewing experience and won the Academy Award as the Best Picture of 1940. Who was going to complain that the ending had been changed?

While writing this book, I followed a set of guidelines: First, I re-read the source novel or story even if I had read it before and felt pretty sure about its contents. Second, I screened the best quality copy of the movie or TV adaptation that I could find.

Naturally, I read and viewed scores more books and movies than I could possibly put into one book. Instead, I chose mostly those examples of books that were substantially altered in some fashion by the filmmakers.

I've broadly defined the boundaries of the mystery genre for this collection to include what many might call suspense thrillers rather than pure whodunit-type mysteries. I've also included a few spy thrillers, like Buchan's *The Thirty-Nine Steps*, because they have a rich vein of mystery in them, plus a few crime novels like Burnett's *The Asphalt Jungle* for the same reason.

Once I settled on a title that I thought should be included in this study, I extended my research to include other works written about both the books and the movies. I sought out autobiographies of actors and filmmakers and searched through them for references to either the books or the films.

In some cases, my background as an entertainment writer for newspapers and magazines helped immeasurably. Several books in this study, for instance, were turned into movies by filmmakers like Alfred Hitchcock, with whom I had talked about his films while he was still making them. My association with the PBS television series *Mystery!*, now absorbed into the PBS *Masterpiece* series, was as the author of the show's official companion book and that gave me the opportunity to talk with several actors, producers and directors of mysteries adapted for that program.

Over the years, I've also interviewed scores of contemporary mystery writers and almost always asked them about their attitudes toward the film versions of their work. Many of their quotes appear in my introduction and, occasionally, in the chapters devoted to their works.

Though I've tried to apply fairly serious journalistic principles to the writing of this book and to keep it as accurate as possible, it was never intended to be an academic thesis, but rather an entertaining look at the ups and downs of the process by which some of the world's most beloved mystery stories have been rendered on the screen.

I hope you will have fun reading this look at 65 classic mysteries and what happened to them on their way to theaters or your living room TV set.

Introduction: Why Can't the Movie Be Just Like the Book?

Mary Higgins Clark was so excited about the upcoming debut of the 1982 movie based on her best-selling mystery novel *A Stranger Is Watching* that she wanted all her friends and family to be there with her for the big night.

"It was opening in 27 theaters in Manhattan," Clark told me in a 1995 interview, "so I bought 90 tickets for my nearest and dearest friends and told them we should go in formal wear because it was The Premiere. We all went traipsing into Cinema One and everybody else was looking at us so weirdly."

Not long after the movie started, she realized *she* was now the one looking at everybody weirdly. That wasn't her book up there on the screen. Even though she had read the script in advance, and thought it was "wonderful," something had gone terribly wrong.

"The language in it was brutal," Clark recalled, thinking back on all the profanity dropped into her story. "I don't use it [profanity] because it's unnecessary, doesn't add anything, gets you an 'R' rating and costs you a part of your audience."

So when the movie was over and the lights went up, Mary Higgins Clark walked to the front of the theater, formal wear and all, and apologized to the crowd.

"I have only one comment," she told them: "*On Golden Pond* is safer!"

In 1982, Clark was still naïve about movie adaptations of her books. That was her first experience and she had no idea what can happen between script and film premiere. Here's what had happened: The director was Sean S. Cunningham, whose most recent film was *Friday the 13th*, a slasher film that had become a box office sensation. He had turned her suspense story into a nasty horror movie.

That was his specialty. He was just doing what he knew how to do best.

Unfortunately, Clark's bad night at the movies is not a rare experience for mystery writers. In this book, you're going to read about many other nightmare scenarios for authors whose proudest literary achievements were treated shabbily by filmmakers. Here are a few choice examples:

- In 1942, RKO became the first studio to film one of Raymond Chandler's acclaimed novels about hard-boiled private eye Philip Marlowe—only the filmmakers left Marlowe out of the movie! The book *Farewell, My Lovely* came to the screen as *The Falcon Takes Over*, a routine entry in a series of low-budget movies about debonair sleuth Gay Stanhope, a character created by writer Michael Arlen.

RKO had kept Chandler's storyline, but turned it over to a character who was the antithesis of a hard-boiled private eye.
- Agatha Christie's Hercule Poirot novel *After the Funeral* was filmed in 1963 as *Murder at the Gallop*, but Poirot wasn't in it. His case had been given to a female sleuth, Christie's other famous detective, Miss Jane Marple (Margaret Rutherford).
- Margery Allingham's *Tiger in the Smoke*, one of her best mysteries featuring sleuth Albert Campion, was filmed in 1956, but Campion never makes an appearance in the movie.
- Ed McBain's novel *King's Ransom*, a kidnap mystery involving McBain's regular series characters (Steve Carella and the detectives of the 87th Precinct), was turned into the movie *High and Low* by famed Japanese director Akira Kurosawa—and the story shifted to 1960s Japan with an all-Japanese team of detectives instead of the 87th Precinct gang.
- Edgar Allan Poe's Auguste Dupin, the first detective character in mystery fiction, was completely left out of the 1971 movie version of *Murders in the Rue Morgue*.
- Actor Paul Newman felt one-word movie titles that began with the letter H were lucky for him, like his hit *Hud*. That's why Ross MacDonald's celebrated detective Lew Archer became Lew Harper when Newman played him in *Harper* (1966), the movie version of the novel *The Moving Target*.
- In Alfred Hitchcock's 1951 *Strangers on a Train*, the hero is a tennis player; he was an architect in Patricia Highsmith's best-selling novel. The book doesn't have the famous merry-go-round climax put into the movie by Hitchcock. Even more upsetting: The 1996 TV remake of Hitchcock's film changed both hero and villain to women and the title to *Once You Meet a Stranger*,
- Dorothy Uhnak's 1977 bestseller *The Investigation*, the stirring story of a detective who falls in love with his chief suspect, came to television a decade later as a movie-length episode of the TV series *Kojak* called "The Price of Justice." Gone was Uhnak's hero. In his place was the bald-headed, lollipop-sucking Theo Kojak (Telly Savalas).

Why do filmmakers do such things? Well, there are as many answers as there are examples. You may wonder why filmmakers buy the rights to a popular novel, then change the story so much that the fans of that novel will leave the theater grumbling. My guess: Most filmmakers think they're "improving" the story, making it more "cinematic."

To be sure, there are some very legitimate reasons why changes are made in the plots, characters and even the outcome of some books.

One can understand, for example, why a Japanese filmmaker might want to re-locate the story to his own environment as Kurosawa did with McBain's *King's Ransom*. One might understand why a reader of James M. Cain's classic Depression Era American novel *The Postman Always Rings Twice* would flinch when finding the story set in France or Italy instead of Southern California in the 1930s. Believe it or not, that actually happened: The first movie version of Cain's novel was *Le Dernier Tourant,* filmed in France in 1939, and the second version was Luchino Visconti's *Ossessione,* filmed in 1942 in wartime Italy. The familiar first American version by Tay Garnett with John Garfield and Lana Turner didn't come along until 1946.

Another reason why a filmmaker might be forgiven for making a mammoth change:

If the book's main character is always alone, the author can tell you exactly what his hero is thinking. But how do you show that on a movie screen?

There are two reliable methods. One is to have the character "think out loud" using a narration by the actor playing the part. Another method: Dramatize the pictures in the character's mind and hope the audience won't think he's been ingesting hallucinogens.

But filmmakers generally feel you can't use those techniques very long or the audience will grow restless and lose interest.

That's why filmmakers often make up a new character for the hero to talk with at those times when he'd otherwise be alone. Some authors do that themselves to avoid having to use interior monologues all the time. That's the main function of "sidekicks" like Holmes' Dr. Watson and Poirot's Capt. Hastings. They all are descended from Poe, who gave his Dupin an anonymous pal in *The Murders in the Rue Morgue*, so Dupin could explain his theories of "ratiocination" to someone instead of sitting around talking to himself.

Sometimes filmmakers make changes to appeal more to the moviegoers they consider their primary audience. For example, producers of the *Inspector Morse* series of British television movies decided that Morse's sidekick, Sergeant Lewis, should be a young man rather than a veteran cop about the same age as Morse, as he is in the original Colin Dexter novels. They thought the stories worked better if there was a sort of twisted father-son relationship between the two detectives. They also thought it would appeal more to younger viewers to have a character they could identify with, someone more their own age.

"They made [Lewis] about half the age I had him," Dexter told me in a 1995 interview. "If I had it to do over again, I think I'd probably do what television did and have that surrogate father-son relationship. It's quite sensible, really."

Dexter is one of a small number of famous mystery writers who don't fret over what the moviemakers do. In fact, Dexter loved the whole process so much that he often hung out with the filmmakers whenever they were filming around Oxford, the natural habitat for both Morse and his creator. Dexter even made frequent cameo appearances in the films, most often seated near Morse whenever the inspector stopped off at a pub.

In contrast to Dexter, best-selling American mystery writer Sue Grafton has consistently declined offers to turn her private eye Kinsey Millhone into a movie or TV character. When asked about it, she usually says she used to work as a television writer, adapting the works of other writers, including the great Agatha Christie, and had lots of personal experience with the compromises that are made with an author's creative works. She doesn't want her work compromised.

The late P.D. James, England's "queen of crime," had the unique experience of seeing almost all her detective novels adapted for television. Though she recognized that the TV shows helped her sell thousands of books, she wasn't always deliriously happy with what she saw on screen.

When they began filming her Adam Dalgliesh novels, they made a fateful decision: They would *not* film them in chronological order. The first to be filmed, *Death of an Expert Witness*, actually was the fourth published. So when they finally got around to filming *A Mind to Murder*, her second Dalgliesh novel, his Scotland Yard career had advanced through seven more novels and a total of about 30 years service.

That meant that Dalgliesh, who had reached the rank of commander at Scotland Yard in the most recent TV movies, suddenly was shown working the kind of case he'd have handled in his youth. To make it all work as a movie, they also added characters, subplots and an uncharacteristic action finale that weren't in James' book.

"I was strongly disapproving of that," she told me in 1995. "I would not have signed the contract if I'd known they were going to do it in that way."

James was even more distressed when her private detective Cordelia Gray turned up pregnant and unmarried in the second season of the TV series *An Unsuitable Job for a Woman*, based on her book of the same name. Because James had only written two Cordelia Gray novels, she permitted the producers to hire other writers to concoct some new stories for the character. But she felt betrayed when they made Cordelia an unwed mother, a change that reflected on Cordelia's moral character.

Why did they do such a thing? Simple: Helen Baxendale, the actress who played Cordelia, turned up pregnant and there was no way her ample dimensions could be concealed. James was so unhappy about this turn of events—they hadn't told her in advance—that she disassociated herself from the TV series. In her 1999 autobiography *Time to Be in Earnest*, she wrote, "The damage, as far as I'm concerned, can't be repaired, since Cordelia with an illegitimate child is no longer my character."

What should the filmmakers have done? They could have re-cast the role or shut down production until Baxendale's figure was back to normal. But both those alternatives would have cost the producers money. In American television, filmmakers might have had their pregnant leading lady stand behind a desk or a chair every time she stood up—or had her carry something that blocked our view of her tummy. In England, they decided it was much easier to make the character as pregnant as the actress.

Sometimes filmmakers make changes for reasons that defy logic. For instance, in Tony Hillerman's 1988 bestseller *A Thief of Time*, Lt. Joe Leaphorn of the Navajo Tribal Police is grieving so deeply for his late wife Emma that he has taken a leave of absence and decided to resign from his job. Yet when the book was filmed for PBS' *Mystery!* series in 2004, Emma was still alive and playing a major role in the solving of a crime.

Why do that? Leaphorn's overwhelming grief is such a crucial motivational issue in the book that there seems no excuse for keeping the wife alive. I finally became so curious that I asked the network to put me in touch with screenwriter Alice Arlen so I could ask her why she let Emma live. Arlen graciously explained: Everybody really liked Sheila Tousey, the actress who played Emma, and didn't want to lose her services. "She's a brilliant actress," Arlen told me.

As crazy as that sounds, it's not an uncommon thing in Hollywood. If the audience really likes a certain character or the actor who plays the part, the writers often are instructed to give the character bigger scenes—or keep him alive, even if the author burned him to death in a fire several books earlier.

Many modern authors feel it's not harmful for filmmakers to make "little changes" in a character's behavior as long as they don't make the really big ones, like turning bachelor girl Cordelia Gray into an unwed mom.

That was made clear to me the first time I chatted with Robert B. Parker, whose Boston private eye, Spenser, was brought to TV in 1985 for the weekly ABC detective series *Spenser: For Hire*. I remember how unhappy I was to discover that Spenser didn't drink the same beer he did in Parker's books. Spenser was finicky about his brew and that was a detail any Spenser fan would notice. How much trouble would it be to put the right bottle of beer in his hand?

But when I asked Parker about it during the initial press hoopla for the TV show, he grinned and explained those were trivialities to him. He said that "a TV show isn't a book" and reminded me that all the little details I loved in the Spenser novels would still be there the next time I looked at his book. Parker later told *TV Guide*, "The business of television is to put on good television, not to replicate my books." That's a liberated attitude few mystery writers share.

When ABC cancelled *Spenser: For Hire*, Parker missed the TV association that had helped drive the sale of his books. A few years later, he and his wife Joan teamed up with a TV production outfit and brought Spenser back in a series of made-for-cable movies, first for the Lifetime network, then for A&E. Parker wrote some of the scripts and his wife became a producer.

How different was Spenser with Parker taking an active role? At first, the only difference seemed to be economic. The original ABC series had been filmed on location in Boston, the genuine Spenser habitat. Now the movies, all of them adaptations of Parker novels, were mostly filmed in Canada, where union rules weren't as rigid and where U.S. dollars went further.

But in A&E's final batch of Spenser movies, they did something really dramatic: They dropped the actor who had always played Spenser—Robert Urich—much to the disappointment of many fans. (Urich was under contract for another series, but also was battling a rare form of cancer that ultimately took his life.)

Though Parker never said anything bad about Urich in our chats, he made it clear to me in a 1999 interview that Urich never was his idea of how Spenser should look— even though, as I pointed out, Joe Mantegna, the actor who took Urich's place, was much smaller and has a more ethnic look than either Urich or the Spenser of the novels. Parker conceded that many people felt that way. "The complaints about Mantegna boil down to the fact he's Italian and doesn't weigh 200 pounds," Parker told me. "The answer to the first complaint is 'I don't care' and the answer to the second is 'Neither did Bogart.'" (The rather small Humphrey Bogart had played the more physically imposing Philip Marlowe from Raymond Chandler's novels without incurring much fan wrath.)

Later, when CBS began to film Parker's novels about Police Chief Jesse Stone, they cast Tom Selleck in the role, though Selleck was much bigger and older than the character in the books. Parker wasn't troubled by that casting either.

American Elizabeth George, whose novels about English police Inspector Thomas Lynley were adapted by the BBC, told me she wasn't bothered by the fact that Lynley isn't blond on TV as he is in her books:

> I've always been very philosophical about this. I'm a novelist. I'm not a television person. I'm interested in writing my novels, not screenplays. I didn't expect my readers to turn on the TV and say, "Oh my god! That person looks just like Lynley!" All I wanted was for a show to be good enough that people who hadn't read the books would say, "Hmm, I think I'll pick up that book at the bookstore." Because of that, I've been able to let a lot of the changes sort of roll off my back.

But George was startled—and far from pleased—to discover the race of Robert Gabriel, a key character in her *Payment in Blood*, was changed from white to black for the TV movie version. That was a shocking change because it automatically changed the dynamics between Gabriel and the other characters. She didn't learn about the switch until she visited the set and was introduced to the actor playing the part.

"That's interesting casting," George said to herself. When she asked why they'd made such a change, the producers explained that they aren't allowed to discriminate when casting roles, hence the change of race.

George accepted that change graciously, but wasn't quite so complacent when she was reading the script for the adaptation of *In the Presence of the Enemy* and saw in the stage directions that there had been another race change that she thought was damaging to the story:

> I got furious. They didn't tell me about it in advance and they pretended it wasn't about what they had to do politically. I told them I understand why they can't discriminate, but not to tell me that they cast a person of another race because they chose the best possible actress in the world for that particular part!

After she realized things like that were going to happen and she wasn't going to be able to do anything about it, George persuaded herself it was no big deal. The books were still the books and maybe the TV shows would inspire more people to try the books.

Names of characters often are changed to soothe the vanity of the actor playing the part. But it usually isn't considered wise to change the name of a famous series detective like Lew Archer just to please the actor playing him. Still, we might want to forgive the producers of the TV miniseries *The Dain Curse*, who decided to give Dashiell Hammett's anonymous detective, known only as the Continental Op in all those early Hammett stories, the name "Hamilton Nash" when they filmed the miniseries. I'd say going through four hours of prime time without a name for your leading character would have stretched the credulity of the TV audience way too far.

Still, let's not forget that Alfred Hitchcock's Oscar-winning film version of Daphne du Maurier's romantic mystery *Rebecca* had a main character without a first name and certainly was successful enough to become a classic among all mystery movies. (While filming the movie, Hitchcock decided to give her a first name after all: Daphne. But producer David O. Selznick vetoed that idea and forced them to keep her nameless, as she is in the book.)

However, in this book's chapter on *Rebecca*, I point out that the ending of the book was changed for the movie, but not because anybody working on the film wanted it that way. In the book, Max de Winter admits he killed his first wife, Rebecca, not knowing at the time that she already was dying of a terminal illness. In the movie, he explains that she fell, struck her head and died accidentally, although he did put her body in her sailboat and scuttle it at sea, hoping her death would pass as a drowning. Why the change? In those days, the Hollywood Production Code wouldn't allow a criminal in a film to escape punishment, so they had to de-criminalize Max to get a Code seal of approval.

In that case, a majority of mystery fans probably felt it was all for the better. They wouldn't have believed the second Mrs. De Winter (Joan Fontaine) was going to live happily ever after with Max (Laurence Olivier) if she knew he had murdered his first wife.

You may understand why some of the changes had to be made by filmmakers, but you'll probably be outraged by others. Is there any way to pressure filmmakers to stop messing up your favorite books when they turn them into films? Personally, I don't think so. Fiction-writing and filmmaking are two different art forms with different requirements. Some books are very cinematic, many others aren't. Good filmmakers will always try to change things to make them work better as films. Sometimes it works, sometimes it doesn't.

Here's my best advice: If you care about such things, read the book before they even start talking about making the movie. Once you know Tom Hanks has been cast as hero

Robert Langdon in *The Da Vinci Code*, you're going to picture Hanks as Langdon all the while you're reading the book and your imagination will never get a chance to start working up the image the author intended you to see.

And then, if you do see the movie and you don't like the way it brings the book to life, at least you'll still have your memory of the way it should have been.

Charlotte Armstrong
The Case of the Weird Sisters

The 1943 novel and the 1948 movie *The Three Weird Sisters*

There are many bizarre stories about how Hollywood bought the rights to a best-selling mystery novel, apparently just to use the pre-sold title as a means of luring mystery fans into theaters to see a movie that had little to do with the book. A classic example: The 1956 British film version of Margery Allingham's *Tiger in the Smoke*, which somehow managed to completely leave out her detective hero, Albert Campion.

Here's another bewildering example: Charlotte Armstrong's 1943 Gothic thriller *The Case of the Weird Sisters*, which was filmed by the British in 1948. Heck, they didn't even hold onto her title. Instead, they called it: *The Three Weird Sisters*.

Armstrong was one of the most popular American mystery novelists of the 1940s, sort of the Mary Higgins Clark of her day. Readers of her books presumably wanted to see her characters come alive on the screen. They were mainly out of luck when they put down their money to see the movie made from *The Case of the Weird Sisters*.

Armstrong set the story in Michigan, her home state. Aging millionaire Innes Whitlock decides to take his secretary Alice Brennan home to his country house in rural Michigan. When they have car trouble, they wind up in Ogaunee, the rural mining town where Whitlock's three spinster sisters live in the old family estate. Whitlock is planning to marry Alice and is about to alter his will to leave most of his estate to her in the event of his death.

Not long after he turns up at the old house, he suffers a sudden bout of food poisoning and is laid low. It doesn't take long for Alice, who's something of a gold digger, to suspect Whitlock's sisters of trying to poison him. Further attempts to kill him start taking place in the spooky old house.

Speaking of spooky, the sisters couldn't be more so if they walked around wearing sheets. Maude is deaf, Gertrude is blind and Isabel has only one arm. Those are just handicaps when the people are normal. Add those qualities to these creepy ladies and you are never sure exactly what is fumbling its way down the dark hall toward you.

While Alice considers giving up her gold-digging ways, she's comforted by Whitlock's chauffeur, a handsome young guy who seems capable of tackling any menace to the beautiful fiancée of his boss. The young town doctor also seems quite attracted to her. Hanging about, ready to provide his services is Armstrong's sleuth, Prof. MacDougal Duff.

It all adds up to a colorful old dark house thriller with way too many characters and a rather unsavory heroine, but somehow it works. It sold a large number of copies to anxious Armstrong fans in the midst of World War II.

Then came the movie, made in postwar England by director Daniel Birt. He assigned the task of adapting the novel to David Evans, then hired Louise Birt to write the screenplay, along with a most unusual helper—the famous Welsh poet Dylan Thomas, now best remembered as the author of the verse play *Under Milk Wood* and the odd prose collection *Adventures in the Skin Trade*.

First they abandoned Michigan and moved the whole thing to a small mining town in Wales. Innes Whitlock was erased and in his place was conceived a much more mean-spirited millionaire, Owen Morgan-Vaughn, played by Raymond Lovell. His secretary is not Alice Brennan but Claire Prentiss, who was trained as a nurse during the war and is most definitely not a gold digger. In fact, she is not engaged to marry her boss and, by the way, does not have a handsome chauffeur standing by, waiting to romance her.

The three sisters are still just as weird. Maude (Mary Clare) is still deaf, Gertrude (Nancy Price) is still blind, but Isobel (Mary Merrall) has grown back her missing arm and instead has two hands that resemble claws. (Moviemakers never were too keen on amputees.) The mysterious Native American heavy who comes in handy in Armstrong's original is gone. (The Oneida tribe is unheard of in Wales.) In his place is a slow-witted houseboy named Thomas (Elwyn Brook-Jones). The amorous doctor is still around, but he's far from romantic.

In the cast, only two names may be familiar to American audiences today. The first is Nova Pilbeam, who played Claire. Pilbeam, as a teenager, was the girl taken hostage by the spies in Hitchcock's original (1934) *The Man Who Knew Too Much*. She then played the romantic female lead in Hitchcock's *Young and Innocent* (1937).

The other familiar name is Hugh Griffith, who plays Mabli Hughes, a character who functions as a sort of Greek chorus, spouting somewhat poetic lines that seem very likely to have been written by Dylan Thomas. Griffith won the Best Supporting Actor Academy Award in 1959 as the sheik in *Ben-Hur*.

The movie begins with the collapse of abandoned mine shafts owned by the Morgan-Vaughn family. The collapse destroys much of the nearby village, leaving many people dead, injured or homeless. The sisters want to rebuild the village, but their nasty older brother holds the family purse strings, which is why he has come to town: He wants to convince them they're getting no money from him for such an act of charity.

While the movie eliminates much of the suspense Armstrong generated in her book, it does have a certain poetic fantasy atmosphere that I'm quite happy to attribute to the talents of Dylan Thomas. Thomas, for a time, wrote screenplays and didn't totally disgrace himself in that field. In this instance, though, most critics seemed to feel the movie would have been better off with more Armstrong and less Thomas.

History has judged both book and film. The works of Charlotte Armstrong are not readily available today outside of used bookstores; the film, though now available from online video dealers, is largely forgotten. Ironically, the major item of interest about the movie today is that Dylan Thomas helped write it. Go figure that.

Charlotte Armstrong
The Unsuspected

The 1945 novel and the 1947 movie

Charlotte Armstrong was one of the most prolific and popular mystery writers of the 1940s. She never created a running series detective, contributing instead to the rising tide of the suspense or thriller genre that stretches back to the old dark house novels of Mary Roberts Rinehart and her many imitators.

One of Armstrong's most successful novels was *The Unsuspected*, which was first serialized in *The Saturday Evening Post* in 1945, then came out in 1946 as a book. Warner Bros. grabbed the film rights and turned it over to one of its most reliable in-house directors, Michael Curtiz, whose previous works included *Casablanca*, *The Adventures of Robin Hood* and many other classic films.

The story is almost impossibly contrived poppycock with plot holes big enough for Godzilla to skip right through without touching the edges. Still, Armstrong was an engaging writer whose dialogue was snappy and her leading character, radio mystery host Luther Grandison, was fascinating. But all the rest of the characters were banal stereotypes.

The novel falls into the "inverted mystery" category because we know from the get-go that Grandison is a murderer and that his "ward" Mathilda, heiress to a large fortune, is in terrible jeopardy the longer she stays around her beloved "Grandy."

If Alfred Hitchcock had been handed the film assignment, he'd have thrown out most of the silliness Armstrong wove into her story, starting with the nonsense about Mathilda being lost at sea and believed dead, then miraculously turning up in mid-plot. Mathilda suffers from amnesia and can't remember the nice young man she met and married just before going to sea.

When Curtiz got busy filming *The Unsuspected*, he left all that stuff in and tried to make the best of it. The result was a film the critics generally disliked with various degrees of intensity. It's now been largely forgotten by movie fans.

My personal feeling is that *The Unsuspected* is a much-neglected gem, despite the dumb plot twists that plague it.

It has two great assets: a bravura performance by one of the all-time great film actors, Claude Rains, as "Grandy" and Curtiz's very stylish production, which imparts to it a seductive 1940s noir look, and also gives us a lot of scenes in the now-vanished world of big network radio, a special attraction to me and, I'm sure, to all old-time radio buffs.

Rains would have been a perfect radio mystery host, so the scenes where we see him doing his broadcasts in the studio are sheer magic. His smooth, cultured voice is soothing and seductive. I can imagine listening to him spin his mystery tales all night, so it's quite easy to picture him as the sort of celebrity host Luther Grandison is supposed to be in postwar America.

Curtiz also gives the film a genuinely creepy look from the start, where we witness the murder of Grandison's secretary by a shadowy figure who strangles her, then hangs her from the chandelier to make it look like suicide.

Grandison has two female "wards." One of them is sexy, naughty Althea, who's played with vigor by the young Audrey Totter. She's married to a lush and is a sharp contrast to

Murderous radio star Claude Rains hovers over his beautiful niece (Joan Caulfield) in *The Unsuspected* (Warner Bros).

the sweet and innocent Mathilda, when she finally shows up. Mathilda is played by the gloriously beautiful young Joan Caulfield, whose primary defender is the "husband" she can't remember, played by Michael North.

"Grandy" has the ego of all great master criminals, so he naturally wants to defy police detective Fred Clark by committing the "perfect crime," then re-enacting it on his radio show without getting caught—the ultimate "in your face" murder that the cops will never realize is the real thing, re-staged.

The Unsuspected also has an exciting ending in which the hero is locked up in a trunk that's about to be dumped into an incinerator at the city dump while the police rush to the rescue.

Armstrong is not much read today because her plots are gimmicky and don't hold enough water for today's "reality"-trained readers. But *The Unsuspected*, flawed as it is by its storyline, remains a fascinating film because of the great Claude Rains performance and the stylish Curtiz direction that moves things along so rapidly that we don't fall into any of the gaping holes in the plot.

It deserves resurrection, the sooner the better.

Charlotte Armstrong
Mischief

The 1950 novel and the 1952 movie *Don't Bother to Knock*

By 1950, Charlotte Armstrong was 45 years old and at the peak of her powers as one of America's most popular authors of suspense novels. She certainly demonstrated that with *Mischief* (1950), a thriller with a psychotic woman as the central character.

The premise put major shivers up the spines of most parents who read it because it was something they all feared could really happen: What if you left your child with a new babysitter you didn't really know—and she turned out to be a nut case?

Though the book contained a plot element that was officially frowned upon by Hollywood censors—it placed a small child in jeopardy—that didn't stop one studio from going after it as an ideal screen property. 20th Century–Fox put it into development as a "B" picture, to be filmed in black and white, using younger stars and a little-known director.

The resulting film, with the new title *Don't Bother to Knock*, exceeded everyone's expectations. A taut thriller, it proved a turning point in the careers of its two leading players, Richard Widmark and Marilyn Monroe, who were cast against type by British director Roy Ward Baker in a film that's been growing in stature year by year.

Today *Don't Bother to Knock* is best remembered as the first movie to star Monroe in a dramatic role. She already was well on her way to becoming the sex icon of the 1950s, but the film is much more than a showcase for her dramatic skills. It's also a highly entertaining suspense film based on one of Armstrong's most enduring novels.

In the book, suburban newspaper editor-publisher Peter O. Jones and his wife Ruth check into a New York City hotel and hurriedly dress for the dinner that night where he's supposed to make an important speech. They have brought their nine-year-old daughter Bunny, but can't take her with them to the dinner because it will run late into the night. Peter's sister was supposed to stay with Bunny, but she pulled out at the last minute. Eddie, the hotel elevator operator, finds a babysitter: his niece Nell.

What Eddie doesn't tell the Joneses is that young Nell has been in a mental hospital; recently released, she stays with her aunt and uncle. Her parents were killed in a fire that sounds as if it might have been set by the disturbed Nell.

Nell, quiet and introverted, lives in a kind of dream world. As soon as the Joneses leave and she puts Bunny to bed, she begins to poke through Mrs. Jones' things, trying on her clothing, applying her makeup, using her perfume. As she slowly dances in front of the hotel window, she's spotted by a man in the room across the courtyard. A bachelor type named Jed, he's leaving the following morning to take a new job out west. He was anxious to have a high time on his last night in New York, but he and Lyn, his girlfriend, quarreled, so he's come back to his hotel room to drink alone and feel sorry for himself. Then he sees Nell dancing and calls her room, inviting himself over to share his bottle of rye whiskey with her.

Nell lets Jed into the Joneses' room and soon they're seriously flirting and taking turns helping to drain his whiskey bottle. When they awaken Bunny, things start to go downhill fast. Nell resents the little girl for interrupting her "fun" with Jed and nearly pushes her out the eighth-story window. When Jed realizes he's making time with a

Marilyn Monroe (right) was the psychotic babysitter to youngster Donna Corcoran in *Don't Bother to Knock*, based on Charlotte Armstrong's novel *Mischief* (20th Century-Fox).

weirdo, he decides to leave, which makes Nell even madder. She threatens to report him for assaulting her if he leaves. While they're arguing, Eddie shows up to check on his nutty niece and finds Jed hiding in the bathroom. Before he can do anything, Nell brains Eddie with a heavy ashtray and he collapses, unconscious and bleeding from the head.

With all the crying, shouting and thumping, other hotel guests begin to complain and the fat's in the fire for Nell. She binds and gags Bunny. Jed slips out while Nell responds to the pounding on the door by an angry hotel guest who wants to know why the child has been crying. Someone asks the hotel detective to check on the room everyone's complaining about.

Mrs. Jones calls to see how Bunny is doing and is perplexed by the strange way Nell answers her questions. She decides to grab a cab and rush across town to the hotel. Will she get there before Nell really loses it and starts pushing Bunny out the window again?

This roller coaster plot keeps the pages turning rapidly in the book, rapidly enough that you don't notice the plot holes you otherwise might break a leg by stepping in if you were going a little more slowly through Armstrong's manipulative storyline.

Screenwriter Daniel Taradash made some worthwhile changes in Armstrong's plot to enhance character development. For one thing, he beefed up the character of Jed (Richard Widmark), making him a thoroughly unpleasant guy who snarls at virtually everybody, including girlfriend Lyn (Anne Bancroft), who's changed into a singer in the hotel's lounge. She breaks up with him because of his sour outlook on life, his unwillingness to really care for anybody but himself. Taradash also makes Jed an airline pilot on layover between flights, rather than the man with no real skills or ambition in Armstrong's novel. The result is a rather nasty character that we watch morph into a reluctant hero.

Armstrong didn't waste lots of time building sympathy for Nell (Marilyn Monroe), using her rather as the demented doll who imperils everyone. Taradash fills in her story, suggesting she was a very young woman who fell in love with a World War II pilot, then went to pieces when he was killed in combat. That permitted him to have Nell mentally confuse Jed with her lost lover, the man she obviously gave herself to because he had promised to marry her. When she learns Jed is a pilot, the connection clicks into place for her. In her twisted mind, he's the dead lover reincarnated.

In the novel, Jed makes a last-minute decision to rush back to the hotel room because he fears Nell will kill the little girl once people start closing in on her. He gets there just after Bunny's mother's arrival and he breaks up a vicious battle between the mother and the babysitter. Armstrong's ironic twist is that Jed is then shot by the hotel detective because Nell has told everybody Jed broke into her room, assaulted her and caused all the commotion.

Taradash comes up with a much more satisfying conclusion, having Jed experience a real change of heart when he risks his own life to save the little girl. That gives the audience a comfortable feeling as Jed learns to care for another person at last—and it enables him to walk off, arm in arm, with reconciled girlfriend Lyn as the cops take Nell away to the psycho ward.

Don't Bother to Knock was a gigantic boost for Marilyn Monroe, who finally proved she was capable of carrying a picture without turning every which way to show off her tight sweater. Her little girl voice and pouty expression were perfectly utilized by her director to convey the mental fragility of Nell. It's a very solid performance that holds up well all these years since we first saw it.

Monroe followed it up with an "A" budget thriller, *Niagara*, which was shot in gorgeous color and gave her yet another vivid opportunity to show she had some dramatic acting chops. By the end of her career and John Huston's *The Misfits*, Monroe had improved to the point where she was an extremely effective dramatic actress, given the right role and quality surroundings.

Richard Widmark also moved closer to full leading man status in Hollywood with his bad-guy-turned-hero performance as Jed. He had a sensational debut in 1947 as the giggling, psychopathic hood Tommy Udo in *Kiss of Death*, but was stuck for the next several years with roles that called for him to giggle or snarl while beating somebody up. *Don't Bother to Knock* afforded him a chance to play a man changed by being forced to look deep within himself.

The rest of the cast is also exceptional. Anne Bancroft, only 21 at the time, played Jed's girlfriend, Lyn. Making her a torch singer in the hotel lounge gave Bancroft the rare opportunity to sing several standards, including "How About You?," "Manhattan" and "There's a Lull in My Life."

Bancroft was in the first year of a Fox contract, trying to find her proper place in Hollywood through a variety of roles in "B" pictures like *Gorilla at Large*. Though she had a respectable part in *Don't Bother to Knock*, she finally decided to stop being a Fox "star of tomorrow" and left for Broadway, where she became a sensation in *The Miracle Worker*. She then starred in the movie version and won the Best Actress Academy Award.

Screenwriter Taradash was on the cusp of greatness when he adapted *Mischief* for the screen. His very next project was to turn James Jones' notoriously sexy and profane *From Here to Eternity* into a screenplay. It was a sensation, winning an Oscar for Taradash, along with Oscars for Best Picture, Best Director and for two supporting players, Donna Reed and Frank Sinatra.

The same year he directed *Don't Bother to Knock*, Roy Ward Baker did another Fox film which is now regarded as one of the best 3-D movies ever made: *Inferno*, a desert suspense drama starring Robert Ryan. Baker didn't get a big career bounce from these two successful thrillers. Back in England, he directed the acclaimed *A Night to Remember* (1958), about the sinking of the *Titanic*, then became a busy director in the New Wave of Horror at Hammer Films. He also directed the marvelous TV miniseries *The Flame Trees of Thika*, shown in the U.S. on PBS' *Masterpiece Theatre*.

The great character actor Elisha Cook, Jr., best known for his memorable performances in such noir classics as *The Maltese Falcon* and *The Killing*, played elevator operator Eddie. Donna Corcoran, who played Bunny, was the first of several Corcoran children to become movie actresses, She made a few more pictures, then retired from show business.

Don't Bother to Knock was remade as a Fox network TV movie called *The Sitter* more than 30 years later.

Though there were significant changes made to Armstrong's story, they aren't silly changes and, in fact, heighten its impact. *Don't Bother to Knock* is a very well-made film and is worth watching today. It's also worth the effort to track down a copy of Armstrong's original novel *Mischief*. One of her very best, it still seems fresh and exciting decades after it was first published.

John Ball

In the Heat of the Night

The 1965 novel and the 1967 movie

In the Heat of the Night is one of the best examples of a good mystery novel being turned into an even better movie. It stands out in Hollywood history as one of the few mystery movies ever to win the coveted Best Picture Academy Award.

In fact, nearly everybody associated with it came away covered in glory.

Veteran actor Rod Steiger, who played Police Chief Bill Gillespie, won the Oscar as Best Actor of 1967 and screenwriter Stirling Silliphant, who adapted the John Ball novel, took the Oscar for Best Screenplay. An Oscar also went to Hal Ashby, who edited the film, and went on to his own successful directing career (*Harold and Maude, The Last Detail, Shampoo, Coming Home, Being There*). The film even won the Oscar for Best Sound. Sidney Poitier, who played detective Virgil Tibbs, cemented his position as Hollywood's No. 1 African-American leading man.

Yet for all its awards and overnight classic status, the truth is that Silliphant and director Norman Jewison made some very dramatic changes in John Ball's story—and not always for the highest and best reasons.

For example, Ball's story takes place in a small Southern town called Wells, but the movie—and the subsequent TV series—changed the locale to Sparta, Mississippi. Why? Well, for a couple of very practical reasons.

First, Sidney Poitier did not want to go on location for several months in the Deep South, where he thought it likely he'd have to deal with harassment from racists on a daily basis. So the picture mostly was filmed in Sparta, Illinois, a rural community that resembled the one described in Ball's novel.

Because so many signs identified the town as Sparta, the filmmakers figured it was easier to change the town's name in the screenplay than to take down all the Sparta signs and put up new ones.

Ball's novel was published in the mid-1960s when the freedom movement for America's black citizens was at its zenith. Newspapers and TV newscasts were awash in coverage of demonstrations by blacks—and liberal whites—against the Jim Crow customs and laws that reduced most Southern African-Americans to second class citizenship.

Detective Virgil Tibbs (Sidney Poitier, left) forms an unlikely alliance with a bigoted Southern lawman (Rod Steiger) in the Oscar-winning Best Picture of 1967, *In the Heat of the Night*. Steiger won the Best Actor Oscar for his performance (United Artists).

The plot was deceptively simple: A white man is murdered, his body dumped in the middle of a street in the early hours of the morning. Police immediately round up a stranger—a black man waiting for a train at the station—and arrest him for the murder. When Bill Gillespie, the town's new police chief, discovers that his men have pounced upon Virgil Tibbs, a highly respected police detective from Pasadena, California, he's embarrassed and eager to release him and get him out of town as fast as possible.

Instead he's pressured to take advantage of the detective's expertise and, with the blessings of Tibbs' boss in California, asks Tibbs to stay on and help him solve the murder. This unlikely pair—a racist white police chief and an angry black detective—eventually team up and, despite lots of racial tension between them, gain a new respect for each other.

From the start, the idea appealed to Poitier, Steiger and co-star Lee Grant, who were all very pro-active in the Civil Rights movement, and to most of the major creative talent involved in making the picture, especially Jewison, Silliphant, Ashby, composer Quincy Jones and cinematographer Haskell Wexler, all active supporters of the black man's struggle for equality in America.

They saw the forging of a Tibbs-Gillespie relationship as a metaphor for the process that would have to happen in the South if the Civil Rights movement was going to succeed. They considered it an "important" project in social terms, even though it was couched in the standard framework of a detective picture.

To maximize the film's impact, Silliphant and Jewison worked on the story with special vigor, trying in every way possible to enhance its power to reach both white and black viewers with its pro-social messages, yet without letting it turn from entertainment into something purely polemic in nature.

They were fortunate in having the services of America's most popular black film star, Sidney Poitier, whose appeal to all races already had been established in such popular films as *The Defiant Ones*, *A Patch of Blue* and *Lilies of the Field*, for which he'd earned the first Best Actor Oscar ever awarded an African-American actor.

Poitier was tall, handsome and imposing, so it was clear that casting him was going to be the first big change in author Ball's concept. His novel's Virgil Tibbs was a small man, always dwarfed by the tall, lean Gillespie. Casting the heavyset Steiger as Poitier's adversary also eliminated the Ball vision of Gillespie. To produce some kind of balance, Jewison decided to make the screen Gillespie resemble the most notorious Southern lawman of the time: "Bull" Connor, the Birmingham police chief famous for setting vicious dogs on black protestors. With the heavy, middle-aged (the Gillespie of the book is only 32), powerfully dramatic Steiger in the role, Jewison made Gillespie the definitive redneck cop.

As he combed through the novel, Silliphant also started making some other fundamental changes. In the book, the murder victim is a well-known musical director who came to the small town to launch a music festival that everyone hopes will draw thousands of tourists in subsequent years. Silliphant changed the victim to an industrialist who was about to start construction of a factory that would mean hundreds of jobs for the town's many impoverished blacks and poor whites.

This seems a more credible situation than the book gives us. Ball's town never seems quite the place where a music festival would flourish.

Silliphant has Tibbs coming from Philadelphia, not Pasadena. This also makes better sense. A major urban police department would be much more likely to have a "homicide specialist" like Tibbs than a department like the smaller, more suburban Pasadena Police Dept.

Silliphant created the entire post mortem scene, a highlight of the film. Though Ball has Tibbs explain some things he discovered while examining the victim's body, he doesn't give us the strong sequence in which white medical officers and policemen stand in awe as Tibbs quite expertly conducts his own examination, discovering so many things they never noticed.

The novel also features a sort of romance between Officer Sam Wood and the daughter of the murdered man. This never makes sense in the book because the young and quite lovely daughter is so much more sophisticated than the crude and uneducated Sam. Changing the victim for the movie gave Silliphant the chance to create a whole new character: the victim's wife, played by that fine actress Lee Grant, giving one of her best performances.

The movie makes the widow a northern liberal appalled at the racism she sees in Gillespie's department. ("My God! What kind of people are you?" she says after listening to some of the racist banter in the chief's office. "What kind of place is this?") She provides another voice in support of the alienated Tibbs, and their scenes together are extremely important to his character. Grant was nominated for a Best Supporting Actress Oscar.

Silliphant's dialogue is exceptionally good and all the central characters have memorable lines to speak. And it seems nobody did mind the changes from the book because *In the Heat of the Night* was a wildly popular movie. Its box office success led to the sequels *They Call Me MISTER Tibbs* (1970) and *The Organization* (1971), in which Poitier reprised his role. *In the Heat of the Night* also became a long-running television series starring Carroll O'Connor as Gillespie and Howard Rollins as Tibbs.

Earl Derr Biggers
The Black Camel

The 1929 novel and the 1931 movie

When Earl Derr Biggers' *The Black Camel* was published, Charlie Chan already was becoming one of the world's most popular fictional detectives. It was the third of Biggers' novels about the pudgy police detective from the Honolulu P.D., each of them serialized in *The Saturday Evening Post*. Chan also had been in four movies by then and there was a heavy demand for more.

Many fans consider *The Black Camel* to be the best of the six Chan novels Biggers completed before his untimely death in 1933, and the film is certainly one of the best of the classy group made by Fox Film Corp.—later 20th Century–Fox—in the 1930s.

It stands out because the story is a rich and complex one that takes place in Chan's own backyard—the island of Oahu—rather than "on the road," where so many of the subsequent Chan stories played out. It also has a fairly lavish look about it, especially compared to the low-budget Chan films made by Poverty Row studio Monogram in the 1940s.

But an even more important reason why Chan fans liked *The Black Camel* is its much greater fidelity to the original novel. That means that the Charlie Chan you see in this film is much more like the one Biggers created as a well-intentioned contrast to the negative Fu Manchu–style images of Chinese characters so prevalent in books and films of the early 20th century.

To be sure, this Chan still spouts bits of philosophic wisdom, such as, "Alas, mouse cannot cast shadow like elephant" and "All foxes come at last to fur store." Both novel and film also contain the embarrassing character of Kashimo, Chan's dull-witted Japanese assistant, who's the butt of much derision by Inspector Chan.

But, in general, this Charlie Chan is a genial, self-deprecating man who's generally liked by most people around him, except, of course, the culprit Chan ultimately exposes as the killer in the final pages of the novel and the last reel of the film.

In *The Black Camel*, a Hollywood movie company arrives in Honolulu to finish shooting a movie that has been shooting on location in the Far East for several weeks.

Inspector Chan is not directly concerned with the movie company when he first appears in the story. Instead, he's posing as a Chinese businessman in order to check up on a mysterious "fortune teller," also recently arrived on the island, whom he suspects of bilking rich tourists.

That sets up one of the best scenes in both the book and the film as the clairvoyant, who calls himself Tarneverro the Great, sees through Chan's false identity and identifies him as a cop. This earns him Charlie's initial respect.

In the film, the scene also brings together two of the most interesting antagonists of early 1930s cinema: Warner Oland, who plays Chan, and Bela Lugosi, fresh from his masterful performance in Universal's box office smash *Dracula* (1931). Oland's Chan is self-confident, disarming and incalculably shrewd while Lugosi's Tarneverro is overwhelmingly mysterious, yet indubitably charismatic. Given Lugosi's piercing eyes and commanding presence, you expect him to be a mighty nemesis even though the air seems suffused with the odor of red herring.

Tarneverro explains he has come to Hawaii at the request of Shelah Fane (Dorothy Revier), a fading Hollywood star who's the leading lady of the film now shooting there. She pays handsomely for his advice—and this time she wants Tarneverro to look into the future and help her decide if she should marry Alan Jaynes (William Post, Jr.), a millionaire she met on the ocean liner that brought her to Hawaii.

Shelah is worried that Jaynes might be dragged into a major scandal if it ever came out that she's linked to one of the most notorious unsolved murder cases in Hollywood history. She tells Tarneverro that she was in the house of Hollywood star Denny Mayo three years earlier—and saw who killed him that night! The case baffled Hollywood's detective bureau, so her admission that she witnessed the killing would be a sensation, if made public.

Shelah is found murdered in her seaside pavilion and suddenly Chan must take on the case. Suspects include her assistant Julie (Sally Eilers); Jaynes, who was furious when she told him she couldn't marry him; her ex-husband Robert Fyfe (Victor Varconi), a stage actor in Honolulu; and, of course, the mysterious Tarneverro.

The Fox film version would be worth seeing if only for the many second unit sequences filmed in 1930-era Honolulu. Modern viewers get to see a relatively unspoiled Honolulu in the days when the Royal Hawaiian Hotel was new and Hawaii was a very exotic vacation spot for Americans. The movie also has an appealing

Warner Oland (left) as detective Charlie Chan confronts the sinister Bela Lugosi in *The Black Camel* (Fox Films).

supporting cast, including a boyish Robert Young, still years from leading man roles, as Julie's suitor, publicity man Jimmy Bradshaw, and sinister Dwight Frye as Shelah's butler. Frye played Renfield, Lugosi's raving mad disciple, in *Dracula*, so this is a reunion for the two film bogeymen.

Though the film follows the general plotline of the novel, it does make a few major changes, chief among them a romance between the butler and Shelah's maid, which provides a surprising bit of action at the film's climax. The script also juggles many of the clues, assigning them to different suspects. For instance, a photo is torn to bits by Shelah in the movie, but by another suspect in the book. In the movie, filming has begun on the Honolulu scenes when Shelah is murdered, but it hasn't yet started when the murder takes place in the book.

The title comes from one of Chan's philosophical aphorisms: "Death is a black camel that kneels unbidden at every gate." It certainly kneels at the gate of Shelah Fane's beachfront pavilion.

One interesting piece of movie trivia: Val Martino, director of the movie being filmed in the story, is played by Hamilton MacFadden, who also directed *The Black Camel*.

For those who have seen the *Black Camel* movie, the 1929 novel will not disappoint. The basic story is the same, but the book fills in the characters in greater depth and includes some who are barely seen on screen.

The Charlie Chan of *The Black Camel* is not the egregious version seen in the films featuring Sidney Toler, who stepped in after Oland died. Still, the Asian community never has been comfortable with non–Asian actors playing a Chinese character created by a non–Asian author. Today Charlie Chan is considered by many to be an example of defamatory racist stereotyping by white Hollywood. Ironically, *The Black Camel* comes from an era when well-intentioned producers were trying to right some wrongs.

If you can look at it that way, *The Black Camel* is still a very absorbing mystery novel—and a highly entertaining film.

John Buchan
The Thirty-Nine Steps

The 1915 novel and the 1935 movie

Back in those nervous days just before the release of *Psycho*, the great film director Alfred Hitchcock granted me an interview at his bungalow at Universal City while I was still a college undergraduate. During that fabulous interview, he happened to mention an author he truly revered: John Buchan.

Though I hadn't read any of Buchan's books, I certainly knew who he was: the famous author, lawyer and statesman who helped start the whole spy novel genre in 1915 with a compact little thriller called *The Thirty-Nine Steps*, then followed it with several sequels.

I also knew and admired the film Hitchcock had made from Buchan's slim novel in 1935, the same year that Buchan, a former member of the British Parliament, had been created the first Baron Tweedsmuir and appointed governor-general of Canada.

Hitchcock talked so fondly of his *Thirty-Nine Steps* that day that I couldn't wait to

Robert Donat finds himself handcuffed to beautiful Madeleine Carroll in Alfred Hitchcock's *The Thirty-Nine Steps*. The protagonist wasn't handcuffed to anybody in the book and her character didn't exist (Gaumont-British films).

see it again and look for some of the amusing things he'd done with the story that still seemed to tickle him so much. But we had no video rental shops in those days and few repertory cinemas. *The Thirty-Nine Steps* was then one of the early British pictures you could find only on the late, late show, and constantly interrupted by commercials for used car dealers. Result: I didn't see it again for another 20 years.

But that was then and this is now. I've owned the video version for years and also went out and bought a copy of Buchan's novel to satisfy my curiosity about the literary origin of yet another classic Hitchcock film.

Well, that was an eye-opener. Though I knew Hitchcock seldom brought any book to the screen without "Hitching" it up quite a bit, I wasn't prepared for the extent that Hitchcock and his frequent screenwriter, Charles Bennett, had gutted the Buchan novel and fabricated all-new contents.

For instance, there's the memorable section of the film in which leading man Robert Donat escapes from the police while handcuffed to glamorous Pamela (Madeleine Carroll). Forced into such close company that they even have to sleep handcuffed together, the romantic sparks soon begin to fly.

As it turns out, Pamela never appears in the book, so there's nobody handcuffed to the hero and no romance.

Then there's the charming British music hall sequence in which the hero discovers that an entertainer called Mr. Memory has memorized all the secret plans the mysterious villains are trying to smuggle out of England. Well, you guessed it: There is no music hall sequence nor any Mr. Memory in Buchan's novel.

Finally, there's the matter of the thirty-nine steps. It was one of the first so-called "McGuffins" that Hitchcock had in his films: non-existent things that everybody's trying to track down or figure out throughout the movie. In the book, there were thirty-nine steps on a staircase leading to the English cove where German spies were planning to take possession of the secret plans. In the movie, it has something to do with the diagrams and plans Mr. Memory has tucked away in his brain, but you never climb any steps and you're never sure what they were supposed to mean.

In Buchan's novel, the hero is young mining engineer Richard Hannay, who has just arrived in London from a long tour of duty in South Africa. One night he's accosted at the door of his apartment by an American journalist who lives in the same building. The man has learned that a secret organization known as the Black Stone plans to assassinate an important European leader during his visit to England. It will have a profoundly negative impact on England in the war (World War I) that everybody believes is imminent in Europe. He wants to pass on what he knows to someone else because he feels the enemy is rapidly closing in on him.

Letting the man stay in his apartment, Hannay goes out, then returns to find the man murdered. Immediately, Hannay becomes the chief suspect and has to flee the police as well as the mysterious foreign agents who now are after him. He runs for the wild and desolate northern country of Scotland, trying to elude capture until the time when he's supposed to reveal what he knows to a government insider.

Hitchcock and screenwriter Bennett liked the notion that an innocent young man suddenly was "caught up" in intrigue that could cost him his life. (This was to become the core situation for dozens of famous Hitchcock films; his *North by Northwest* is the one that most resembles *The Thirty-Nine Steps* in flavor. His 1942 *Saboteur* is another fine example.) But they also noted that Buchan's story had virtually no female characters and was devoid of romance.

Bennett remedied that in part by turning the American reporter into "Miss Smith," a sexy spy with a Russian accent, and having her murdered in Hannay's apartment. Going further, he then added a character dreamed up by Hitch and himself: the beautiful Pamela, who initially takes a firm dislike to Hannay, but is accidentally swept up with him when police catch and cuff him. Along the way, Hitch and Bennett also decided that Hannay should be newly arrived from Canada rather than South Africa.

Another Buchan gimmick that Hitch and Bennett altered and used to much better effect involves the criminal mastermind. Buchan warns us early that the Black Stone's double agent in Great Britain is rumored to have a pronounced lisp, although his name isn't known. Perhaps Hitch thought too many young British leading men had lisps and that would confuse the audience. More likely, though, he went looking for something a little more visual than a lisp.

So in the movie, we're told that the villain has part of a finger missing. Hitch used that secret to great effect when Hannay is telling one of his contacts that they must look out for a man with part of one finger missing.

"You mean, like this?" the man says, holding up his own hand to show the missing digit.

It's a showstopper moment and, of course, Hannay immediately knows he's just stepped into a giant bear trap.

Hitch and Bennett also adapted another of Buchan's gimmicks to delightful effect. In the book, Hannay is helped by Sir Harry, a young man running as the Liberal Party candidate for Parliament. He's a very nice and resourceful fellow, but he's a dreadful public speaker, so he persuades Hannay to pose as a visitor from Australia, and Hannay gives Sir Harry's campaign speech.

Buchan made little of that incident except perhaps to show readers how capable Hannay was in many different ways. But in the movie, Hitchcock makes something truly special of that sequence by having Hannay nearly cornered by his pursuers when he's suddenly dragged into a meeting hall because he's been mistaken for the candidate scheduled to speak that night. Rushed up to the stage, Hannay has to deliver a speech in order to continue to befuddle his pursuers. It's a beautifully orchestrated scene, one that would be imitated many times over by many other filmmakers, not to mention Hitchcock himself.

The Thirty-Nine Steps was a huge success as a novel, even though Buchan wrote it while recovering from an illness and purposely conceived it as a "penny dreadful" to prove he could write a cheap thriller. His immediate sequel *Greenmantle* was also very popular; he followed it with three more Hannay spy novels.

Hitchcock's film helped propel him out of the ranks of "British directors" into what the French critics might later have described as an auteur—a filmmaker so original that he seems to become the "author" of the material he's adapting to the screen. It was his first really big international smash hit and put him in the "suspense" category for the remainder of his career.

Hitchcock's *Thirty-Nine Steps* doesn't wear quite as well as some of his later films. It seems rather disjointed at times and the story is told in such a shorthand style that you're often left wondering if something is missing. Yet it has those signature scenes that still retain their punch, most of them made up by Bennett and Hitch. It also has a lively "action" performance by Robert Donat, who went on to become a star in American films and won the 1939 Academy Award for his immortal performance as the endearing schoolteacher Mr. Chips in MGM's *Goodbye, Mr. Chips*.

Hitchcock disciples cite *Thirty-Nine Steps* as a film in which he submits his "cool blonde" female star, Madeleine Carroll, to any number of on-camera indignities. I've read that Hitch and Carroll got along quite famously, despite the pratfalls and soakings he puts her through.

Also of considerable interest to modern film fans is that *The Thirty-Nine Steps* includes a rare early screen appearance by Peggy Ashcroft, later to become Dame Peggy Ashcroft, one of England's most esteemed stage actresses, and a Best Supporting Actress Oscar winner five decades later for *A Passage to India*. (Viewers of PBS's *Masterpiece Theatre* will never forget her marvelous work in *Jewel in the Crown*.) In the movie, she plays the "crofter's wife" who befriends Hannay—and seems to be sexually stirred by his attentions—even though her miserable husband turns the fugitive in.

Both film and book are now easily found in most any community, so I strongly suggest that fans of the movie seek out the very brief, action-packed book and read it to get an even greater understanding of how the inventive Hitchcock digested literary material and metabolized it into something extraordinary for the screen.

Buchan's novel has been filmed several more times since Hitchcock did it first, some of them borrowing more from Hitchcock's film than they do from the original novel. None of the subsequent versions can hold a candle to the Hitchcock version.

W.R. Burnett
The Asphalt Jungle

The 1949 novel and the 1950 movie

W.R. (William Riley) Burnett was one of the most influential American novelists during Hollywood's Golden Age—roughly the 1930s through the 1950s. He exercised a profound influence on the development of the noir school of motion picture crime drama.

His 1929 novel *Little Caesar* was turned into the first great American gangster movie in 1930 by director Mervyn LeRoy, propelling star Edward G. Robinson to fame overnight. Burnett also worked on the screenplay for another epic gangster film, the original *Scarface* (1932), a thinly disguised portrait of Al Capone. His 1941 novel *High Sierra* was filmed that same year by director Raoul Walsh, helping establish actor Humphrey Bogart as the film world's reigning anti-hero.

Then, in 1949, he wrote the definitive caper crime film of its time, *The Asphalt Jungle*, which director John Huston turned into a searing noir classic in 1950. It survives as one of the all-time greats in that genre and served as the model for three MGM remakes in different cinema genres: *The Badlanders* (1958), which turned the story into a Western; *Cairo* (1962), which shifted the locale to Egypt, and *Cool Breeze* (1972), which spun the story with a mostly African-American cast for the profitable blaxploitation market. ABC also tried a 1961 *Asphalt Jungle* TV series, which lasted only 13 episodes and used none of the characters from the novel or first movie.

In retrospect, the 1949 novel was a trendsetter in that it plunged the reader into the shadowy world of big city criminals and yet portrayed them with a certain nobility. It's about the carefully planned burglary of a major jewel company and how it eventually comes apart because of the character flaws of the key figures involved. Its ability to convey the code by which the scheme's crucial players operate foreshadowed the character-rooted construction of Mario Puzo's *The Godfather* and the films it inspired.

The story's focus is on a "surefire" plan to break into the ultra-secure jewelry store, worked out by a brilliant, middle-aged German immigrant named "Doc" Riemenschneider, who has just finished a prison term and is anxious to pull off one great job that will net him enough to live comfortably in retirement in Mexico for the rest of his life. He needs the help of a talented safecracker, an armed "hooligan" to handle any trouble that may develop, a getaway car driver and, most of all, a backer who will put up the seed money to get the job done, then pay everybody a share of the estimated $500,000 haul by finding a fence to handle the stolen gems.

"Doc," a calm, reassuring intellectual, prizes loyalty above all and has only one obvious character weakness: an appetite for sexy young women. He shares this weakness with his backer, a wealthy criminal lawyer named Emmerich, whose wife is an invalid with an illness that may be more imagination than reality. Emmerich has taken up with a beautiful young redhead named Angela who's costing him a fortune. He hopes to cut his losses by double-crossing the burglars and taking the loot for himself.

Meanwhile, the cops are looking to crack down on big city criminals because new Police Commissioner Hardy is trying to root out corruption on the force and demanding a roundup of all shady characters, including Dix, the strong-arm specialist recruited to be the burglary team hooligan.

Dix and "Doc" form a bond right away, seemingly because each man is a seasoned professional and both realize that they need to keep the team working together smoothly if the job is going to succeed. Like "Doc," Dix has ideas of making enough from this job to get out of the racket and go back home to his rural country roots where life is much less complicated.

When the time came to turn Burnett's taut novel into a movie, the filmmakers were well served by the author's rich background as both a screenwriter and an author whose books had been filmed many times. The book moved like a film scenario already and the dialogue was terse and cinematic. Director Huston, an experienced screenwriter himself, adapted the novel with Ben Maddow.

Sam Jaffe (left) was the mastermind of the burglary plot at the center of the 1950 thriller *The Asphalt Jungle*. With him is Sterling Hayden as the gang's muscle man (MGM).

The movie sticks closely to the novel much of the way, making only a few cosmetic changes. Gus, the hump-backed café operator who helps bring Dix and "Doc" together, is referred to as a hunchback a couple of times, but actor James Whitmore, who plays Gus, has only the mere suggestion of a hump on his back. Perhaps the filmmakers thought a bigger hump would be tasteless.

Angela, Emmerich's red-haired mistress, is turned into a blonde, but that's no deficit since Huston cast the very young and incredibly sexy Marilyn Monroe in the part. For Monroe, this was a big step up the ladder to leading lady status.

Safecracker Louis Bellini gets a name change to Louis Ciavelli, but that affects nothing in the story. As for "Doc" Riemenschneider, he gets an extra "d" added to his name, making him Riedenschneider. My guess is that somebody made a typographical error on the screenplay and nobody bothered to correct it. "Doc," who's played by the marvelous character actor Sam Jaffe, is also a little taller and considerably trimmer than Burnett describes him in the novel.

By keeping the film character-based, like the novel, Huston was able to avoid casting any high-profile Hollywood stars whose established personas might have clashed with the Burnett characters. Dix, who becomes the leading man in the story, is played by Sterling Hayden, who was just then developing into a masterful character actor, specializing in tough guys. Jean Hagen plays his loyal but tawdry girlfriend "Doll" perfectly. She would go on to her best ever film role as the silent screen star whose voice was too awful for talking pictures in 1952's *Singin' in the Rain*. Today she is best remembered as Danny Thomas' first TV wife in *Make Room for Daddy* (1953–56).

The most enduring performance in the film may be that of Louis Calhern as Emmerich. Calhern generally played likable upper class people, but in *Asphalt Jungle* he's a smooth but utterly corrupt conniver. But this first film version of *The Asphalt Jungle* is a tightly edited, beautifully acted movie that even makes you feel a little sympathy for a conniver like Emmerich, who still loves his pitiful wife and also wants to protect his airhead mistress from the fallout from his misfortune. Likewise, you feel for "Doc" when he finally meets his Waterloo after spending too much time ogling a pretty young girl when he should be getting the heck out of town. And when Dix finally makes it to the horse ranch he knew and loved as a kid, you groan when you realize he's not going to survive to smell the roses again.

The alterations in Burnett's absorbing crime novel are minor and it remains a riveting read today, more than half a century after its first arrival in bookstores. Because the film has survived as a cinema classic, it should continue to drive fans back to the source novel by a great American writer.

James M. Cain
Love's Lovely Counterfeit

The 1942 novel and the 1956 movie *Slightly Scarlet*

In between *The Postman Always Rings Twice* (1934) and *Double Indemnity* (1943), James M. Cain's two towering classics of crime fiction, he wrote a rather neglected little crime novel called *Love's Lovely Counterfeit* (1942), which was turned into the equally neglected movie *Slightly Scarlet* (1956).

In retrospect, it's easy to understand why both book and film were neglected. First, the novel has a god-awful title that isn't remotely intriguing. Like his two classics, this novel has an unsavory character for its protagonist, but is missing the searing realism that still marks both *Postman* and *Indemnity* as icons of the "hard-boiled" school of American fiction and the films made from them as immortal film noir classics.

Still, because Cain is such an important figure in the history of mystery-crime writing in America, many curious fans still may seek out *Love's Lovely Counterfeit* and *Slightly Scarlet*.

The book's "hero" is big Ben Grace, a sort of public relations man for urban racketeer

Sol Caspar. Ben's one of those well-spoken, cleaned-up guys who often front for gangsters and keep busy smoothing things out for them.

Ben at first seems like a new kind of protagonist for Cain—a man who works for criminals, but is really above their crooked dealings and is longing for a decent life on the right side of the law. When he starts to fall in love with June Lyons, the sharp-witted aide to the reform mayoral candidate who sweeps the rascals out of office, we naturally assume he'll team up with her and, with his deep knowledge of the local underworld, help bury the city's criminal rats for good.

Well, that's where we're wrong. Ben turns out to be a bigger, smarter rat than the others. He really wants to turn Julie toward the dark side as he prepares to take over Sol's operation, finding new ways to make it pay even more money during the reign of the clean new mayor. And it seems to be working—until Julie's younger, nastier sister, Dorothy, turns up.

Dorothy, a bad apple who's been in trouble with the police, continues to live dangerously once her older sister attempts to take charge of her life. When Ben starts to pay close attention to the lovely Dorothy, his master plan comes apart at the seams.

Love's Lovely Counterfeit purports to give us an inside view of a big city's criminal underbelly, but its edges aren't hard enough to convince us that what Cain is showing us is real. Still, the unconventional plot, pitting two sisters against each other, is vintage Cain. Like most of his novels, it's tersely written and rockets along nicely.

By 1956, when Hollywood finally got around to filming the book, the age of gritty realism was upon the film industry. Among the revolutionary crime films we'd already seen were John Huston's movie version of W.R. Burnett's novel *The Asphalt Jungle*, Jules Dassin's startling prison film *Brute Force* and his ultra-realistic police procedural *The Naked City*, Laslo Benedek's tough biker gang thriller *The Wild One*, Fritz Lang's fiercely cruel *The Big Heat* and Elia Kazan's grim *On the Waterfront*. There was no going back from the hard-edged crime movies of the late 1940s and 1950s.

The studio that gave us *Slightly Scarlet* was RKO, which was in the throes of economic chaos: Howard Hughes had left and the new owner, General Teleradio, was struggling to keep the studio competitive. The year 1956 would be RKO's last as a viable studio. The following year, all employees were terminated and the studio's remaining films had to be distributed by rival companies.

That partially explains the poor judgment that resulted in RKO producing *Slightly Scarlet*, which came from busy producer Benedict Bogeaus, who made many of the studio's disappointing "A" pictures in its final years. The director was 70-year-old Allan Dwan, a Canadian-born veteran who had made his first picture in 1911. Dwan didn't make "gritty" crime pictures and the studio required him to shoot this nasty story in color and in SuperScope, the studio's knockoff version of Fox's widescreen process, CinemaScope.

RKO and Bogeaus also assigned Dwan a set of second-tier stars. John Payne played Ben with the proper smoothness, but lacking the visceral toughness the character needs. Payne had made the same sort of career transition that Dick Powell had made from juvenile male lead in musicals to playing anti-heroes in crime films. (Payne actually sang "Twinkle, Twinkle, Little Star" in the 1936 musical *Hats Off*.)

They probably thought of Payne for *Slightly Scarlet* because he'd just done a series of crime films with director Phil Karlson, starting with the acclaimed *Kansas City Confidential*. In color, though, he just didn't look tough enough to double-cross rackets

Rhonda Fleming (left) and Arlene Dahl as sisters involved with crime in *Slightly Scarlet*, the film version of James M. Cain's novel *Love's Lovely Counterfeit* (RKO).

boss Caspar, played by classic heavy Ted DeCorsia. (The following year, Payne started playing a hard-edged cowboy hero in the TV series, *The Restless Gun*.)

The Robert Blees screenplay also diminished the role of June, who was played by buxom redhead Rhonda Fleming, and built up the role of her wicked sister, played by yet another blazing redhead, Arlene Dahl. In fact, the film begins with June meeting Dorothy as she gets out of prison (for shoplifting?) while Ben (Payne) photographs them from a distance, obviously gathering dirt with which to smear June and her boss, the reform mayoral candidate.

Cain's novel spends considerable time building up the budding romance between Ben and June, but it never really gets going in a convincing manner in the movie. There's no particular chemistry between Payne and Fleming, but the film cranks up the passion between him and Dahl quite a bit. Dahl, who would specialize in more ladylike characters later in her career, is allowed to turn on the heat in *Slightly Scarlet* and comes close to stealing the picture from her more-experienced co-stars.

Slightly Scarlet preserves the downbeat ending of *Love's Lovely Counterfeit*, but it really has no impact because Dwan and his screenwriter never really make us care about these people—admittedly a difficult job for any director and screenwriter. The fact that *Slightly Scarlet* always looks like it's happening on a well-lighted Hollywood soundstage in color and SuperScope also doesn't help set much of a proper mood for the nastiness going on in Cain's story.

End result: Cain's so-so crime novel was turned into a so-so crime movie with a hohum cast in the final days of RKO, the studio that was perhaps Hollywood's greatest source of tough films noir.

Vera Caspary

Laura

The 1942/43 novel and the 1944 movie

Whenever I think of Waldo Lydecker, my favorite character from 20th Century–Fox's 1944 mystery classic *Laura*, I always picture Clifton Webb in his bathtub, making sardonic remarks to police detective Dana Andrews while writing his acerbic newspaper column on his portable typewriter, mounted on a platform over the sudsy water.

No wonder. Webb turned in one of Hollywood's greatest screen performances as Lydecker, earning a Best Supporting Actor Oscar nomination in the process. (He lost to Barry Fitzgerald of *Going My Way*.) Thanks to Webb, Waldo is vividly remembered by most of us as the epitome of the effete urban columnist, a cold-blooded, self-centered bachelor who tells young advertising sales rep Laura Hunt (Gene Tierney) he won't endorse a fountain pen because "I write with a goose quill, dipped in venom."

But the image we retain of Lydecker isn't the image first created by writer Vera Caspary, whose novel *Laura*—which first appeared in Collier's magazine as a seven-part serial—was a bestseller in 1942–43 and is still regarded as one of America's classic mystery novels.

In that still-entrancing novel, Waldo is an enormously fat man, fashioned more along the lines of actor Laird Cregar (*The Lodger*, *Hangover Square*), who also was under contract to 20th Century–Fox in 1944. I don't know if director Otto Preminger ever considered Cregar for the role of Waldo, but it might have been his final role anyway since he died late in 1944 at age 28 while undergoing radical dieting to shed some pounds off his 6'3" inch frame.

Does it make any difference that Waldo is reed-thin in the movie and fat in the book? That's a judgment call, but in the book, Waldo's enormous girth makes his fatal attraction to Laura all the more hopeless. In the film, you might imagine the beautiful, streamlined Gene Tierney being attracted to the fussy, suave Clifton Webb—but you wouldn't have bought it if Preminger had cast Cregar or Sydney Greenstreet as Waldo.

There's another element of Waldo's character that comes out much more openly in the book than the movie: the fact that Waldo is rather obviously homosexual. I'm guessing you couldn't come right out and describe someone as gay in a work of popular fiction in the early 1940s, but planted in Caspary's novel are all kinds of major hints at Waldo's sexual orientation.

Preminger tiptoes around the issue, although it probably was considered a bold stroke among Hollywood insiders to cast Webb as Waldo. There was little mystery around town about Webb's sexual orientation and Preminger surely knew Webb would bring that sensibility to the character even if the script didn't call for it.

With Clifton Webb (right) looking on, Detective Dana Andrews talks with glamorous Gene Tierney in the 1944 film version of Vera Caspary's thriller *Laura*. In the book, the Webb character was enormously fat, but the slim Webb wowed critics and earned an Oscar nomination (Fox Video).

Film historian Leonard Maltin has reported that Fox studio boss Darryl F. Zanuck initially opposed the casting of Webb as Waldo because he considered the actor "too effeminate." Preminger was right, though, in insisting upon Webb, who dazzled everyone who saw the film. His performance turned him into a golden commodity at the studio, leading to his immortal Mr. Belvedere character in *Sitting Pretty* and many other hits for Fox.

Waldo's size and sexual orientation weren't the only things the movie changed. In the book, Waldo is known around New York for his swaggering style—and for his rather affected habit of carrying a walking stick wherever he goes. The movie changes that walking stick to a simple cane—and eliminates a major plot surprise in the process.

In both movie and book, the murder is committed by a killer armed with what appears to have been a sawed-off shotgun that fired a blast of BB shot directly into the face of the victim. The murder weapon isn't immediately found, but suspicion falls upon Laura's fiancé Shelby Carpenter, who owned a shotgun that turns out to have been fired recently.

Those who read Caspary's novel, though, may have forgotten that Lydecker had carried the murder weapon all along: a shotgun built into his walking stick!

The movie changes this key gimmick and diverts our attention to an antique grandfather-style clock in Laura's apartment—a gift on loan from Waldo. As improbable as it sounds, the movie has Waldo conceal the shotgun in a secret compartment in the clock after committing the murder.

Caspary's gimmick is the better one because it allows the arrogant Waldo to carry the murder weapon all through the story; detective Mark McPherson handles it on one occasion. This is very Waldo-like. He'd love to flaunt the weapon like that under the very nose of the detective, further establishing his intellectual superiority over the dumb cop.

What's more, I can't imagine an effete man like Waldo ever using a sawed-off shotgun, which strikes me as a sort of gangster weapon. He's a born swordcane-type killer, so Caspary's lethal walking stick seems absolutely perfect for him.

Still, I'm betting most of us remember what the movie showed us, even if we read the original novel and loved it. That's the film medium: Its visual imagery is so much more powerful than the written word that we can't get those images out of our mind even when we try.

For example, Caspary certainly does her best to make us understand that Detective McPherson is falling in love with Laura, a woman he has never seen in person, but who seems to embody everything he wants in a woman: beauty, thoughtfulness, intelligence and success.

But Preminger's film wallops us with that core story point in just one vivid sequence in which McPherson, played in laconic style by Dana Andrews, spends an evening alone in the dead girl's apartment, staring at the portrait of Laura on the wall, drinking her liquor and playing her music on her phonograph. (To nobody's surprise, the record on the turntable is a lush instrumental version of David Raksin's haunting "Laura," one of the most memorable of all movie themes.)

In fact, a still photo from the movie that shows Andrews gazing up at Tierney's painted likeness seems to capture the whole essence of *Laura* in a single visual image. If you ever doubt the power of film imagery, just look at that photo and you'll think you know everything you need to know about the movie and the book.

If you've seen the film, but never read the book, please correct that situation as soon as possible. The book is a quick read and it's loaded with wit and colorful 1940s New York urban lore. You may be surprised at how different Waldo comes off in the book, but I think you'll decide Tierney and Andrews were the perfect Laura and McPherson.

As for the movie, I can't imagine anyone who hasn't yet seen *Laura*. It's a noir classic from the very moment Waldo begins his narration with the words, "I shall never forget the weekend Laura died…"

I dare say none of the rest of us will forget it either.

Raymond Chandler
The Big Sleep

The 1939 novel and the 1946 and 1978 movies

If Raymond Chandler was a little gun-shy when he learned that Warner Bros. was going to start filming a movie version of his first Philip Marlowe detective novel, *The Big Sleep*, in 1944, you could hardly blame him.

Hollywood already had twice filmed his second Marlowe novel, *Farewell, My Lovely*—and showed no respect for it either time. The first version didn't even have Philip Marlowe in it!

But there were some good signs about the plans for a film of *The Big Sleep*. For one thing, it would be made by Howard Hawks, who had a reputation as one of Hollywood's best directors of tough, male-oriented films. For another, acclaimed novelist William Faulkner was going to help write the screenplay. Finally, it would star Humphrey Bogart as Marlowe—the same actor who was so convincing as Dashiell Hammett's hard-boiled private eye Sam Spade in John Huston's 1941 adaptation of *The Maltese Falcon*.

First published in 1939, *The Big Sleep* was immediately recognized as something new and exciting in the mystery world. Chandler brought a sense of realism and a nearly irresistible style to the genre. Some readers

Private eye Philip Marlowe (Humphrey Bogart) gets up close and personal with his client's daughter (Lauren Bacall) in the 1946 version of Raymond Chandler's *The Big Sleep*. They were also getting pretty personal in their private lives at the time (Warner Bros. and the James Bawden Collection).

even dared to suggest that Chandler was lifting the mystery up to the level of "literature." Today there's hardly any debate about that, which is why Chandler's books are still widely read and deeply admired.

Much has been made about the convoluted plot of *The Big Sleep*, in which so many murders are committed. Legend has it that even Chandler wasn't sure who was responsible for all of them. Well, forget the plot. The immortality of *The Big Sleep* comes from the creation of the Marlowe character, a cynical "righter of wrongs" whose profession simply happens to be private investigator rather than priest, judge or frontier sheriff. We see his world—mostly a seedy 1940s-era Los Angeles—through his eyes, and it's his point of view that puts the magic in those mystery novels.

In *The Big Sleep*, Marlowe introduces himself to us as he arrives at the mansion of a former military general, Sternwood, who wants Marlowe to get a blackmailer off his back. The blackmailer's target is Sternwood's youngest daughter, Carmen, a twisted 20-year-old who thinks she can seduce any man. Before Marlowe has even met her father, he gets a dose of Carmen's torchy style.

"She bit her lip and turned her head a little and looked at me along her eyes," Marlowe tells us in his first-person narration. "Then she lowered her lashes until they almost cuddled her cheeks and slowly raised them again, like a theater curtain. I was to get to know that trick. That was supposed to make me roll over on my back with all four paws in the air."

Marlowe resists her—and he *keeps* resisting her, even when she turns up stark naked in his bed one night. The guy isn't gay, though. He's just smart enough to avoid getting involved with a client's daughter before the case is wrapped up. He also is a very good judge of character. He seems to realize that Carmen has a screw loose upstairs as well as downstairs. That early observation serves him well by the time the complicated knots in his case finally are sorted out in the final chapters.

Chandler also put some of the wittiest dialogue we'd ever heard in Marlowe's mouth—so witty, in fact, that movie producers rarely wanted to mess with it. After that first steamy encounter with Carmen, Marlowe tells the family butler, "You ought to wean her. She looks old enough." The three writers who first adapted that scene to the screen pretty much left that line alone, along with many, many more.

A fresh reading of *The Big Sleep* today will reward any reader. Though the plot wanders all over the place, you won't lose interest because Chandler makes you Marlowe's shadow, so you go everywhere with him. And he never has a dull moment.

When Hawks began to prepare his film of *The Big Sleep*, he vowed to pay plenty of respect to the novel he admired greatly. He wanted to hire a screenwriter who had high regard for what Chandler had accomplished, so he turned to Leigh Brackett, a woman who had written a mystery novel called *No Good from a Corpse* that Hawks also liked. To co-write the screenplay, he then hired a man who at the time was considered possibly America's greatest living novelist: William Faulkner, the author of *The Sound and the Fury*, *As I Lay Dying* and the best-selling *Sanctuary*.

At first, that may seem to be an odd choice. Faulkner hailed from the Deep South, and most of his stories were set there. He also was the composer of some of the longest sentences in contemporary literature, filled with compound phrases and complex thoughts. Why choose him to adapt a terse writer whose milieu was Los Angeles, Hollywood and the western suburbs?

But it doesn't seem so goofy a plan once you remember that Faulkner also loved detective stories and had written a bundle of them, many collected in his book *Knight's Gambit*. Like Chandler, Faulkner had a great eye for odd characters, so it figured he'd feel at home with some of the weirdos that populated Philip Marlowe's world.

Right off the bat, Brackett and Faulkner faced a challenge: Chandler's plot revolved around the fact that Carmen had posed nude in some salacious photos while stoned on booze and drugs. That was the source of the blackmail scheme. But Hollywood filmmakers weren't free to deal with that sort of subject matter in 1944, when production was scheduled to start. They had to change that pronto.

They also faced a more typical Hollywood problem: Bogart had been romancing beautiful model Lauren Bacall, who had made a sensational screen debut opposite Bogart in *To Have and Have Not* (1944), a film adapted from an Ernest Hemingway novel and also directed by Hawks. Warner Bros. wanted to capitalize on the headline-making chemistry between Bogart and Bacall, so they cast her as Carmen's older sister Vivian. Result: Vivian's role in the plot had to be built up, so Bogart and Bacall could heat up the screen in some scenes not in the book.

Brackett and Faulkner solved the problems hastily. They dumped the pornographic photo angle and never discussed what sort of photo Carmen was being blackmailed with, leaving the impression it was just compromising enough to be worth some money to the family. Then they made a bold move to make Vivian more available for romance with Marlowe.

In the novel, Vivian is married to a former crook named Regan, who has been missing for several months. Since her wealthy father was very fond of Regan, Marlowe also looks into his disappearance and discovers that Regan was having an affair with the wife of a major Los Angeles racketeer. The assumption: The mob guy had Regan killed.

But the movie makes Vivian into Mrs. Rutledge, a fast-living woman who once was married, but now is free to dally with private eyes. Regan stays in the story, but he's changed to a missing friend of General Sternwood, who wants to find him.

Brackett and Faulkner actually remained pretty faithful to Chandler's original story, though the film's ending is different. In the book, Carmen takes Marlowe out to a remote part of the family's acreage—theoretically for him to give her a lesson in pistol marksmanship—and then attempts to shoot him and dump him down the same deep sump where Regan, her sister's missing husband, has been deposited. But Marlowe, who suspected something of the sort, has put blanks in Carmen's pistol.

In the movie, there's no such scene between Marlowe and Carmen. Though there's vague talk about Vivian getting Carmen some therapy, the screenwriters were more concerned with leaving the impression that Marlowe and Vivian were about to embark on a torrid love affair now that the case was solved.

"What's wrong with you?" Marlowe asks Vivian in his last line of the picture.

"Nothing you can't fix," says Vivian as their lips come together, just before "The End" flashes on screen.

Raymond Chandler didn't want to get his sleuth tied up with any woman in his very first novel, so the book ends with Marlowe heading for a bar, where he downs three Scotches and fantasizes about the handsome blonde gangster's wife that Regan was romancing before Carmen sent him to "the big sleep." Even then, Chandler has Marlowe assure us he wasn't going to take up with the blonde, saying, "I never saw her again."

Like Chandler's novel, the Hawks version of *The Big Sleep* today is regarded as a classic. It still holds your attention for all 114 minutes, for a variety of reasons. The film is very stylish and Bogart was never better. He was the perfect Marlowe, even though he was short and Chandler described Marlowe as tall. In the book, Marlowe's first wisecrack line of dialogue comes when Carmen looks him over and tells him, "You're tall, aren't you?" and Marlowe replies, "I didn't mean to be." In the movie, she tells Marlowe he's "short" and he has a similar rejoinder.

Though the film was completed in 1945, it wasn't released until a year later. At first, it was assumed that its release was delayed so Warners could release all the war-themed movies it was stuck with when World War II ended in 1945. Now it's known that the original version of *The Big Sleep* was rejected and a second one, slightly shorter, was prepared.

In the DVD released by Warner Bros. in 2001, both versions are presented for the first time, along with a short documentary explaining why a second film was made. In that documentary, we learn that Bacall's performance in *Confidential Agent*—made after she finished *The Big Sleep*, but released first—was almost universally condemned by critics. Fearful that the critics would savage *The Big Sleep*, studio boss Jack Warner listened to Bacall's agent, Charles Feldman, who pleaded with him to rewrite her part and re-shoot her scenes. After looking at Hawks' final cut of the film, Warner agreed that the high voltage hostility that Bacall showed Bogart in *To Have and Have Not* was missing and her performance suffered. He ordered the rewrites and the retakes.

Jules Furthman was brought in to doctor the Brackett-Faulkner screenplay and the actors reassembled to shoot the new scenes, which resulted in a much tougher Vivian character—and a lot more chemistry between the stars, who were married while the film was being re-edited. The heat they generated in these two scenes is obvious when you see the film that finally came out in 1946 and earned rave reviews.

The Big Sleep remains one of my all-time favorite mystery movies. The beautiful Max Steiner score—with its haunting love theme for Bogart and Bacall—is worth the price of the DVD alone. But the movie itself is a grabber and it's loaded with lots of great little performances, including Martha Vickers as sexy Carmen and then-unknown Dorothy Malone, a future Oscar winner (for Best Supporting Actress in 1956's *Written on the Wind*), as a horny bookshop clerk who takes off her eyeglasses so Marlowe will realize what a babe she is. (He does and she was!). Also very special is Elisha Cook, Jr., as a small-time hood who helps Marlowe. Bogart fans will remember Cook as the incompetent gunman easily disarmed by Bogart in *The Maltese Falcon*. Former cowboy star Bob Steele is also a standout, playing against type as a gangland killer who shoots it out with Marlowe, much to his misfortune.

Howard Hawks' *The Big Sleep* is another case of a classic book becoming a classic film, even though some fundamental story changes were made. Both book and film still hold up very well.

Making another version of such a classic is always a risky affair, but English director Michael Winner—best remembered for his three Charles Bronson *Death Wish* films (1974–85)—took the challenge in 1978, casting durable Hollywood tough guy Robert Mitchum as Marlowe, but moving the detective all the way from his familiar 1940s Los Angeles digs to contemporary London in the age of Carnaby Street and British 1970s *chic*.

Winner's *Big Sleep* actually followed on the heels of Dick Richards' 1975 British film *Farewell, My Lovely*, the third movie version of Chandler's second Marlowe novel and the first to actually use its original title. It, too, moved Marlowe to England in the person of Robert Mitchum.

For years, film fans had talked about Hollywood "bad boy" Mitchum as the ideal Philip Marlowe. He was big, appropriately tough and looked like he could take care of himself in a scrap a little better than the small, rather runty Bogart. Those who really knew Mitchum also saw in him the sort of pessimistic poet figure that Marlowe often seemed to be in his more philosophical moods, often after consuming a few too many drinks. Mitchum was known to consume more than a few too many drinks in his day and could be quite

Robert Mitchum demonstrates his well-worn private eye persona as Raymond Chandler's Philip Marlowe in the 1978 version of *The Big Sleep* (ITC Entertainment and CBS).

effusively philosophical any time he was at least half awake. (Mitchum was drinking heavily the first time I met him and was virtually comatose with drink at our second meeting, both times in conjunction with his 1983 TV miniseries *The Winds of War*.)

But Mitchum in the late 1970s was not what he used to be physically. By the time he got around to playing Marlowe in *The Big Sleep*, he was in his 60s, considerably overweight and no longer very credible as a romantic hero. His vaunted "sleepy-eyed" look was still there, but it now seemed to be less attitude than actual tiredness. In the scene where Carmen—now called "Camilla" (Candy Clark)— shows up naked in his bed, taunting him to make love to her, his lack of interest seems genuine—no doubt because she figures to be more of a workout than he'd be able to handle.

The 1978 *Big Sleep* is a curious mixture of respectfulness for Chandler's original coupled with a ludicrous premise: a handful of American characters involved in a quintessentially American 1940s mystery plot that takes place, for no good reason, in 1970s England. For example, why the obviously American General Sternwood (James Stewart) has an obviously English older daughter, Charlotte (Sarah Miles), and an equally obvious American daughter (Candy Clark, fresh from George Lucas' *American Graffiti*) is never explained.

Still, the film does hew much closer to the Chandler story than Hawks' more famous film. The missing Regan is restored to his proper place in the plot. The book's ending is preserved and no attempt is made to fashion any kind of interesting romance between Marlowe and the general's older daughter. And the relaxed screen code of the 1970s allows the pornographic photos of Camilla to be a plot element, and permits us to see Candy Clark naked as often as possible.

Mitchum's reading of the famous Marlowe lines is disappointing. He seems too arch and literary. He looks world-weary enough, but doesn't seem to invest much sincerity in what he's saying. It might be too harsh to suggest he walks through the role, but the thought does come to mind.

Co-star Miles, always a little eccentric with her characters, makes Charlotte a bit too kooky for my taste and Candy Clark is way overboard for Camilla, who should be a libertine and a tease, but not an outright mental case who needs immediate incarceration.

Among the supporting players, only Stewart as Gen. Sternwood and Oliver Reed as gangster Eddie Mars are really memorable. Joan Collins, just two years before her explosive turn as Alexis Colby on TV's *Dynasty*, already had her reputation as a screen sexpot, so there was no point in trying to make us believe she was the prim bookstore lady who was smoldering inside. Collins would smolder playing a nun—and *did* in the 1957 movie *Sea Wife*.

Even more out of place is American Richard Boone as a sadistic English gangster. The bearded, limping Boone uses a twisted laugh that's supposed to suggest he's dangerously wigged out, but it's so forced that one wonders if director Winner didn't give him a shot of laughing gas before each take. Other major British actors, including the great John Mills, are largely wasted in token parts.

It was a mistake to try transplanting Marlowe and the original Chandler storyline to contemporary London, circa 1978. The British-set versions of *Farewell, My Lovely* and *The Big Sleep* also effectively ended the notion that a Mitchum version of Marlowe would be superior to the Bogart rendition. Bogart remains the essential Marlowe, at least for the first half century-plus after the immortal gumshoe's creation.

Raymond Chandler
The Lady in the Lake

The 1943 novel and the 1946 movie *Lady in the Lake*

By almost any standard, Raymond Chandler's fourth Philip Marlowe novel, *The Lady in the Lake*, is a classic. Published in 1943, it finds Marlowe working for a husband who wants to locate his missing wife. She may or may not be the woman whose body is found on the bottom of a remote mountain lake, near a cabin the couple owned. It might be the body of another missing woman, the wife of the caretaker of the mountain cabin.

The poster for *Lady in the Lake*, the 1946 film where the camera stood in for detective Philip Marlowe (Robert Montgomery), who was seldom seen in the picture (MGM).

The Lady in the Lake

Audrey Totter faces a mirror in *Lady in the Lake*, one of the few moments in the movie where the viewer actually sees her co-star Robert Montgomery as detective Philip Marlowe (MGM).

This is a clever, action-packed novel with the cynical Marlowe giving us another satisfying dose of his opinions about Los Angeles and the mixed-up people who lived there in the turbulent 1940s. It might have been one of the best mystery movies of its era, but, regretfully, it fell into the hands of actor-director Robert Montgomery, who was eager to stun Hollywood by doing something truly memorable with the film.

Well, he certainly did. His *Lady in the Lake* was a precedent-setting abomination, still painful to watch today. It's not that *everything* in the movie is awful. It does have some fine moments. What makes it a disaster is the terrible waste of talent and material that it represents overall. Montgomery's self-indulgent desire to be daring and original ruined one of Chandler's greatest novels.

Montgomery's major act of imbecility was to film the story with an experimental "subjective camera" approach. Using that technique means the camera represents a character in the story. The camera is Philip Marlowe, making us see everything through his eyes. That means the only time we ever see Marlowe himself is when he happens to step in front of a mirror or some other reflecting surface.

Yes, we do also see Montgomery as Marlowe at the beginning and end of the movie— but only in a pair of awkwardly staged sequences in which Montgomery talks directly to the audience.

"You'll see it exactly as I saw it," he tells us, speaking as Marlowe, as if he's our teacher, explaining his great cinematic experiment to a bunch of halfwits.

This ludicrous—and totally unnecessary—gimmick does nothing beneficial for the enjoyment of the film. Rather, it creates problems that hinder our enjoyment of the movie. For example, all the other actors seem to be talking to the camera instead of a real human being when Marlowe is around. Meanwhile, Montgomery speaks his Marlowe lines as if he's reading them from a radio script. It distracts us and irritates us. At times it even infuriates us because it slows down what ought to be a fast-moving story, making it crawl.

There are times when the subjective camera is an interesting way to put the audience in a character's shoes. A classic example: the opening sequence of *This Is Cinerama* (1952), in which the camera is placed in the front car of a roller coaster and everybody in the audience feels like they're in that car as the roller coaster starts its downhill ride.

Delmer Daves, one of Hollywood's most inventive directors, used the subjective camera brilliantly in his *Dark Passage*, made the year after *Lady in the Lake*. In that film, Humphrey Bogart plays a prison convict who escapes, then has plastic surgery to alter his appearance. The camera stands in for Bogart for the first third of the film—while he's supposed to have another face. As soon as his bandages come off, the camera becomes a detached observer, as it usually is in all movies, and we see Bogart head-on.

But Montgomery was determined to shoot the whole movie with a subjective camera and that's what he did, to heck with what moviegoers might think about it.

Montgomery the director also should have realized that Montgomery the actor wasn't the right guy to play Marlowe, a shopworn, pessimistic private eye. In real life, Montgomery was a sophisticated man of considerable means, a political conservative who, after he retired from acting, served as the chief media consultant to Republican President Dwight Eisenhower. He also was an activist in the anti-communist movement that eventually led to the notorious Hollywood blacklist. If he ever turned up on Chandler's famous "mean streets," it most likely was in a chauffeur-driven limousine.

Though Montgomery was a fine actor who had played dark characters quite well upon occasion (the serial killer in 1937's *Night Must Fall* may be the best example), he just didn't have the bearing of a Philip Marlowe, and he wasn't very convincing in the role.

Once Montgomery saddled himself with the awkward story-telling device, he must have realized that the story would have to be altered so that Marlowe not only was in every scene, but also had to be the central figure in every scene.

We can only lament the fact that if Montgomery had just been a little respectful of the great material at hand and tried to put it on the screen without messing it up badly, one of Chandler's best mysteries might have become one of Hollywood's best mystery movies.

Lee Child

One Shot

The 2005 novel and the 2012 movie *Jack Reacher*

After 17 novels and the formation of a solid literary cult over a couple of decades, author Lee Child's popular Jack Reacher character finally reached the screen in 2012 in a big-budget movie based on the ninth novel in the series, *One Shot*. They called the movie *Jack Reacher*.

Fans of suspense and mystery novels by now should be used to the idea that Hollywood likes to change titles, so I doubt if anybody was too upset that *One Shot* became *Jack Reacher*. They may have been more upset that Tom Cruise was picked to play the title character because, at first glance, Cruise seems an unlikely choice as the screen's Jack Reacher.

In the books, Jack Reacher is a giant of a man, built along the lines of a young James Arness—a towering, muscular guy who could snap Tom Cruise's neck with his bare hands and drop kick him through the goal posts of life. I have great respect for Cruise as an actor, though he doesn't get a chance to show off his talent much these days. He brings just the right attitude of cold competence to this role and seeing him as Jack Reacher didn't bother me an iota. In fact, the movie, written and directed by Christopher McQuarrie, is a superb suspense-adventure.

The DVD cover for *Jack Reacher*, the film version of Lee Child's *One Shot* (Paramount).

I discovered Reacher some 20 years ago in the first novel in the series, *Killing Floor*. He's a most unusual sort of modern action hero: a former military policeman, an expert in firearms *and* a superb detective. More importantly, he's a total iconoclast whose life seems to resemble that of Richard Kimble (TV's *The Fugitive*) more than it does, say, Sherlock Holmes.

Reacher now and then winds up with a home address, but seldom actually stays there. He's constantly on the move, carries no papers, doesn't own a car, doesn't carry credit cards and would be very hard to trace if you wanted to find him. Nobody's very likely to steal his identity because hardly anyone really knows who he is.

In the movie, Reacher arrives on the scene in order to make sure that an accused sniper-killer actually meets with justice. Back in the day, during his years in the military, Reacher helped prosecute the man for a similar crime but wasn't able to put the guy away. To Reacher's surprise, the more he looks into the mass shooting the man is charged with, the more he comes to believe the man was set up.

Ultimately, Reacher discovers that a sinister group is behind the mass shooting and many of the victims were killed just to confuse the authorities about who the real target was. As usual, Reacher is operating more or less outside the law, calling upon his own very advanced skills as a soldier and a sleuth.

One of the great things about the movie is the casting of Robert Duvall as the gun expert who helps Reacher figure out who the real bad guys are, then actually chips in to help Reacher in the big climactic shootout between good and evil.

The movie does make quite a few changes to Lee Child's original storyline, but they aren't terribly disturbing. The shooting suspect's sister, a key character in the book, never appears in the movie, and a local TV news reporter who plays a big role in the book is also bleeped out of the central action pretty thoroughly.

In exchange, the film gives us some very strong sequences where Cruise's Reacher re-establishes his credentials as a cinema tough guy. Yes, he's close to the same guy he plays in all those *Mission: Impossible* movies, but he makes Reacher much more credible.

What a fan of the books really wants, I think, is to have the movie version respect the literary vision. That happens with *Jack Reacher*. It's not like the awful change that came over Ross MacDonald's Lew Archer when Paul Newman played the role in *Harper* and *The Drowning Pool*, molding the detective character to his own star image and even changing his name to Lew Harper.

For that reason, I highly recommend *Jack Reacher* to fans of the book and hope that we'll see the same respect for Child's marvelous literary character in any future movies made about him. (Cruise reprised the role in 2016's *Jack Reacher: Never Go Back*.)

Agatha Christie

4:50 from Paddington

The 1957 novel and the 1961 movie *Murder, She Said*; the 1987 TV movie; and the 2004 TV movie *What Mrs. McGillicuddy Saw*

One of the best of Agatha Christie's later Miss Marple novels is *4:50 from Paddington*, known in the U.S. as *What Mrs. McGillicuddy Saw*. It also must have been considered the most dramatically interesting because it has been filmed several times, all with distinctly different Jane Marples.

It has a deceptively simple plot gimmick that wasn't all that original, even in 1957: Someone riding in a railroad car witnesses what seems to be a murder taking place in another railroad car as two trains pass, going in opposite directions on closely parallel tracks.

In the novel, the witness is Elspeth McGillicuddy, an old friend of Miss Marple. Mrs. McGillicuddy is coming to visit Miss Marple in St. Mary Mead before leaving for a trip overseas. Still in shock from what she's seen—and the railroad's apparent indifference to her story—Mrs. McGillicuddy is comforted by Miss Marple, whose own curiosity is piqued by the story. The real puzzler is this: If there was a woman strangled on the train, why was no body found on the train nor on the railroad tracks along its route?

Working with her friend to reconstruct what happened, Miss Marple concludes that the body must have been pushed off the train in the vicinity of the large private estate known as Rutherford Hall, property of the wealthy Crackenthorpe family. She reasons that the killer must have returned quickly and moved the body, possibly hiding it somewhere on the estate, where investigators would not have looked.

Without a corpse to inspire them, the police aren't interested in pursuing the matter. In fact, they treat Miss Marple and Mrs. McGillicuddy pretty much as dotty old ladies who got all worked up about some bit of nonsense on the train that surely wasn't a murder. In other words, if anyone is going to find out about the murder, it will have to be a busybody sleuth like Jane Marple.

The most important thing to remember about Christie's original concept is that she was portraying a much older Jane Marple in *4:50 from Paddington*, one whose doctor has urged her to slow down. She realizes she's physically unfit for the challenges of investigating the murder herself, so she enlists the help of 32-year-old Lucy Eyelesbarrow to handle the leg work.

A handsome, well-educated young woman, Lucy specializes in taking short-term positions as a housekeeper for some of England's wealthiest people. Jane knows her because her nephew Raymond West, the famous novelist, once hired Lucy to take care of Jane as she recovered from a bout of pneumonia. Jane contacts Lucy and asks her to take a job at Rutherford Hall, so she can look for the hidden corpse in her spare time.

Lucy agrees and lands the job—she's young, pretty and absurdly over-qualified, making her a bargain at any price. She reports regularly to Miss Marple, who is staying nearby at an inn run by a former maidservant of hers. Marple digests the information Lucy supplies and soon enough Lucy finds the body of a woman who had been strangled and hidden in a storage building.

So, in *4:50 from Paddington*, Marple functions very much like Rex Stout's armchair detective Nero Wolfe, while Lucy does the on-site detective work, much like Wolfe's sidekick Archie Goodwin.

In the first film version of the novel, MGM's British-made *Murder, She Said* (1961), that whole concept went into the rubbish bin. There is no Lucy because Miss Marple (Margaret Rutherford) does all the detective work herself, getting the housekeeper job so she can skulk around on her own. There is also no Elspeth McGillicuddy because Marple herself saw the strangulation on the passing train. That, of course, meant that Marple had no Elspeth to scout around with before getting her housekeeper job.

Enter a new character: Jim Stringer, a doddering old bookstore clerk and "boyfriend" for the spinster sleuth. Stringer, played by Rutherford's real-life husband Stringer Davis, appears in all four of Rutherford's Marple films. Call it nepotism if you like, but Davis was an agreeable old chap and seemed perfectly suited for Rutherford, if not for the Miss Marple we all cherish.

Rutherford was not the screen's first Miss Marple. That distinction goes to Dame Gracie Fields, the beloved English singer and comedienne who played the part in "A Murder Is Announced," a 1956 episode of America's *Goodyear Television Playhouse*. Rutherford was the first Miss Marple in any feature film—and a radical departure from the Miss Marple of the printed page.

Rutherford was short, rather stout and did lots of mugging for the camera, including many double-takes done in an exaggerated fashion. While the literary Marple was a quiet, even meek-appearing village busybody, Rutherford was like a giant stone rolling down a hill. Her presence almost by itself turns *Murder, She Said* into more comedy than mystery.

In one sequence, Miss Marple and Mr. Stringer find the spot by the railroad tracks where they think the body was dumped. Marple is sure the killer hauled the corpse to a nearby stone fence and pushed it over. She wants to climb up and see what's beyond the wall, which leads to an embarrassing bit of slapstick in which the hapless Mr. Stringer has to hold her up high enough to peek over the wall, her rear end nearly in his face. It never fails to get a big laugh from any audience, even though the real Miss Marple would never do such a thing—nor generate such laughs.

When Miss Marple finally goes to Rutherford Hall to apply for the job, she's greeted by the manor's chief housekeeper, Mrs. Kidder, who takes her into the kitchen for a brief chat. This is a historic moment in mystery trivia since Mrs. Kidder is played by Joan Hickson, who would play the role of Miss Marple two decades later on the acclaimed British television series *Agatha Christie's Miss Marple*. (Once when Hickson was appearing in a play in London's West End, Agatha Christie approached her backstage after a performance. Christie told her she would be an ideal Jane Marple "when you're a little older.")

Though the storyline otherwise resembles Christie's original, eliminating the Lucy character probably was quite jarring to readers who enjoyed the book and understood where it fell in the long saga of Jane Marple's many cases. But it's best to remember that *Murder, She Said* was the first film about Miss Marple and it was based on a book that occurs in the late stages of Marple's life. If they had followed Christie's story faithfully, those not familiar with the book might have wondered why the famous "detective" wasn't taking a more active role in solving the case and instead was turning it over to a stand-in. Still, *Murder, She Said* was enormously popular and led to three more feature films starring Rutherford as Marple, so perhaps the end justified the means in MGM's eyes.

Veteran actress Rutherford employed lots of comic schtick that was totally out of place for Jane Marple. Ron Goodwin's infectious musical score wasn't

Margaret Rutherford as Agatha Christie's elderly sleuth Miss Jane Marple. She played the role in four films starting with *Murder She Said* (1961), based on Christie's novel *4:50 from Paddington* (MGM).

subtle either, making sure moviegoers didn't forget they were watching a comedy. But the four Marple films brought about a great career revival for Rutherford, who went on to win an Academy Award for a supporting part in MGM's *The V.I.P.s*.

The next version of *4.50 from Paddington* was a 1997 television adaptation with Joan Hickson as Miss Marple. It kept Christie's original title and hewed much more closely to the novel. Elspeth McGillicuddy (Mona Bruce) witnesses the murder and Jane Marple takes up her case after the authorities frustrate her attempts to identify the victim or her attacker. Screenwriter T.R. Bowen replaced the book's Inspector Craddock (played by Charles Tingwell in *Murder, She Said*) with Detective Inspector Slack (David Horovitch), who serves as Marple's eternally perturbed police ally-adversary through several of the Hickson films. (Slack refers to Marple, not exactly affectionately, as "quite the local busybody.") Lucy (played by Jill Meager) also makes her first appearance on screen and, because she's very attractive, creates quite a stir among the males at Rutherford Hall.

Hickson's Marple is older, drier and much less demonstrative than Rutherford's. Neither Hickson nor, we expect, the real Marple of Christie's imagination would ever be caught dead climbing over a stone wall, Rutherford-style, with some man helping to heft her rear end. There are no pratfalls nor comedy gags in the Hickson version. Those who favor the Rutherfords have been known to refer to the later Hickson versions as much slower in pace.

Like the others in the Hickson series, *4.50 from Paddington* was beautifully filmed in color around English village locales and featured a superb cast, including Maurice Denham and Joanna David. In contrast, the Rutherford *Murder, She Said* was a black and white film and had some casting peculiarities, such as American actor Arthur Kennedy as the story's *bête noire*, Dr. Quimper.

After Hickson's 1998 death, there were no Marple films until 2004, when the BBC decided to remake all the classic Marple novels. Geraldine McEwan was a younger, more stylish Jane Marple, who colors her hair and avoids the dowdy look that Hickson always affected for the character, in keeping with Christie's vision of her.

The McEwan version of the story, which uses the American title *What Mrs. McGillicuddy Saw*, also follows the Christie novel fairly closely. Mrs. McGillicuddy (Pam Ferris) witnesses what she believes is a murder just as her train pulls out of a station and passes another train. Marple persuades Lucy (Amanda Holden) to become a Rutherford Hall maid, as in the book. One significant change: Marple takes up temporary lodging near Rutherford Hall, not with a former servant but with a local constable, who shows considerable romantic interest in the fetching Lucy.

The McEwan version also starts with a major change in the Christie narrative: a flashback showing a deathbed sequence that later turns out to have profound significance in terms of the murder case. It's not effective, though, because we don't yet really know who the people are in that flashback and it only serves to confuse what should have been a straightforward story, letting us meet the major players as the story unfolds in real time. This version has no Inspector Craddock or Inspector Slack. It gives us Inspector Awdry (Rob Brydon).

Another peculiarity is a strange London party sequence near the start of the film where we see Lucy hobnobbing with Noël Coward (Pip Torrens), which seems rather extraneous to say the least. Lucy's romantic leanings also seem to take a lot more time than justified.

For a purist, the Joan Hickson version is closer to Christie's vision than the others, but, truthfully, they're all quite entertaining films—even the clownish Margaret Rutherford edition. So, your enjoyment may depend upon how seriously you take your Christie and how sacrosanct you feel Miss Marple ought to remain as a character.

Mary Higgins Clark
The Cradle Will Fall

The 1980 novel and the 1983 and 2004 TV movies

This clever suspense novel was one of the early bestsellers that helped make Mary Higgins Clark America's "queen of suspense" in the last few decades of the 20th century. Clark's specialty was the "woman in jeopardy" storyline that linked her to a fine tradition in the American mystery genre that stretched all the way back to 1908 and Mary Roberts Rinehart's *The Circular Staircase*.

By the 1980s, the "woman in jeopardy" storyline had become a much relied upon formula for the modern made-for-television movie, which most often aimed for female viewers who especially enjoyed watching women as leading characters in tense suspense dramas with romantic undertones.

That made *The Cradle Will Fall* a very valuable commodity for a TV network anxious to find an already popular novel with female readers who might relish seeing it turned into a movie the network could load up with commercials for woman-oriented products.

In Clark's novel, Katie DeMaio, an assistant county prosecutor, unravels the mystery behind a series of deaths of women all linked to a single physician, Edgar Highley, who was secretly using his patients as guinea pigs in experiments with drugs he hoped would prolong youth indefinitely.

Katie was recently widowed, but involved in a new romance with Richard Carroll, the local medical examiner, who ultimately joins her in searching for clues to the deaths. The harrowing climax comes when Katie herself is being treated for a blood disorder by Dr. Highley and suddenly finds her own life in immediate jeopardy.

Once the *Cradle Will Fall* film rights were sold, the book's journey to the screen took a most unusual route that could not have given author Clark much cheer. It wound up in the hands of producer Joseph Cates, who partnered with the CBS network and Proctor & Gamble, the soap manufacturer. They decided to turn the book into a TV movie for airing on May 24, 1983, as an "event" for the May ratings "sweeps," a time in which intensive local ratings surveys are taken so local stations can set advertising rates for the next sales period. The networks put on lots of special programming during "sweeps" in order to help their affiliated stations get the highest possible ratings, so they could charge higher ad rates.

The master plan was truly off the wall. Proctor & Gamble wanted to move some of the most popular characters from its daytime soap opera, *The Guiding Light*, into the cast of *The Cradle Will Fall*. CBS liked the idea, because it figured fans of the daytime show would flock to the movie in prime time, increasing its rating, while prime time viewers might be intrigued by the soap opera characters enough to start watching them on *The Guiding Light*, thereby increasing *that* show's ratings. It surely was viewed at CBS as a win-win proposition. (*The Guiding Light* ran for an amazing 57 years on television, finally coming to an end in 2009. Its legacy was even longer if you count radio, where it began to weave its stories in 1937 on NBC before switching over to CBS Radio a decade later.)

But how could you take daytime soap opera characters who live and work in a mythical community called Springfield and suddenly have them appear in Chapin River, the mythical town where Clark's mystery takes place? Well, that was easy: You just take Clark's story and characters and move them into the soap opera setting of Springfield.

But there were other changes that had to be made. Katie DeMaio worked for Valley County District Attorney Scott Meyerson in the novel, but he had to be eliminated when filming began because Katie now had to work for the Springfield D.A., Ross Marker. He was one of the soap opera characters, played by Jerry Ver Dorn, and they wanted him to be in the movie.

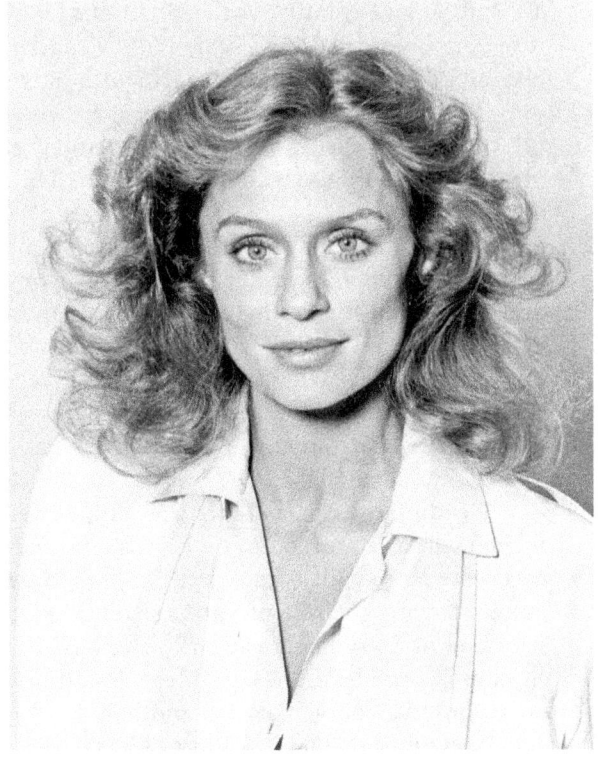

Lauren Hutton was the star of NBC's 1983 TV movie version of Mary Higgins Clark's *The Cradle Will Fall* (NBC).

Another major soap personality had to be worked into the movie storyline: "Bert" Bauer, played by longtime *Guiding Light* regular Charita Bauer. They solved that by making her the close friend and confidant of Edna Burns, a key witness in one of the mysterious deaths, who's murdered in order to keep her quiet. They also gave Katie a new personal physician—Springfield's Dr. Ed Bauer (Peter Simon)—and added a Springfield police detective, Larry Wyatt (Joe Ponazecki), to the mix of characters. Two other prominent soap people made unexpected appearances in Clark's story: Hope Spaulding (Elvera Roussel) and Lesley Ann Monroe (Carolyn Ann Clark).

The effort to cross-pollinate the Clark novel with daytime soap opera characters wasn't a one-way street. The producers cleverly took a character from the novel—Katie's romantic interest Richard Carroll—and wrote him into the soap opera for several episodes leading up to the movie's premiere to help whet the daytime viewers' appetite for seeing him in the prime time movie. And it probably helped that the actor who played Dr. Carroll in both movie and soap opera was Ben Murphy, a veteran TV player who had starred in several TV shows, including *Alias Smith and Jones.*

Though the attempt to soap-opera-ize Clark's novel may have irritated fans of the book, it didn't negatively impact the movie too badly. The film had two very appealing lead actors in Lauren Hutton, the famous model-turned-actress, as Katie and seasoned

TV star James Farentino as the villainous Dr. Highley. Hutton had worked mostly in feature films before making *Cradle Will Fall* and her performance is quite capable. Farentino also nicely balanced sinister charm with outright nastiness.

There's also a special bonus for those who seek out the 1983 *Cradle Will Fall*: a youthful William H. Macy, now widely regarded as one of America's best character actors, playing a pathologist who helps uncover Dr. Highley's use of the deadly experimental drugs.

In 2004, a new *Cradle Will Fall* was filmed by a Canadian company for American cable TV showing. It was then the latest in a new wave of Mary Higgins Clark adaptations, first by the Family Channel cable network and then the Lifetime cable network. This new version, directed by Rob King, featured Clark's original characters, including Katie's real boss, although District Attorney Scott Meyerson now has a new first name (Alex) and spells his surname Myerson. The 2004 version also turns down the heat between Katie and Richard Carroll as if their romance hadn't quite flowered yet. The local signs no longer say "Springfield."

Heading the cast as Katie was Angie Everhart, playing a part not that far from her former role as a prosecutor on NBC's *Law and Order: Special Victims Unit*. Others in the cast were largely little known TV actors, mostly Canadian. The big exception was the actress playing the role of Katie's sister, Molly: Carol Higgins Clark, the actress-novelist daughter of Mary Higgins Clark, who has appeared in several of the TV versions of her mother's bestsellers. The daughter has authored many popular mysteries of her own and co-authored a couple with her mother.

Though the 2004 version of *Cradle Will Fall* may be slightly more faithful to the novel and doesn't contain the embarrassing soap opera connection, it's nowhere near as suspenseful as the 1983 version, which benefited from a better screenplay structure and the more reliable direction of John Llewellyn Moxey, who was quite skilled in the suspense genre.

Wilkie Collins

The Woman in White

The 1860 novel, the 1940 movie
Crimes at the Dark House and the 1948 movie

Wilkie Collins' *The Woman in White* first appeared in serial format in the English magazine *All the Year Round*, which was owned by Collins' close friend, author Charles Dickens. Its opening segment appeared in the same issue that contained the final segment of Dickens' *A Tale of Two Cities*, a very popular success already—and it gave *Woman in White* a great sendoff.

The Collins serial built an even larger readership than Dickens' book and quickly became the rage of London. It helped Collins on his way to becoming one of the 19th century's most successful writers of "sensational stories."

His story was "sensational," all right. It's about the efforts of two colorfully corrupt villains—Italian Count Fosco and Sir Percival Glyde—to strip lovely young heiress Laura

Sydney Greenstreet, one of Hollywood's all-time great bad guys, takes command of Alexis Smith in the 1948 version of Wilkie Collins' *The Woman in White* **(Warner Bros).**

Fairlie of her wealth and family properties through a bizarre scheme. Fosco is a monumental heavy—erudite and mannered, yet grossly fat and in the habit of playing with his personal collection of white mice, which he permits to crawl over his immense bulk, in and out of his clothing, at will.

Fosco plans to marry Laura to Sir Percival, a bounder unfortunately chosen as her future husband by her late father. They easily gain full approval of her guardian, her distracted uncle Frederick Fairlie, a neurotic invalid. Once that's done, they then intend to fake Laura's death by killing her nearly exact double, insane asylum escapee Anne Catherick, and burying her in the family plot. Even before the false Laura is buried, they'll turn the real Laura over to the asylum, passing her off as the fugitive lunatic. Locked up in the nuthouse, where nobody will believe she's really the late Lady Glyde, Laura will be unable to stop Sir Percival and Fosco from ransacking her bank accounts and plundering her estate.

Complicating their master plan are Laura's cousin Marian Halcombe, who lives with Laura at Limmeridge, the Fairlie estate, and Walter Hartright, a young painter working as an art instructor for the two women, who has fallen in love with Laura.

This elaborate romantic mystery with Gothic trimmings was inspired by a real-life courtroom case that Collins had read about in Mejan's *Recueil des Causes Célèbres*, a book that Collins had found in a Paris bookstall in 1856. In that case, Adelaide, the Marquise de Douhault, had been the victim of a similar scheme to drain her assets.

But perhaps an even more profound influence was Collins' real-life encounter with his own "woman in white" in 1859, the year he began writing the novel. Collins and his brother Charles were walking party guest John Everett Millais to his home through the semi-rural roadways of northern London when they heard a woman's scream and stopped to investigate. The gate of a nearby villa opened and a beautiful young woman, dressed all in white, came running out, briefly stopped in front of the three men, then ran off into the darkness. Collins alone followed her.

The frantic lady turned out to be 25-year-old widow Caroline Elizabeth Graves, who told Collins she'd been held as a prisoner for several months by a man with whom she'd been romantically involved. She had fled when he approached her with a poker, threatening to bash her brains out. Collins, about 35 and never-married, was instantly entranced by the beautiful stranger.

Thus began the most compelling romantic relationship of his life. Collins and Mrs. Graves became lovers and for years she lived with him—or in lodgings he provided close by—as his mistress. Though Caroline later married another man and Collins took up with Martha Rudd, who bore his children, the author and his "woman in white" were reunited in subsequent years. He legally adopted Harriet, her daughter by her first husband, and provided for both of them in his will. Caroline Graves lived with him for the last 20 years of his life and, upon her own death in 1895, was buried with Collins at Kensal Green Cemetery.

Hailed as a mystery classic from the start, *The Woman in White* was destined to be turned into a motion picture as soon as filmmakers began to make adaptations of famous books in the early days of the new medium. In 1912, two different versions were filmed, the first by the Gem Corp. with distribution by Universal Film Manufacturing Co., and the second by Thanhouser Pictures, featuring James Cruze as Count Fosco. Cruze would become more famous as a film director with his silent classics *The Covered Wagon* (1923) and *Old Ironsides* (1926).

Two more silent versions were made, a 1917 American version about which little is known and a 1929 British version by director Herbert Wilcox. The latter featured the popular silent pictures star Blanche Sweet as Laura Fairlie.

The first notable sound movie version was England's *Crimes at the Dark House*, one of a series of *grand guignol*–style horror movies made by director George King with actor Tod Slaughter, who plays Sir Percival Glyde. Slaughter certainly was one of the least subtle film actors of all time, employing broad gestures and grotesque cackles as he went about his villainy on the screen. When he advances upon the terrified Laura (Sylvia Marriott) to have his brutal, drunken way with her on their wedding night, he's even shown in immense close-up, growling "Heh, heh, heh!" in the manner of "Oil Can Harry" villains of the early silent pictures.

It's easy to understand why they didn't use Collins' book title for the movie: Screenwriter Edward Dryhurst gave it a massive rewrite, turning Sir Percival into the archvillain of the piece and Count Fosco, the real *bête noire* of Collins' novel, into little more than an ineffectual sidekick. From the shocking opening sequence, we know we're in for a major overhaul of the original: Sinister Slaughter creeps up behind the real Percival Glyde, who's visiting Australia, and hammers a spike into his skull, killing him instantly. Chuckling like a maniac, he then assumes Glyde's identity.

When the False Sir Percival turns up at the Fairlie estate in England, he checks first to make sure there are no surviving servants who might remember the real Sir Percival. When he is introduced to the newest chambermaid, he actually licks his lips in anticipation of the fun he'll have with her! (She ends up being strangled and dumped down a well.)

Though Sir Percival pretty much takes his orders from Count Fosco in the novel, the movie makes it clear that Fosco (Hay Petrie), who's a small, unimposing fellow on screen, operates in constant fear of Percival. Little wonder. Actor Slaughter was a huge man and Percival sounds like he means business when he tells Fosco, "Fail and I'll feed your entrails to the pigs!"

He doesn't twirl his moustache when he lumbers toward the slim Laura in their bridal chamber, but he chuckles loudly, enjoying the sight of her trembling with fear at the thought of his monstrous bulk descending upon her, and tells her, "Come, my little bride. Cheer up! This is your wedding night!"

Collins' story is so chewed up by the movie that by the climax hardly anything remains unchanged. In the book, Sir Percival burns to death when he accidentally locks himself in an old church where he's attempting to burn records that would reveal his past villainy. But Fosco lives on to threaten Lady Glyde for quite a few more chapters until he's finally forced to flee England by Walter Hartwright (called "Paul" Hartwright in the movie), who has found evidence to prosecute him.

In the movie, Sir Percival strangles Fosco after they quarrel—and then he dies in the fire, the story's true villain to the end.

Eight years later, a new version of *The Woman in White* was made by Warner Bros. Directed by Peter Godfrey, the 1948 production was lavishly mounted, filmed on atmospheric sets and given a rousing musical score by the great Max Steiner. Oddly, the cast was loaded with quintessentially American actors, not one of them attempting a British accent: Eleanor Parker in the dual role of Laura Fairlie and Ann Catherick; Alexis Smith as Marian; Gig Young as Walter Hartright; John Emery as Sir Percival Glyde and Agnes Moorehead as the Countess Fosco. The two British-born actors in the cast—Sydney Greenstreet as Count Fosco and John Abbott as Frederick Fairlie—were so familiar to American movie fans that *they* almost seemed American, too.

Though the 1948 film is much more faithful to Collins than the grotesque 1940 version, it also makes wholesale story changes. For example, just when it appears that poor Laura is about to lose her mind—and her good looks—from her stay in the asylum, Walter starts falling in love with cousin Marian—and eventually winds up marrying her!

Collins had underscored the fact that Marian was plain-looking and wholly dedicated to the idea of helping her beloved Laura find happiness with Walter, even though we readers always suspected she had a yen for him, too. But the movie sabotages that notion by having the young, lively and extremely attractive Alexis Smith playing Marian. Still, Gig Young's Walter comes off as somewhat callow once we see him start responding to Marian as soon as Laura is out of sight.

The 1948 film also ditches the Dickensian flourishes Collins gave the Fosco character. Gone are the pet white mice and their antics, along with his collection of canaries. In their place, we get a monkey that sits on Fosco's shoulder like a parrot. Perhaps director Godfrey couldn't find a reliable "mice wrangler" to control the rodents on a soundstage. Alas, the age of digital mice was still half a century away.

Another mammoth change involves Countess Fosco. She sniffs out his real secret plan: He wants to grab Marian for himself once Laura is put away. Mrs. Fosco is so ticked at this betrayal of her loyalty that she ends up saving Marian from the fate worse than death, plunging a dagger into Fosco's back and finishing him off for good just moments before hero Walter arrives with help.

Altogether, the 1948 *Woman in White* isn't a bad film, though it does seem a little too Hollywoody for its own good. Gig Young, who gives the most embarrassing performance as the very un-romantic, un-dashing and un-heroic Walter, went on to win a Best Supporting Actor Oscar 21 years later as the sleazy dance promoter in *They Shoot Horses, Don't They?* (1969).

As good as Greenstreet is as Fosco, he still seems to be playing his *other* famous fat man, Casper Gutman from *The Maltese Falcon*. Probably the best in this cast is John Abbott, whose shaky-quaky Frederick Fairlie was the best of them all until Ian Richardson came along to own the role a few decades later in a British TV remake.

All the subsequent English-language versions of *The Woman in White* have been made for television, starting with the BBC's 1966 version, shown in six 25-minute chapters with Jennifer Hilary as Laura and Ann.

Much more memorable was the 1982 BBC version in which Laura Fairlie was played by the young and lovely Jenny Seagrove, best known in America for her starring role in the TV miniseries *A Woman of Substance*. Diana Quick was Marian, Alan Badel was Count Fosco (complete with hordes of mice) and the incomparable Ian Richardson played an effete and fast-failing Frederick Fairlie, deathly afraid of the slightest noise or ray of excessive sunlight. (This version had its American premiere in 1985 on PBS' *Mystery!*)

Still another British TV version premiered in 1997. Under the direction of Tim Fywell, Tara Fitzgerald was Marian, Justine Waddell was Laura, James Wilby was Sir Percival Glyde, Ian Richardson reprised his classic Frederick Fairlie portrayal and Simon Callow played Count Fosco. It was the most faithful adaptation of Collins' novel.

Sir Arthur Conan Doyle
A Study in Scarlet

The 1887 novel and the 1933 movie

It would be natural to assume that *A Study in Scarlet* would be exactly the right place to start any discussion of the films made from the Sherlock Holmes stories of Arthur Conan Doyle. After all, it was the very first Sherlock Holmes story, appearing in an 1887 edition of *Beeton's Christmas Annual*.

But for this 1933 film, the filmmakers pretty much just kept the title and threw away the story. Produced at Tiffany studios by the KBS Co., it was from an original storyline dreamed up by writer-director Robert Florey and actor Reginald Owen, who played Sherlock Holmes in the film. Though they borrowed a few bits and pieces from other Holmes stories, there's virtually nothing in the movie that connects it to the first Holmes adventure.

Why would they do that? It's believed they felt the original story was no longer filmable because of its controversial contents—a rather virulent attack against the Church of Latter-Day Saints (LDS), depicting its Mormon followers as unsavory villains who belonged to a cult that practiced polygamy. And they probably were right: Any film that made the Mormons out to be villains surely would have been widely protested by members of that faith worldwide.

Instead, Florey and Owen concocted a story about the systematic murdering of the members of a secret London-based organization known as the Scarlet Ring. Holmes is drawn into the affair when he's contacted by the daughter of one of the murder victims, seeking the truth about the fate of her father.

Holmes eventually discovers that the killings were motivated by greed because the group's seven original members had agreed that the others would share the fortunes of any member who dies. We never are told exactly what sort of investments these conspirators were involved with, but one can assume they were not totally legal.

Reginald Owen as Sherlock Holmes in the 1933 *A Study in Scarlet*. Owen had played Dr. Watson in an earlier Sherlock Holmes movie (World Wide Pictures).

In the literary canon left behind by Conan Doyle, *A Study in Scarlet* is important because it portrays a younger Holmes and how he gets started in the private investigating business with his old friend and partner, Dr. John Watson. The movie skips all that and just shows us Holmes and Watson doing business as usual at their Baker Street lodgings in London. (Purists will blanche when Holmes runs a classified ad in the newspaper and lists his address as 221A Baker Street. Even a beginner at Holmes lore knows he lives at 221B.)

One of England's finest character actors, Owen spent most of his long career working in America in MGM movies, most notably the 1938 version of Dickens' *A Christmas Carol*, in which he played Ebenezer Scrooge. I met Owen when he was in his 80s and doing community theater in Northern California. At that time, he had no particular fond memories of playing Sherlock Holmes, but did remind me that he was one of the few actors who could claim to have played both Holmes and, a year earlier, Dr. Watson to Clive Brook's Sherlock Holmes in the 1932 Fox film *Sherlock Holmes*.

Owen's Holmes is perhaps the least eccentric of all the Sherlocks. He seems like a nice, gentlemanly fellow with an incredibly sharp mind. His Dr. Watson was the undistinguished Warburton Gamble. Inspector Lestrade was played by Alan Mowbray, who's best remembered today for the many English butlers and servants he played. Anna May Wong plays a sinister widow, and the *bête noire* is a lawyer named Thaddeus Merrydew, played with relish by Alan Dinehart.

If Robert Florey had directed *A Study in Scarlet*, it might have been a more enjoyable picture, despite its lack of fidelity to the original. A specialist in *outre* themes and atmospheric sets, Florey's films included Universal's *Murders in the Rue Morgue* (1932) with Bela Lugosi and two memorable films with Peter Lorre—Columbia's *The Face Behind the Mask* (1940) and Warners' *The Beast with Five Fingers* (1946). Unfortunately, he was called away to another project and *A Study in Scarlet* was directed by newcomer Edwin L. Marin, who had only done one prior film.

If you come to this movie expecting to compare it to the book, forget about it. As an example of an early Sherlock Holmes movie, it's too talky and you're not likely to rank Reginald Owen among your favorite Sherlocks.

Sir Arthur Conan Doyle
The Hound of the Baskervilles

The 1901 novel and the 1939 and 1959 movies

One of only four Sherlock Holmes novels that Conan Doyle wrote, *The Hound of the Baskervilles* is the most famous of them all and has been the one most often filmed for the movie screen and for television. There have been at the very least 20 screen adaptations.

There are several reasons why this Holmes tale stands out. It has the most outrageous plot, bordering on the supernatural: Holmes must solve the mystery of a series of ghastly deaths in the Baskerville family, stretching back centuries, in which the most recent heir to the family fortune is always killed by a gigantic red-eyed hound, fulfilling a family curse.

It also has perhaps the most mysterious setting: A lonely estate on the fog-shrouded moors of Devonshire near Dartmoor Prison. This dreary setting is also a dangerous one because of the quicksand-like "mires" scattered through the moors.

The story is also noted as the one in which Holmes' assistant, Dr. John Watson, plays the largest role—actually starting the investigation himself at the remote Baskerville estate because Holmes says he's engaged elsewhere. Holmes appears in the early chapters, but is missing for a large part of the novel before returning to solve the mystery.

Finally, *Hound* is important for the significant role it played in Conan Doyle's career. He had decided to quit writing about the detective and, in the short story called "The Final Problem," actually killed Holmes off in a tumble over Switzerland's Reichenbach Falls during a stirring battle with criminal mastermind Prof. Moriarty. Conan Doyle went eight years without publishing another Holmes story, then was intrigued when his friend Bertram Fletcher Robinson told him of the Devonshire legend of a giant killer hound. Conan Doyle began writing the story and realized it was a perfect mystery for Sherlock Holmes to solve.

Even though Holmes was supposedly dead, Conan Doyle marketed the novel to eager publishers as an "untold story" from Holmes' past, dating back before his "death."

Published first in 1901 as a serial in the magazine *The Strand*, then later as a book, *The Hound of the Baskervilles* became a huge bestseller. Its success finally persuaded Conan Doyle to declare that Holmes hadn't died after all, so he could bring him back for a whole new series of adventures.

The poster for the 1939 *The Hound of the Baskervilles* (20th Century–Fox).

Basil Rathbone (right) as Sherlock Holmes and Nigel Bruce (left) as Dr. Watson find the body of the escaped convict on the English moors in *The Hound of the Baskervilles*. **In the movie, the convict was played by the slender Nigel de Brulier, but in this photo it's a younger, stockier and unidentified actor.**

Movie versions of the story began as early as 1915 and many others followed in the silent and early sound era in England, America and Germany. The best-known, most widely seen movie version was made in 1939 by 20th Century–Fox, introducing English actors Basil Rathbone as Holmes and Nigel Bruce as Watson. The studio made two elaborate and costly Holmes films back-to-back, *Hound* and *The Adventures of Sherlock Holmes*. They surely were intended as the start of a series to run along with the studio's other two established detective series featuring Chinese-American sleuth Charlie Chan and Japanese secret agent Mr. Moto.

But the series didn't continue at Fox. A few years later, Universal signed up Rathbone and Bruce and starred them in another dozen Sherlock Holmes movies, a series that lasted until 1946. Rathbone (1892–1967) is often cited as the best of all the movie Sherlocks, although a great many Holmes fans prefer the late Jeremy Brett (1935–95), who played the role only on television. Rathbone's 16 Holmes movies and his large number of radio performances as Holmes may give him the deeper legacy, but Brett appeared in TV versions of 41 different Holmes stories, the largest slice any actor has ever taken of the total Holmes canon of 56 short stories and four novels.

Still, Rathbone was electrifying as Holmes in his debut in the 1939 *Hound*. His lean, athletic figure, sharp aquiline nose and resonant, booming voice made him seem almost the personification of Conan Doyle's detective. He even resembled some of the most famous drawings of Holmes used to illustrate Conan Doyle's original stories.

Rathbone was one of the movie industry's best swordsmen, a skill Holmes had also perfected, and the actor's intense persona made him one of Hollywood's most effective villains. In fact, just the year before *Hound*, Rathbone gave one of the screen's great villainous portrayals as Sir Guy of Gisbourne in *The Adventures of Robin Hood*, losing out to Errol Flynn in an epic swordfight still considered one of the movies' all-time action sequences.

If Rathbone was the quintessential Holmes, his co-star Nigel Bruce was far from an ideal Dr. Watson in the opinion of many Holmes purists. Though a wonderfully endearing actor, Bruce played Watson as a rather bumbling old fool rather than as the admiring partner to Holmes that Conan Doyle created. Holmes and Watson were about the same age in the stories, but Bruce's Watson seems so much older than Holmes that he often seems like his dotty grandfather. Still, if you can set aside your memories of the Watson that Conan Doyle gave us, there's a lot of humor and affection in Bruce's Watson that probably helped make the series so popular with moviegoers for so long.

The 1939 movie begins with the visit of Dr. Mortimer to Holmes and Watson's 221B Baker Street flat. It's one of the most memorable Holmes-Watson sequences in all the stories because it so vividly demonstrates Holmes' uncanny ability to deduce things through careful observation. Dr. Mortimer had already stopped by, while they were out, and left behind his walking stick. Holmes and Watson examine it in an attempt to deduce the character of their visitor. Watson draws a series of conclusions that seem quite logical until Holmes makes his own deductions, which prove most of Watson's wrong.

In the book, for example, Holmes notes the tooth marks of a dog on the walking stick—and when Mortimer returns, he has his dog, a small Spaniel, with him, proving Holmes right. (In the 1939 movie, Mortimer tells Holmes, "I used to have a dog—a small Spaniel—but it died.")

Mortimer leads Holmes into investigating the Baskerville mystery, so he's an important character. He's played in the 1939 movie by Lionel Atwill, an actor who was much older—and stouter—than the man Conan Doyle describes in the book. For the film, though, it was ideal casting because Atwill came to the project with a well-established sinister bearing from his portrayals in such classic 1930s horror films as *Mystery of the Wax Museum* (1933), *The Vampire Bat* (1933) and *Murders in the Zoo* (1933). Also in 1939, he co-starred with Rathbone in *Son of Frankenstein*. So moviegoers naturally were suspicious of Atwill from the start, which made him especially useful to the filmmakers as a red herring and, for a while, the chief suspect. (Atwill played Holmes' No. 1 adversary, Prof. Moriarty, in 1942's *Sherlock Holmes and the Secret Weapon*, the first of Universal's Holmes films.)

Holmes agrees to look into the mystery of the hound and the potential threat to the latest heir, Sir Henry Baskerville (Richard Greene), but sends Watson ahead to start the investigation while he remains in London to clear up a prior case. (In reality, Holmes goes on ahead of Watson and watches the Baskerville estate from a hideout on the moors, disguised as a peddler.)

The 1939 film largely stays with the Conan Doyle story, but does make some interesting changes. Mr. and Mrs. Barrymore, the husband-and-wife caretakers at Baskerville Hall, become the "Barrymans" in the movie. Several sources suggest the name change was made because the three famous acting Barrymores—John, Lionel and Ethel—were then still big names in Hollywood and it might prove distracting to moviegoers to have their surname bandied about in the film. (The movie uses Mr. Barryman as a red herring, casting yet another actor known for his screen villainy—John Carradine—in the part.)

A more conventional reason was probably behind the decision to make the other most obvious alteration to the original story: The studio surely thought the public would appreciate a happy ending for Sir Henry's romance with Beryl Stapleton (Wendy Barrie), so she is not revealed to be the secret wife of the villainous John Stapleton (Morton Lowry), as she is in the book. Guilty of no crime, she is free to marry Sir Henry and share in his good fortune. Romance was never part of the program for Holmes, a dedicated bachelor, so it made sense for the movie to build up the romance between Greene and Barrie, then two very attractive young stars.

For 20 years after the success of the widely praised 1939 version, no really outstanding new versions were released. But in 1959 the English company Hammer Films produced a new *Hound of the Baskervilles*, the first in color, which immediately drew many supporters because of its expensive look, its action-packed pace and the casting of Peter Cushing as Sherlock Holmes and Christopher Lee as Sir Henry Baskerville.

Beginning in 1957, Hammer specialized in lavish new color versions of great horror classics: *The Curse of Frankenstein* (1957) starred Cushing as Dr. Frankenstein and Lee as his monster. Hammer followed that with *Horror of Dracula* (1958), a remake of the 1931 *Dracula* with Lee as Count Dracula and Cushing as his nemesis, Prof. Van Helsing. In 1959, Hammer remade Universal's *The Mummy's Hand* (1940) as *The Mummy* with Lee as Kharis, the living mummy, and Cushing as famous archeologist John Banning. These films established Cushing and Lee as potent box office names in the horror field.

Obviously that was the reason Hammer's *Hound* was conceived more as a horror film than a detective mystery. The fog-shrouded moors gave it the perfect horror environment and the bloodthirsty hound its "monster." The scholarly looking Cushing is a convincing Holmes, though he's not the physical match that Rathbone was. For Lee, cast against type as Sir Henry, it was a rare chance to play a romantic role, which included genuine love scenes with the leading lady.

The 1959 movie's Dr. Watson, Andre Morell, is most definitely more the Conan Doyle character—a clever, thoughtful man who doesn't dither about the way Nigel Bruce did in the 1939 version. Many have judged him the best of all the screen Watsons.

Peter Cushing (right) as Sherlock Holmes with Andre Morell as Dr. Watson in Hammer Films' 1959 version of *The Hound of the Baskervilles* (United Artists and Hammer Films).

If there is a major departure from Conan Doyle, it comes in the character of Beryl Stapleton, who becomes Cecile Stapleton, a much more impulsive and earthy version of the character, especially as played by sexy, voluptuous Marla Landi. She has the look of the rebel about her, a distinct move away from the canny gentlewoman of the original story and the 1939 film.

At the film's climax, Cecile reveals her unsavory attitudes as the hound comes running for Sir Henry and tells him she has waited for this moment all her life. Holmes and Watson shoot the hound before it can tear Sir Henry apart. Then, departing sharply from the book, Cecile runs off into the moors and drowns when she slips into the Grimpen Mire. In the book, it's her husband, Stapleton, who dies in the mire. In the movie, he's shot and then falls prey to his own devil dog's fangs.

Though neither the 1939 nor the 1959 films are totally faithful to Conan Doyle, they're both rousing entertainments that certainly capture the essence of the famous story and remain worthwhile viewing today.

Hound of the Baskervilles may, in fact, be the most often filmed mystery story of all time. There have been versions filmed in several non–English-speaking countries and there was a 1978 parody starring comedians Peter Cook and Dudley Moore as Holmes and Watson.

And television has tackled the story many times, including a 1972 American version with Englishmen Stewart Granger and Bernard Fox as Holmes and Watson, with William Shatner of *Star Trek* in a supporting role. Other TV versions include the 1982 English miniseries with Tom Baker of *Doctor Who* fame as Holmes; a 1983 English version with Ian Richardson as Holmes; the 1988 English version with Jeremy Brett as Holmes and Edward Hardwicke as Watson; a 2000 Canadian version with Matt Frewer of *Max Headroom* fame as Holmes and Kenneth Welsh as Watson, and a 2002 British version with Richard Roxburgh as Holmes and Ian Hart as Watson.

Michael Connelly
Blood Work

The 1998 book and the 2002 movie

It's usually good policy to read the book before you see the movie or TV program they make from it. Reason: Even if the movie is a good rendition of the book, your imagination will be short-changed because you'll see the actors from the movie instead of the characters your mind would picture for you.

I'd make exceptions for certain filmmakers, such as Alfred Hitchcock. Hitch often changed major elements from any book he was turning into a film, but he often changed them for the better. Result: You might spoil a good movie if you were holding it to the plot and characters you first discovered in the book. Example: John Buchan's *The Thirty-Nine Steps*, which was a much better Hitchcock movie than it was a book.

I'd also add Clint Eastwood to that list of directors whose own judgment about stories and characters is pretty reliable. However, that's not the way it turned out when I saw *Blood Work*, adapted from Michael Connelly's popular 1998 crime novel.

I loved Connelly's novel, which I read just before seeing the film so that it would be fresh in my mind. In the final analysis, the book is a much more intelligent and suspenseful thriller than the movie, which is uncharacteristically slow for a film directed by Eastwood and gives away too many clues to develop any genuine suspense.

In Connelly's novel, former FBI agent Terry McCaleb, recovering from heart transplant surgery, intends to sail his boat to Santa Catalina island, his ultimate retirement destination, as soon as his doctor okays it. But he's drawn into working on one last murder case—the shooting of a customer during a convenience store robbery—because he's learned that the victim was the donor of the heart now beating in his chest. The case becomes a crusade once he gets to know the victim's sister Graciela and his young son. The boy is now being raised by his unmarried aunt, who works in a hospital emergency room. McCaleb finds himself falling in love with Graciela.

It's an engaging premise for a mystery, even though you know how unlikely it is that a former FBI "profiler" specialist like McCaleb would ever get involved with a local robbery-shooting carried off by a masked man who left behind no clues. Connelly's genius, though, is in figuring out a way to turn this simple shooting into a major criminal case quite worthy of the sort of deep investigation McCaleb is used to carrying out when tracking down serial killers and the like.

Because Connelly wanted to keep his story as plausible as possible, it necessarily becomes a lot more complex than a movie could afford to get in the conventional two-hour running time. For one thing, he gets into the jurisdictional problems between the Los Angeles Police Dept. and the Sheriff's Office and the petty jealousies between them and "the feds." He also gets into the problems McCaleb would face conducting an investigation without a private eye's license or any formal connection to the official police investigation, which has already come to a halt when McCaleb gets into the case.

But that detail keeps Connelly's novel quite lively and quite credible—and it gives us time to accept the fact that McCaleb is falling in love with the woman who got him into the case, over his doctor's strenuous objections.

Eastwood's film deals with the complexities in Connelly's story by eliminating most of them. For one thing, he jettisons the killer who's finally revealed in the novel and instead uses one of Connelly's "innocent" supporting characters as the movie's killer. Viewers are asked to believe an awful lot of nonsense in order to buy into this "surprise" killer—and, in my opinion, it doesn't fly.

There's also the problem that McCaleb is supposed to be in his late 40s while Eastwood was 72 when the film came out. Though Eastwood has kept himself remarkably fit, he's obviously a little old for most of what we see him doing in the picture. Frankly, that didn't trouble me as much as it has troubled other critics. Personally, I think Eastwood really could do most of the stuff we see him doing in the movie, including making love to Graciela (Wanda DeJesus).

The film also turns the character of Arrango, a Los Angeles police detective who resents McCaleb's interference, into a comic character by casting standup comic Paul Rodriguez. In the book, there's nothing funny about the mean-spirited Arrango, who really typifies the sort of cop who doesn't want anybody messing with his "cold" cases for fear they'll show up faults in his own work.

The book's exciting finale in Mexico also is dumped in favor of a more routine finale aboard a wrecked cargo boat near San Pedro Harbor. Connelly kept the action to a believable level; McCaleb didn't perform extraordinary feats not long after heart transplant surgery. Eastwood prefers keeping McCaleb on the verge of cardiac arrest.

Eastwood fans may not be let down by *Blood Work*: Despite its slowness and its other shortcomings, it's still a pretty good movie. But anyone who enjoys a taut literary thriller will much more enjoy Connelly's novel than they will Eastwood's pale movie version.

Daphne du Maurier
Rebecca

The 1938 novel and the 1940 movie

When Alfred Hitchcock came to the U.S. in 1939 to make his first American movie, he was already England's most sought-after filmmaker. He had established an international reputation as the stylish director of the British thrillers *The Man Who Knew Too Much* (1934), *The Thirty-Nine Steps* (1935) and *The Lady Vanishes* (1938) and already had turned down several offers to make his American debut.

RKO, for instance, wanted to hire him to make *The Saint in New York*, but Hitchcock wasn't that interested in a series detective movie. (Little known director Ben Holmes took the job.) MGM desperately wanted to hire him for much bigger things, but balked at his then very lofty price: $35,000 a picture.

In the late 1930s, he was approached by his agents to consider an offer from American producer David O. Selznick to make a big-budget film about the sinking of the *Titanic*. One of Hitchcock's agents was Myron Selznick, David's brother, who arranged a meeting between Hitchcock and producer Selznick. Hitchcock was very interested in the *Titanic* movie and was impressed with Selznick, who offered him $40,000 a picture on a four-picture contract.

What really clinched the deal was the fact that Selznick had just bought the movie rights to Daphne du Maurier's best-selling English suspense novel *Rebecca*, which Hitchcock had been trying to buy on his own. In their conversation, Selznick suggested that *Rebecca* might be Hitchcock's second film in America. Hitchcock thought it would make a great movie and he also had a personal connection: Daphne du Maurier was the daughter of his good friend George du Maurier, author of the bestseller *Trilby*. What's more, Hitchcock's last English film had been the 1939 *Jamaica Inn*, which also was based on a Daphne du Maurier novel.

So, Hitchcock signed for the deal and came to America.

But by the time Hitchcock arrived in the States, England was at war with Germany, Selznick's *Titanic* had been cancelled and the producer was up to his neck in details regarding the completion of his Civil War epic *Gone with the Wind*. Hitch, a very patriotic Englishman, was deeply concerned about being stuck in America at his nation's time of greatest jeopardy. Still, the movie he really wanted to do, *Rebecca*, was now going to be his first job in America.

Rebecca was an incredibly popular novel; its storyline and very offbeat narrative style remain fascinating today, more than 75 years later. The heroine is a very shy and backward young woman. When we first meet her, she's a paid companion to a wealthy middle-aged woman who's taking a holiday at an English coastal resort. The girl is forced into the company of widower Max de Winter, a casual acquaintance of the wealthy lady. Suddenly and very shockingly, the wealthy Max falls in love with the girl, marries her and takes her home to Manderley, his ancestral manor on the Cornish coast.

At no time do we ever learn the girl's name. Du Maurier clearly wanted to diminish the young bride's persona so thoroughly that she virtually has no identity of her own. That sets up what happens when she becomes the mistress of Manderley: She lives in the shadow of Max's dead wife, the beautiful, mysterious Rebecca, whose presence remains powerfully strong in the great manor house she once ruled. From that point on, our heroine is known only as "the second Mrs. de Winter."

Hitchcock quickly discovered that producer Selznick did nothing halfway. He wanted Hitchcock to have the very best of everything and so *Rebecca* went into production with elaborate sets, top-notch cinematography and musical score, etc. But the director also discovered that Selznick was a hands-on producer who wanted to make the final decisions about nearly everything concerned with his films.

Fortunately, Selznick was deeply engaged with the final editing of *Gone with the Wind*, the most expensive, elaborate and carefully hyped film in Hollywood history. Consequently, he had little time to micro-manage *Rebecca*, which probably saved his already very tense relationship with Hitchcock.

Still, Selznick imposed his will on Hitchcock at a level the English director never had endured before. Hitchcock worked on the script with his personal assistant, Joan Harrison, and the famous playwright Robert E. Sherwood. He was used to being in charge of how the story would be developed in his films and he was notorious for making sometimes radical changes in even the most beloved novels in order to make them work better on the screen. As a matter of fact, Hitchcock's first draft of the script contained lots of little changes he thought necessary to make *Rebecca* a "Hitchcock film."

Hitchcock and his collaborators felt it would confuse the audience to have a main character with no name of her own. They caucused and decided to name her "Daphne." Selznick was furious when he heard that one and put an end to that quickly. She would be "anonymous" just as she is in the book.

Hitchcock also wanted a flashback sequence that would include Rebecca herself. The book purposely keeps her at a distance, so she never becomes anything but a phantom in the storyline, although a most intimidating one. Selznick vetoed that, too.

Hitchcock also was a believer in having comic relief in his suspense films to relieve the tension for the audience, so he could build it up again. He had added several comic sequences that weren't in the book. Selznick was livid about all these changes. He believed you don't pay a small fortune to buy movie rights to a novel, then write your own different story and throw away the author's work. He insisted there be no fundamental changes in the storyline of *Rebecca*, so the comic relief went out along with nearly everything else Hitchcock wanted to add.

But the biggest change Hitchcock was required to swallow was the new ending demanded by Hollywood censors. In the book, Max really did kill Rebecca. The Hollywood Production Code didn't allow killers to go unpunished in movies, no matter how the story went in the book. So the book's ending had to be altered. That was something

Selznick had to accept, too, like it or not.

So, in the movie, we learn that Rebecca had been diagnosed with a terminal illness and was going to die anyway. Though Max is angry at her for a love affair and gets rough with her, she actually trips in their struggle, falls down and is killed when she strikes her head. Max then puts her body in her sailboat and scuttles it at sea to fake a drowning incident.

When it came to casting, Hitchcock lost the fundamental battles, too. Selznick really wanted Vivien Leigh to star in *Rebecca*. She already was playing Scarlett O'Hara in *Gone with the Wind* after a much-hyped international search for just the right star. Selznick thought she should be back on the screen right away in another showcase role. Hitchcock, who was familiar with Leigh's work in England, believed she was all wrong for the part of the timid wife. Leigh was radiantly beautiful and no amount of messing with her could make her plain like the nameless girl had to be.

Joan Fontaine (left) with Judith Anderson as her nemesis, Mrs. Danvers, in Alfred Hitchcock's *Rebecca*, the Oscar-winning Best Picture of 1940 (United Artists).

Hitchcock at first wanted Robert Donat to play Max de Winter, then favored Ronald Colman. But Leigh, who was then having a love affair with Laurence Olivier that ultimately led to their marriage, wanted him to get the part. Selznick wanted to keep her happy and told Hitchcock he'd signed Olivier.

Scheduling complications came along and Leigh no longer was available for *Rebecca*. Dozens of other actresses were tested or interviewed for the role; Selznick was smitten with young Joan Fontaine and she got the part. (It's generally believed that Selznick never got anywhere with Fontaine, who was in love with actor Brian Aherne and later married him.)

Though Fontaine was a beautiful woman, she could be made to look rather plain without much cosmetic wizardry. So far in her career, she hadn't played anything quite like this complex character, so some feared she might be in over her head. (She had been Fred Astaire's dancing partner in the 1936 musical *A Damsel in Distress* without getting anybody too excited.) But there couldn't be any further delay, so *Rebecca* rolled into production with Fontaine playing opposite Olivier.

Hitchcock was a gentleman who hated arguments and did not intend to get into any big ones with Selznick. So when Selznick demanded the right of final cut on the picture, Hitchcock quietly agreed. What Selznick didn't know was that Hitchcock cut his films in the camera, meaning he didn't take any alternate angles or let an actor "try it one more time" just to satisfy his or her ego.

Hitch had been an artist and designer before he turned to directing, so he carefully storyboarded his entire film in advance, sketching out exactly how the scenes would

Joan Fontaine with Laurence Olivier in Alfred Hitchcock's *Rebecca*. She played his second wife in the picture, living in the heavy shadow of his dead ex-wife (United Artists).

look. He liked to shoot only on indoor sets, even if the scene took place outdoors in the script, because that way he could control the lighting and avoid sound glitches when planes flew over or trains rolled by in the distance.

That's why Hitchcock was so happy to let Selznick go into the editing room every day, look at the footage from the previous day and make any changes he liked. Typically Selznick would look at a scene and say, "That looks pretty good," and then ask to see the alternate takes. There never were any. He surely dropped in on the set now and then to be sure Hitchcock wasn't hiding anything. Once he was satisfied that his director was saving him lots of money by not taking forever to get a scene right, he stopped going into the editing room at all.

When the picture was finished, Selznick told Hitchcock he had come up with a fabulous final scene: As Manderley burned in a huge fire, Selznick wanted the smoke to form a giant "R" in the sky to indicate that the hovering memory of Rebecca was going up in smoke along with her mansion. Hitchcock came close to gagging on that ridiculous thought, but politely told Selznick he'd go ahead and do it.

But the following day, according to Rudy Behlmer's marvelous book *Memo from David O. Selznick,* Hitchcock broke the news to Selznick that the scene with the "R" in the sky was going to cost a large sum and wanted to clear it with the boss before starting the costly process work to get that "R" effect. Hitchcock had, of course, made the whole thing up, but it convinced Selznick it would be foolish to spend so much money for just one scene—and he told the director to forget all about it.

What sort of film did Hitchcock turn out for Selznick? Though perhaps not rated as highly as the Hitchcock classics *Notorious*, *Strangers on a Train*, *Vertigo* and *Psycho*, *Rebecca* is a magnificent film that just keeps getting better every year. I've seen it countless times and I always find something new to admire with each new screening.

First is the underrated performance of Joan Fontaine, who was nominated for Best Actress of 1940 and lost to Ginger Rogers, who got enormous credit from Academy voters for going from chorus girl in *42nd Street* to romantic dancing partner to Fred Astaire and then establishing herself as a fine dramatic actress with her 1940 performance in *Kitty Foyle*. Fontaine didn't wait long for her Oscar: She won the Best Actress award the following year as the heroine of Hitchcock's *Suspicion*.

This luminous beauty makes us believe, mostly with her acting skills, that she's a shy, plain girl overwhelmed by the rich life she suddenly is plunged into and traumatized by the endless comparisons she thinks people are making between the first and second Mrs. de Winter.

In her first scene at Manderley, she arrives in an open convertible during a sudden rainstorm, her hair wet and stringy. She looks, as they say, like something the cat dragged in. When she enters the grand hall, she finds a small army of servants waiting to greet their new mistress. Suddenly, the film's *bête noire*, housekeeper Mrs. Danvers (Judith Anderson), looms up in front of the camera and in that very first moment begins the intimidation of the drab young woman who dares to try taking the place of her beloved Rebecca.

Fontaine stammers and stumbles, drops things and bumps heads with Danvers trying to pick them up, not understanding that Danvers is supposed to pick up after her. She visibly seems to regress to childhood whenever she's around Danvers, who is the female equivalent of a well-trained attack dog, never actually growling, but always giving you the impression she'd like to tear your leg off.

In the film's most psychologically twisted sequence, the second Mrs. de Winter finally determines that she's going to enter Rebecca's wing of the house, closed since her death, but maintained as a shrine to her dead mistress by Danvers. As Danvers gives her new mistress a tour of Rebecca's boudoir, she takes special care to show how much classier Rebecca was than her replacement. When Danvers runs her own hands through the lingerie of Rebecca, urging her new mistress to feel how soft the undergarments are, Fontaine's face takes on a look of such awesome repugnance that you know exactly what she's thinking: Exactly what services did you perform for Rebecca, you twisted old lesbian?

In 1940, Hitchcock couldn't get away with opening the homosexuality door, but there's simply no doubt what he's telling you. One day Fontaine asked Hitchcock, "What ever happened to *Mr.* Danvers?" Hitchcock supposedly answered, "I believe she ate him."

Judith Anderson, one of America's leading stage actors, played Danvers with real gusto, tightened down as firmly as her lank hair was tied down to her skull. She, too, earned an Oscar nomination, but lost out to Jane Darwell, equally memorable in her own way as Ma Joad in John Ford's adaptation of the John Steinbeck novel *The Grapes of Wrath*.

Rebecca is, at heart, a Gothic romance in what were then modern times. Max really loves his lovely young bride and part of her allure is the fact that she isn't outrageously beautiful, isn't flirting with every man in sight and doesn't have a soul as dark as Hades. Olivier gives Max an often off-putting severity, but his moments of romantic charm certainly make up for it. Meanwhile, Fontaine lets us see how this simple young and inexperienced girl grows up and finally stands on her own as she takes control of her destiny for the first time in her life.

Rebecca has an almost supernatural quality to it and George Barnes, who would become Hitchcock's favorite cinematographer, captures this mystical quality in what is one of the all-time most artfully photographed movies of the black-and-white era. Franz Waxman's haunting score embellishes that effect. In my opinion, you can enjoy *Rebecca* even if all the dialogue blew out a window because it's such a good-looking and musically satisfying work of art.

When *Rebecca* won the Best Picture Oscar, it also must have convinced Selznick he'd done well by signing Hitchcock. One year after sweeping the 1939 Oscars with *Gone with the Wind*, Selznick came right back and won the top prize again, thanks to Hitchcock.

Hitchcock himself never won an Oscar for directing. (He earned a special Oscar for career achievement before he died in 1980.) Though nominated for *Rebecca*, he lost to John Ford for *Grapes of Wrath*. The only other Oscar won by *Rebecca* was the one George Barnes took home for his cinematography.

Public television has remade *Rebecca* twice and, though both were respectable productions, nobody seriously thinks they merit comparison to this Hitchcock-Selznick masterpiece. Anyway, there's no need to do it again. The 1940 version is one for the time capsule—a cinema classic that's as good today as the day it premiered.

Dick Francis
Dead Cert

The 1962 novel and the 1974 movie

In 1962, Dick Francis, one of England's most renowned steeplechase jockeys, published his first novel, *Dead Cert*, a taut murder mystery set in the world of competitive steeplechase racing. A rousing success, it launched the second career of Francis—this time as one of the world's most popular mystery writers, a status that continued into the 21st century.

In 1974, United Artists released *Dead Cert*, the first motion picture adapted from any Francis story. It was directed and co-written by Tony Richardson, the acclaimed stage and screen director. Richardson, a pioneer in England's "New Wave" of filmmakers, had a list of credits which included such instant classics as *Look Back in Anger* (1959), *The Entertainer* (1960), *A Taste of Honey* (1961), *The Loneliness of the Long Distance Runner* (1962) and *Tom Jones* (1963), a Best Picture Oscar winner.

By the time *Dead Cert* reached theaters, Francis had proved many times over that his initial success was no fluke and he already had become one of the world's most respected mystery authors. That's why it probably seemed bewildering to many of his fans that *Dead Cert*, the movie, showed so little respect for *Dead Cert*, the novel.

In the book, the hero is Alan York, an amateur steeplejack jockey from Kenya who has been taken under the wing of well-known jockey Bill Davidson and lives with Davidson, his wife Scilla and their children. When Davidson is thrown from his horse Admiral during a race and dies from his injuries, Alan discovers that someone had strung a wire across the track, causing Admiral to fall, By the time Alan can alert track officials to the criminal sabotage, the wire has been removed and nobody believes his story.

Alan vows to find out who targeted Davidson. Following up a number of leads, he starts uncovering a racing gambling conspiracy, but is savagely beaten by a band of hooligans who warn him to stop probing. Later, he's able to tie the hooligans into the mysterious Marconicars taxi firm located in Brighton. Police Inspector Lodge begins to realize that Alan has sniffed out something significant, which leads to the exciting conclusion as Alan, riding Admiral cross-country, attempts to dodge dozens of armed men pursuing him in radio-equipped cars.

Richardson's screenplay, written with John Oaksey, ravages the author's carefully plotted storyline. The movie concocts a simmering love affair between Alan (Scott Antony) and Davidson's widow (Judi Dench), who's re-named Laura, and suggests they'd been sexually involved before Davidson's death. The movie also eliminates Kate, Alan's love interest in the novel, and fabricates a new temptation for him, a would-be-actress called Penny (Nina Thomas). Penny's really the mistress of Cliff Tudor, an unsavory bookie who sends her to seduce Alan and find out what he knows about the conspiracy. Tudor is not a bookie in the novel and has no mistress.

Davidson's horse isn't brought down by a wire in the movie, but rather by a drug administered by a character who's not in the book. The Marconicars taxi outfit is re-titled "Whiteley's" in the movie and, most shocking of all, the arch criminal behind the conspiracy turns out to be—Police Inspector Lodge! (John Glover). The real villain of the book isn't even in the movie! And who does Alan ride off into the sunset with? Improbably, it turns out to be Penny, now a reformed seductress.

The great cross-country ride of the book becomes a brief and not very exciting sequence in the movie, often played for laughs.

The film was a major letdown to Francis fans and was little seen in the U.S. However, some of the steeplejack racing scenes are well done, some of them shot from the horseback point of view.

Scott Antony, who plays Alan without much emotional conviction, had made a splash as the leading man in Ken Russell's 1972 *Savage Messiah*, but was not heard from much again after 1974.

But, of course, *Dead Cert* offers a rare chance to see the young Judi Dench, who would go on to become one of England's most respected stage, screen and television performers, eventually being honored as a Dame of the British Empire. In her long and distinguished career, she has won nine British BAFTA awards and a Best Supporting Actress Oscar for *Shakespeare in Love* (1998), and for years co-starred in the hit British comedy series *A Fine Romance* with her real-life husband Michael Williams, who plays treacherous jockey Sandy Mason in *Dead Cert*. More recently, Dench took on the role of "M," 007's boss in the James Bond movies.

No other feature film has yet been made from a Dick Francis mystery, though a few more have been adapted for the TV screen. Francis died in 2010; his son Felix has continued to write mysteries under both their names.

Dick Francis
Blood Sport

The 1967 novel and the 1989 TV movie

At the peak of Dick Francis' popularity in the late 1980s, a new effort was made to bring his mysteries to TV. A series of two-hour telemovies would be based on actual Francis bestsellers, if the filmmakers could get past one huge problem: The novels had no running series character.

In the TV industry, it's common knowledge that viewers will flock to watch a character they like, week in and week out, but it's very difficult to entice them to watch any program regularly if it has no recurring characters. That's one reason why anthology programs have virtually vanished from TV network schedules.

By the late 1980s, the only really distinctive recurring protagonist in the Francis novels was Sid Halley, the handicapped hero of *Odds Against* and *Whip Hand*. (The third and fourth Halley novels, *Come to Grief* and *Under Orders*, hadn't been written yet.) But Halley had already been given a shot at a TV series: *The Racing Game*, which had run its course. So where could the filmmakers find another worthy Francis hero?

They'd chosen three novels they wanted to film—*Twice Shy*, *Blood Sport* and *In the Frame*—but they all had different leading characters, some of them not very appealing. For instance, *Blood Sport*'s leading character Gene Hawkins is an investigator with suicidal impulses. At 38, he's a disillusioned man, worn down by the grueling undercover work his job requires and troubled over his failure in affairs of the heart. He carries a handgun wherever he goes, promising himself to end his misery as soon as he gets his affairs in some kind of order.

It doesn't take a genius to figure out that Hawkins wasn't the sort of TV hero the filmmakers wanted. Still, the storyline of *Blood Sport*, in which Hawkins hunts for an extremely valuable race horse that's gone missing in America, seemed more than ideal for the TV project. The story had plenty of action, strong characters and an American locale. That translated to potentially strong TV ratings on both sides of the Atlantic, where Francis' novels were steady bestsellers.

Likewise, the heroes of *In the Frame* (an artist who paints pictures of horses) and *Twice Shy* (a young race track manager)—seemed to lack a certain something for the TV audience.

That's when the filmmakers came up with a novel idea: Why not take David Cleveland, the leading character in Francis' 1973 novel *Slay-Ride*, and transplant him into the other three novels? It might just work. Cleveland's job was investigating equine mysteries for the British Jockey Club. If they could squeeze him into *Twice Shy*, *Blood Sport* and *In the Frame*, he might become a Dick Francis TV hero with much more basic appeal than Sid Halley, the ex-jockey with the bionic hand.

Would the purists raise the roof? Perhaps, but they would only comprise a small part of the TV audience. Maybe the movies would appeal to millions who'd never read any of Francis' mysteries—viewers who wouldn't know if David Cleveland belonged in the stories or not.

As special insurance, the filmmakers signed one of England's most popular actors to play Cleveland: Ian McShane. McShane had just played the starring role in *Lovejoy*, a

1986 British detective show, which would become a long-running TV series (more than 70 episodes). He had just the right sort of dashing *bon vivant* charm the filmmakers wanted for their David Cleveland.

But the major compromise that lifted Cleveland out of *Slay-Ride* and plopped him into the movie versions of three other Francis novels was just the beginning of the compromises ahead. Let's take the case of *Blood Sport*.

In the novel, Hawkins is asked to help wealthy horse owner David Teller find his missing horse, but the idea doesn't appeal to the depressed Hawkins. He changes his mind after an accident on a river-boating trip in England with Teller and his family: As their boat approaches a system of locks, they see a young couple struggling to keep their small boat from tipping over right at the point where the water is rushing through the locks. As they try to reach the couple, Teller is accidentally knocked into the water by the pole the young people are using to keep their little boat from being sucked into the cascading water.

Instinctively, Hawkins jumps into the river and dives down in a valiant attempt to save Teller. The awesome power of the rushing water nearly drowns both Hawkins and Teller, but Hawkins manages to bring Teller to the surface, badly banged up, but still alive.

Something about the "accident" intrigues the investigator in Hawkins and he eventually concludes that the young couple in trouble intentionally tried to drown Teller. When he learns they're from America, he begins to wonder if the missing horse episode isn't really part of something far more serious. He decides to take the assignment Teller is offering.

In the movie, the "accident" occurs after Cleveland agrees to help Teller—and it happens in Canada, not England. In fact, the mystery never reaches America's shores, no doubt because the project could be filmed more cheaply in Canada, with Canadian partners. The "accident" is also completely different: The young couple try to run Teller over with their power boat on a lake filled with holiday sailors. The gripping excitement of the river locks is missing and the rescue of Teller is nowhere as dramatic as it was in the book.

Andrew Payne, who adapted *Blood Sport* for the screen, also took the Francis characters and threw them into a blender. David Teller becomes Harry Teller (Kenneth Welsh). In the book, Hawkins develops a love affair with Lynnie, the daughter of his English boss Simon Keeble. In the movie, Lynnie becomes Lynne (Carolyn Dunn) and her father is now *Harry* Teller. Simon Keeble becomes *Geoffrey* Keeble and the filmmakers hired a British TV icon—actor Patrick Macnee, the beloved John Steed of *The Avengers*—to play the part.

The highlight of the book's second half is the section in which Hawkins, working undercover, poses as a customer at a mountain dude ranch run by Matt and Yola, the young couple involved in the river incident, and discovers they have Chrysalis, Teller's missing race horse, hidden on the property.

In the book, Matt and Yola are brother and sister, but they're husband and wife in the movie. They're working for Culham James Offen, another millionaire horse breeder, who becomes James Culham Offen (Lloyd Bochner) in the movie.

The movie junks the book's exciting finish, in which Hawkins' ally, insurance detective Walt Prensela, is killed. Instead, the movie plays Walt (Heath Lamberts) as a fat, food-addicted comic character who lives happily ever after. The movie's totally different final showdown takes place during a secret attempt to swap Chrysalis with a disappointing look-alike horse owned by the villainous Offen, who covets the stud fees he'll get from the stolen horse's superior blood lines.

Did the filmmakers ruin *Blood Sport* with all these changes? Not really. The basic mystery premise is fundamentally unchanged and McShane's David Cleveland is a much more appealing hero than the embittered, suicidal Hawkins of the book. On the other hand, the movie's hero is much more conventional and, perhaps, not quite as intellectually interesting.

The three Francis movies featuring McShane as David Cleveland were not terribly successful, so no more were filmed. They're not bad movies, though, and I'm sure they're quite enjoyable if you haven't read the books. However, if you see the movies first, *then* read the books, you may be wondering what the heck ever happened to that dashing David Cleveland fellow. He'll be nowhere to be found.

Erle Stanley Gardner
The Case of the Velvet Claws

The 1933 novel and the 1936 movie

Lawyer-turned-author Erle Stanley Gardner provided a milestone in the history of the mystery genre in 1933 when he first published *The Case of the Velvet Claws*. It was the first of 82 full-length novels about the now iconic criminal defense lawyer Perry Mason, nearly all of them bestsellers.

Writing from his own experience as a trial lawyer, Gardner had such success that he almost single-handedly created a new subgenre within the mystery: the courtroom mystery. Today it has many practitioners from John Grisham and Scott Turow to Linda Fairstein and Steve Martini.

Perry Mason became the hero of a popular CBS radio program that ran from 1943 to 1955; the Raymond Burr CBS-TV series, which lasted from 1957 to 1966; a second CBS series, *The New Perry Mason* with Monte Markham (1973–74); and a series of NBC-TV movies with Burr as Mason, which ran from 1985 to 1993. There was even a *Perry Mason* comic strip syndicated in the U.S. and Canada from 1950 to 1952.

But before all that, shortly after the publishing success of *The Case of the Velvet Claws* in 1933, Warner Bros. made a deal with Gardner to bring Perry Mason to the movie screen. The money was good (Gardner had an escalating contract that began at $10,000 and rose up to $25,000 per novel filmed), but he was not at all happy with the results. "Warners proceeded to ruin Perry," he complained repeatedly over the years.

Seven of Gardner's Perry Mason novels were filmed, starting with *The Case of the Howling Dog* in 1934. The novel that started it all, *The Case of the Velvet Claws*, was the fourth to go before the cameras and the last to feature smooth, slick Warren William as Mason.

If you want a lesson on how to wreck a "detective" hero, this abominable film would be an ideal place to start. Gardner was right: It does seem as if the studio and screenwriter Tom Reed set out to frustrate all of Gardner's millions of fans by turning Perry Mason

Claire Dodd was loyal secretary Della Street and Warren William was lawyer Perry Mason in the 1936 film version of Erle Stanley Gardner's *The Case of the Velvet Claws*. Perry and Della were married in the movie, but never in any of the Perry Mason books (Warner Bros. and Turner Classic Movies).

into a wisecracking *bon vivant* in Depression-era America, the exact opposite of the character Gardner created.

It's now considered very likely that Warners was trying to find a detective hero to match Dashiell Hammett's Nick Charles, the main character in MGM's box office sensation of 1934, *The Thin Man*. As portrayed on the screen by William Powell, Nick was a hard-drinking playboy who just happened to solve mysteries, usually in the company of his beautiful wife Nora. The public was crazy about Nick and Nora, and MGM was busily engaged in making a series of *Thin Man* movies by the time *The Case of the Velvet Claws* reached theaters.

In the novel, Perry Mason is a brash young lawyer willing to get his hands dirty helping his client, the beautiful Eva Belter, avoid being identified as the "other woman" in an affair with Congressional candidate Harrison Burke. A scandal sheet is about to expose them and she's afraid of her wealthy husband's reaction. Mason agrees to try paying off the tabloid, but then is drawn deeper into the case when her husband George is murdered.

One can only imagine Gardner's shock when he saw how the movie version of his first Perry Mason novel begins: Not with Eva Belter coming to Mason's office with her sob story, but rather with Mason and his secretary, Della Street (Claire Dodd), being married in a courtroom by a judge!

This was, of course, heresy to readers. Perry and Della worked together for more than 40 years and never went anywhere near saying marriage vows. Gardner must have been apoplectic.

Things continue going downhill. Eva Belter does show up, but not at Perry's office. Instead, she arrives at his apartment on his wedding night as he and Della are packing to leave on their honeymoon. She doesn't bother to ask Perry to represent her, just sticks a gun in his ribs and orders him to join her for a taxi ride. The ride he's taken on gets him involved in the murder of his client's husband and his eventual place on the list of leading suspects.

The plot meanders further and further from Gardner's original story and eventually even leads us to a different killer than the one in the book!

The Warner Bros. screen version of Mason severely diminishes the character for the sake of making him more "fun." He drinks way more than he does in the books and he's much more likely to step outside the law to win his cases. Gardner was also most uncomfortable with the movie version of Della. He felt they never portrayed her as a reliable working girl, but made her into a playmate for Perry. He once observed, "Della was so dazzling, I couldn't see her for diamonds."

Likewise, Gardner's original concept for detective Paul Drake was that of a solid professional all the way. But Drake, as portrayed by comic actor Eddie Acuff (brother of hillbilly singer Roy Acuff) in *Velvet Claws,* is a goofy guy. His name is even changed to "Spudsy" Drake as if he were a Mason sidekick like "Gabby" Hayes was to cowboy star Roy Rogers.

By the time they had finished the first six films in the *Perry Mason* series, finally casting Latin Lover–type Ricardo Cortez as Mason, followed by insipid Donald Woods, the public no longer was interested in what the studio was doing with the Gardner novels.

A final indignity was yet to come. In 1940, the studio took the last of the Perry Mason novels it had acquired, *The Case of the Dangerous Dowager* (1937), and eliminated the Perry Mason character completely, turning it into a comedy starring elderly character actress May Robson and released it in 1940 as *Granny Get Your Gun*.

Little wonder that when Gardner finally agreed to let Hollywood try again with Perry Mason a couple of decades later, he formed his own production company rather than accept a $1 million offer for the TV rights to the character. The end result was the hit CBS *Perry Mason* series with Raymond Burr, an unqualified success in Gardner's opinion—and the opinion of mystery fans, too.

David Goodis

Down There

The 1956 novel and the 1960 film
Shoot the Piano Player (*Tirez sur le Pianiste*)

David Goodis was one of the American crime novelists, like Cornell Woolrich and Jim Thompson, who were adopted by French New Wave filmmakers in the late 1950s and early 1960s as fathers of *roman noir*, the dark genre of writing that inspired the cinematic genre those critics dubbed film noir. These young French filmmakers then began to make their own films noir, drawing their inspiration from American crime and mystery movies based on similar noir novels.

Film critic François Truffaut wrote the story for Jean-Luc Godard's 1959 *Breathless*, one of the very first French films noir. He turned to feature film directing that same year with *The 400 Blows*, an autobiographical story of his youth. For his second film, he decided to adapt a 1956 Goodis novel called *Down There*.

Goodis was a novelist who had done some screenwriting, but was best known as the original author of the novel *Dark Passage*, which was turned into an acclaimed Humphrey Bogart–Lauren Bacall suspense film in 1947 by director Delmer Daves. His novel *Down There* is about a former concert pianist who travels a path of self-destruction following the suicide of his wife. His despair leads him to a futureless job playing background piano in a neighborhood saloon in Philadelphia.

Truffaut was moved by the story of a ruined man who's nearly redeemed by love, but then is drawn into the miserable criminal life of his two brothers. They're both being stalked by gangsters they've ripped off.

In the novel, piano player Eddie is an unlikely hero. He has learned to avoid trouble by keeping the lowest of profiles. Nobody at Harriet's Hut, the café-bar where he works, knows much about him except that he seems to be a decent enough guy. He has no intimate friends and, as far as anybody knows, no family. Clarice, the prostitute who lives across the hall in his tenement apartment house, is sweet on him, but his relations with her are perfunctory and require no commitment from either of them.

An attractive waitress named Lena works at Harriet's, but Eddie never shows any signs of interest. She's coveted by Plyne, a former wrestler, now the bouncer at Harriet's Hut. Eddie certainly doesn't want to get on his bad side.

Everything changes one night when Eddie's brother Turley comes into Harriet's, bedraggled and exhausted, and asks Eddie to help him hide from two men who are after him. Eddie refuses to be drawn into the situation until the men finally arrive at Harriet's, obviously determined to kill Turley. Eddie creates a distraction that gives Turley time to escape through the back door.

From that point on, Eddie is thrown together with Lena the waitress, and they begin what might be a romance in any other context. But they barely have time to get to know each other before the hit men start coming after them, figuring they know where Turley is hiding.

Along the way, we learn why Eddie fell to his current low station in life: His wife had slept with Eddie's mentor in the music world in order to get Eddie his first break as a concert pianist. When Eddie learned about this, he freaked and she killed herself. His life spun totally out of control after that and he lost everything.

When Truffaut began to pull all the elements of Goodis' novel into a movie storyline, he also started making some changes. Eddie is now called Charlie and is played by actor-singer Charles Aznavour, one of France's great anti-hero specialists of the New Wave, a sort of singing Bogart. Eddie's brother Turley becomes Chico (Albert Remy) and the other brother, Clifton, becomes Richard (Jean-Jacques Aslanian). Truffaut, who wrote the script with Marcel Moussy, also added another brother, the teenage Fido, pronounced "Fee-doe" (Richard Kanayan).

Truffaut also shifted the location from Philly to Paris. The saloon proprietor is no

Charles Aznavour is a former concert pianist caught up in an underworld manhunt in François Truffaut's *Shoot the Piano Player*, based on David Goodis' novel *Down There* (Bravo network).

longer Harriet: Truffaut promoted the club's bouncer, a beefy ex-wrestler named Plyne, to club owner. Though his name is still Plyne, he's no longer quite so beefy and there's no mention of any wrestling background. He's played by Serge Davri. Lena (Marie Dubois) is still Lena, but Clarice the hooker is now Clarissa and we get to see the pianist have sex with her, which he never gets around to doing in the book.

In both book and film, the pianist and Lena run off together after Plyne, who covets Lena, engages in a furious struggle with the pianist over her and Plyne is killed. In the book, Goodis goes to great lengths to show us that the pianist is a pretty tough guy who can take care of himself physically, even though he never seems a fair match for the huge Plyne. Truffaut makes us believe the slim and short Aznavour can handle Plyne by making Plyne much less a brute than he is on the printed page.

The film uses the book's same action finale at the mountain cabin where the pianist and Lena find his brothers, who are hiding there from the mob with their stolen loot. However, the action isn't as furious on screen as it becomes in the book when the gangsters show up with automatic weapons. In the film, the outcome, as far as the brothers are concerned, is inconclusive. Truffaut's film retains Goodis' book's cynical ending, which fits neatly into the noir sensibility of the movie genre Truffaut was celebrating.

Shoot the Piano Player is a good movie, but it's not as edgy and real as the Goodis original. On the plus side, though, the international appeal of the movie, which helped cement Truffaut's place in the French New Wave of filmmakers, spurred sales of the Goodis novel, which had never amounted to much since its publication in 1956.

Graham Greene
A Gun for Sale

The 1936 novel and the 1942 movie *This Gun for Hire*;
the 1957 movie *Short Cut to Hell*;
and the 1991 TV movie *This Gun for Hire*

In the 1930s, English novelist Graham Greene began to designate certain new works as "entertainments" to separate them from his more "serious" works of fiction. He listed his 1936 novel *A Gun for Sale* as an entertainment and, perhaps as a consequence, it isn't regarded quite as highly by critics as his more serious novels.

And yet it was a tremendously popular book and so far has been filmed three times. None of the films has very closely resembled the original novel.

The first version, called *This Gun for Hire*, was released by Paramount in 1942 just months after America went into World War II. Today critics call it one of the great films noir of the 1940s. It made unknown actors Alan Ladd and Veronica Lake stars. After that film together, they became one of the most potent romantic star duos of the period.

Greene's novel was adapted for the screen by American crime novelist W.R. Burnett, whose own novels *Little Caesar* and *High Sierra* had both

Fugitive assassin Alan Ladd puts a restraining hand on the arm of Veronica Lake in *This Gun for Hire*, Paramount's version of the Graham Greene novel *A Gun for Sale* (Universal).

become classic crime films. Working with Burnett on the script was Albert Maltz, who later was blacklisted after being smeared by the McCarthy era's Commie-hunting House Un-American Activities Committee.

This Gun for Hire took extravagant liberties with the original Greene story, which was a cynical thriller about Raven, a soul-dead mercenary killer who only briefly knows the touch of human kindness before he meets his grim end.

The first big change was shifting the setting of the film from pre-war England to America, trading London for San Francisco and, eventually, Los Angeles. With England's film industry severely curtailed by the war and many of its actors and directors working in America at the time, it made sense to switch the locale, which surely made it more appetizing to American moviegoers.

Greene's main character, the hit man Raven, also got an overhaul in the American screenplay. In the novel, he's a grotesque-looking man with a harelip, which makes it much harder for him to hide from the police. His deformity and the hints Greene gives us of Raven's terrible childhood—his father was a criminal who was hanged—make it easier for readers to understand why he might have turned into a hate-filled adult who trusts nobody.

But the movie's Raven is, of course, quite handsome because he looks just like Alan Ladd. To make up for tossing out the harelip, the screenwriters gave Raven a badly scarred wrist, which is spotted regularly by witnesses who report his whereabouts to the police.

Robert Wagner played the hired killer known as Raven in the TV remake of *This Gun for Hire,* based on Graham Greene's novel *A Gun for Sale* (USA Network).

Greene gave Raven one humanizing quality: He loves the stray cat he's been feeding in his shabby tenement apartment. When the slovenly maid kicks the cat one day, Raven whacks her upside the head. He worries what's going to happen to his kitty while he's the object of a manhunt.

The screenwriters weren't content to leave it there. They also have a little crippled girl with leg braces spot him as he leaves the scene of his murder assignment. Rather than shoot the kid—his normal reaction when a witness spots him—he actually says a few nice words to her, then reluctantly lets her live. As mean as he gets later in the movie, that gives him a good heart that Greene never quite gave him.

In the novel, Raven was hired to kill England's Minister of War, which he does rather cold-bloodedly for money, killing the old man's secretary, too, because she would be a witness if allowed to live. Though

Greene doesn't come right out and tell us so, I think we're supposed to believe the people behind the killing are Nazi sympathizers and the assassination nearly plunges England into war with Germany.

But the 1942 *This Gun for Hire* was conceived and filmed before the December 7, 1941, attack on Pearl Harbor by the Japanese, when America finally was drawn into World War II, lining up with England against the Germans, Italians and Japanese. Once the locale of the story was switched to America, that made it difficult to maintain the same sort of "brink of war" climate of the 1936 novel.

So the American version of Raven is hired to kill a chemist who has some evidence that would incriminate the archvillain of the American movie, a wheelchair-bound corporation kingpin who is apparently supplying America's foreign enemies with secret formulas. The chemist is apparently blackmailing the kingpin. Raven kills the chemist and, out of necessity, the blackmailer's girlfriend. "They said he'd be alone!" Raven grumbles as the girl runs into an adjacent room to hide from him. He shoots her through the door and doesn't seem much bothered by it either.

In the book, Raven's contact man is "Chumley," who's also known as "Davis." He's a grossly fat corporate lackey who invests in local theater productions for his amusement—and as a way of connecting with good-looking young women looking for some way to get ahead in show business. This "hobby" puts him in the right place to meet the book's heroine, Anne, a young actress who just happens to be engaged to marry the Scotland Yard detective who's assigned to investigate the Minister of War's murder.

In *This Gun for Hire*, Anne becomes Ellen (Lake), a nightclub performer who does a song and magic act. The contact man is now Willard Gates (Laird Cregar), who owns a Los Angeles nightclub where she works. The movie still has her engaged to the chief investigator (Robert Preston), whose character name is changed from Mather to Michael Crane. The screenplay also has her working undercover for Senator *Burnett* (perhaps an in-joke referring to screenwriter W.R. Burnett), head of a Senate committee gathering evidence against the treasonous corporate kingpin.

In Greene's novel, Raven is betrayed by the men who hired him (they pay him off in marked bills from a robbery). The numbers of the bills have been widely circulated just before the murder, so Raven suddenly finds himself hunted by the police, but unable to use any of the money he's been paid for the job. Angry, he vows to kill not only Chumley but whoever Mr. Big turns out to be.

The movie makes the betrayal even more personal because the corporation puts lots of pressure on the cops to catch the man who robbed their company and killed the paymaster, adding yet another layer of motivation to not only catch Raven, but to perhaps kill him on sight. The book makes it clear that Raven is a hardened villain who deserves the unhappy end that comes for him. But by giving us a glimpse into his prior life and showing us how he begins to see things differently while in the company of Anne, who becomes his hostage at one point, we do eventually understand him and care about what happens to him.

But *This Gun for Hire* goes further, turning Raven into a movie anti-hero. We go along with him because most of the people he's killing are worse villains than he is and we sense he might have had a completely different kind of life if he'd been treated better as a youngster. We don't even root for him to have cosmetic surgery to eliminate his deformity because the screenwriters removed his deformity (without need for anesthetic) before we even met him.

Directed briskly by Frank Tuttle, *This Gun for Hire* still holds up quite well and is worthy of its towering reputation as a noir classic.

The second version of *A Gun for Sale* came in 1957 and it's best-remembered today as the only film directed by actor James Cagney. *Short Cut to Hell* kept the story in America, but changed all the names of the characters. Raven becomes Kyle Niles (played by Robert Ivers), Anne becomes Glory Hamilton (Georgann Johnson) and Detective Mathers becomes Sgt. Stan Lowery (William Bishop). It has even less connection to the Greene novel than *This Gun for Hire*.

In 1991, the telefilm *This Gun for Hire* starred Robert Wagner as Raven, Nancy Everhard as Anne and Fredric Lehne as Mather. Raven now bears a facial scar and the locale was again switched, this time to New Orleans. It was basically a remake of the first movie and not a new adaptation of the book.

In retrospect, some of the changes made for the 1942 *This Gun for Hire* don't seem so high-handed. Giving Raven a harelip, as Greene does in the book, would have made it all the more difficult to build audience sympathy for him. A leading character's visual deformities can be more unsettling in a movie than in a book, where the imagination can be toned down by the reader. You need to imagine that something romantic might occur between Alan Ladd and Veronica Lake to retain your interest in what happens to them. If he looked like Quasimodo, it would be harder to go along with him as he hunts the men who betrayed him and his country.

But Graham Greene was a masterful storyteller and *A Gun for Sale* retains its potency all these years later because you understand why Raven has been turned into a cold-blooded killer and accept the fact that he's a doomed man from the moment we meet him.

Patrick Hamilton

Hangover Square

The 1941 novel and the 1945 movie

One can understand why 20th Century–Fox executives felt they needed to mess about with the plot and characters and practically everything else about Patrick Hamilton's 1941 novel *Hangover Square* when they brought it to the screen in 1945.

After all, the principal character was a socially backward, mentally ill hulk of a man who seems destined to commit murder. The leading female character, though quite beautiful, was self-centered, a thoroughly reprehensible exploiter of men. There are no other major characters in Hamilton's book who aren't unsavory.

And filmmakers, of course, really don't much like to try and interest moviegoers in stories that have no likable characters—for good reason: People usually don't buy tickets to films like that.

On the other hand, Hamilton's novel wasn't a cheesy paperback thriller. It takes a hard look at a decadent segment of young London life just before the start of World War II. These are hard-drinking non-achievers who live off others and don't care about anyone but themselves. One can only imagine how useful any of them will be to their fellow

Sinister Laird Cregar seeks out lovely Linda Darnell in *Hangover Square* (1945). Cregar died right after completing the film (20th Century–Fox and the James Bawden Collection).

countrymen once the blitz begins and people start suffering all around them as German bombs fall. You naturally wonder how many of them will be changed for the better by some higher call to duty. It's a serious novel with only the veneer of a thriller.

And yet the Hamilton story, as written, would have been a hard sell as a movie in 1945 when the whole world still was reeling from the horrors of a global war. It must have seemed more intelligent to just nudge Hamilton's story in the direction of a terrifying thriller and ashcan all the sociological elements specific to English class society, things studio execs figure Americans wouldn't care much about anyway.

Marketing rationale surely entered the decision-making process. MGM had done major business in 1944 with *Gaslight*, its thriller based on another dark Patrick Hamilton story. Ingrid Bergman had won the 1944 Best Actress Academy Award playing the wife being driven mad by her sinister husband (Charles Boyer) so he could be free to go after jewels hidden in their spooky old London house. Hamilton's reputation in America had been growing after the success of *Angel Street*, the stage version of *Gaslight*, and a 1940 British film version of *Gaslight* had been very successful overseas.

So, naturally, the Fox executives would hope an overhauled *Hangover Square* could tap the same market vein as *Gaslight*.

Also supporting that reasoning was the recent popularity of Fox's *The Lodger* (1944), which had elevated the studio's contract player Laird Cregar to star billing with his frightening performance as Jack the Ripper. Why not bring Cregar right back in a similar role—the psychotic George Harvey Bone of *Hangover Square*, a man of huge proportions just like Cregar?

I'm also guessing that's why John Brahm, the German immigrant filmmaker who made the gloomy, chilling *The Lodger*, also was assigned to direct *Hangover Square*. Fox wanted it to be a dark thriller in the German noir style, Braham's specialty. But first the story would have to be totally overhauled. And indeed it was.

Hangover Square, the novel, takes place mostly in 1939 as Germany starts its march across Europe by invading Poland. But Barre Lyndon's screenplay pushes the time period back to the turn of the century and the gaslit London of *The Lodger*.

In the book, Bone lives on a dwindling amount of money given him by his aunt. He does no real work. He's drifting in life, like most of his pub acquaintances. But, for the movie, he becomes a composer and pianist, verging on fame, needing only that one great work to put him over at the concert hall.

Large and ungainly, the George of the book is socially inept. He has no females even remotely interested in him. But the movie gives him the lovely, sweet Barbara (Faye Marlowe), the daughter of a renowned symphony conductor (Alan Napier) who's been mentoring George and urging him to complete the concerto he believes will make George's reputation in the world of serious music.

As in the book, though, George has a nagging problem: his frequent blackouts. He fears he "does things" while he's not himself and, in the book, he has a growing conviction that his destiny is to kill Netta, the sexy woman he loves, even though he knows she's just been toying with him for the money she can wheedle out of him. He doesn't act on these homicidal urges until the very end of the novel.

But the movie makes us instantly aware that George is a walking time bomb because it opens with him murdering an antique dealer and setting his victim's lodgings on fire. This is something that never happens in the book.

Hamilton's original story finds George hanging out with a group of hard-drinking men whose primary focus is Netta, a beautiful young movie bit player whose career is going nowhere fast. She survives by sweet-talking George and making him think that, if he plays his cards right, he'll be able to have her soon. George wants her, of course, but not just for a bed partner. He wants her for his wife and hopes to go live in the countryside with her, behind a picket fence.

In the movie, Netta (Linda Darnell) is a music hall singer who meets the doting George when he composes a song for her act and presents it to her. Once she works it into her act, giving George no credit for it, she then starts pleading with him to forget about finishing his concerto and just write new tunes for her.

The person who brings George and Netta together is her pal Mickey (Michael Dyne), who serves as a kind of agent for her. There *is* a Mickey in Hamilton's book, but he's a minor player. Screenwriter Lyndon took a character called Johnnie, George's only male friend in the book, and turned him into Mickey, giving him the additional function of career adviser to Netta.

The ambitious movie Netta connives in several directions at once, making her a true multi-tasker of the gaslit era. Her real goal is to seduce Eddie Carstairs (Glenn Langan), a powerful theater producer who runs the agency where Mickey works. (Trivia note: Langan's career took a nosedive in the late 1940s; he's now best remembered for playing the title role in the drive-in sci-fi classic *The Amazing Colossal Man*.) This also happens in the book, but Carstairs is wary of Netta and figures her for a gold digger from the start. Yet the movie has Carstairs fall for Netta and plan to marry her. This is the final straw that sends George into his ultimate blackout experience.

In *The Lodger*, the young music hall performer who's the object of Jack the Ripper's desire is the girlfriend of a police detective, who begins to suspect that the strange man renting a room in her house may be the serial killer who's terrorizing Whitechapel. That idea obviously resonated with the *Hangover Square* producers, who decided to add such a character to the story, even though Hamilton has nobody like him in the book.

Enter George Sanders, another star name to go above the title. Sanders plays Dr. Allan Middleton, a specialist in criminal psychology; George consults him about his "blackouts." Naturally, Middleton is attracted to George's loyal but rejected "girlfriend" Barbara, so he remains close to the heart of the drama building around the troubled mind of George Harvey Bone.

The ending of Hamilton's novel and the movie aren't alike at all, but I'll leave that for you to discover if you want to experience them both.

Both the novel and the movie are quite involving, the movie even more so if you have no prior knowledge of the story as Hamilton originally told it.

Many critics consider Laird Cregar's performance as George to be his best-ever in his short film career. He most definitely turns in a fascinating portrait of this basically decent but terribly disturbed man. Fox thought Cregar would develop into a great screen "heavy" like Warner Bros.' Sydney Greenstreet, but Cregar desperately wanted to avoid that sort of typecasting.

Cregar never saw the completed *Hangover Square*. He had been placed on a severe weight-loss regimen and took it further on his own because he deeply desired to re-shape himself into a Hollywood leading man. He was taking diet pills and may have overdosed by accident, dying of heart failure at age 29.

Fox developed Vincent Price the way it wanted to develop Cregar, especially in films like *Dragonwyck* (1946) , but Price didn't really become a box office draw until he left Fox and segued into the horror genre with *House of Wax* at Warners, *The Mad Magician* at Columbia and his long string of Poe films at American International. In later years, many thought another immense actor of great skill, Victor Buono, was going to be the new Laird Cregar, especially after Buono's Oscar-nominated performance in *What Ever Happened to Baby Jane?* (1962). Buono also died young (his early 40s) and never became a real headliner.

Hangover Square also was important in moving Linda Darnell up to leading lady roles in "A" pictures. Personally, I'm not blown away by her performance, which I find unconvincing and shallow. The rest of the cast, though, is uniformly good.

Brahm's stylish direction and the beautifully lighted black and white rendering of gaslight-era London also are very strong plus values for the movie, but the other great reason to see *Hangover Square* today is the musical score by Bernard Herrmann, the great film composer whose score for Orson Welles' *Citizen Kane* had already put him on the map, along with his 1941 Oscar-winning score for *All That Money Can Buy*. Herrmann soon would become the favorite composer of the Master of Suspense, Alfred Hitchcock, and scored some of the greatest Hitchcock films, including *Psycho*, *Vertigo* and *North by Northwest*.

So, in *Hangover Square*, it was Bernard Herrmann, not George Harvey Bone, who finally completed the concerto that is played in one of the film's most mesmerizing scenes.

Hangover Square, the novel, is now riding the crest of a renewal of interest in the works of Patrick Hamilton. (Hamilton, by the way, also wrote the play that Hitchcock adapted in 1948 for one of his most unusual—and commercially disappointing—thrillers, *Rope*.)

In retrospect, I think *Hangover Square* suffers because of the effort to make it almost like a companion film to *The Lodger*. But if you haven't yet discovered any of the great performances by Laird Cregar, this is a great place to start—with his last and best performance.

Dashiell Hammett
The Maltese Falcon

The 1929 novel and the 1931 movie, the 1936 movie *Satan Met a Lady* and the 1941 movie

You can be sure that Warner Bros. wasn't wasting any money between 1930 and 1940. The Great Depression ate away at the U.S. economy until the recovery finally began to take hold in the mid–1930s. Then war broke out in Europe, threatening our foreign markets and creating new doubts about America's economic prospects.

At cost-conscious Warners, it seemed a smart idea to start a recycling program, so it became common to buy a literary property as cheaply as possible, then use it over and over. That probably explains why they filmed *The Maltese Falcon* three times in an 11-year period.

Dashiell Hammett's cynical detective novel, published in 1929, was immediately popular. Read today, it's still easy to understand why: It's a taut, fast-moving detective story with strikingly original characters.

With the perspective of almost 90 years, it's also easy to understand why it's regarded as a mystery classic: It took all the creative steam Hammett had been building up with his pulp magazine action hero, the Continental Op, and pumped it into the new character, private eye Sam Spade—the first enduring American "hard-boiled" detective hero.

Hammett's novel seemed a natural for the movies. In the early 1930s, Warner Bros. was working hard to establish itself as the place where the best and toughest crime pictures were made—pictures like *Little Caesar* (1930) with Edward G. Robinson and *The Public Enemy* (1931) with James Cagney. So, it was almost preordained that *The Maltese Falcon* would join the Warners lineup of tough guy pictures.

But somehow Warners missed the boat when they put together the talent behind the first version of *The Maltese Falcon*, which was released in 1931 while the book was still fresh in the minds of its first eager readers.

Hammett's novel is about San Francisco private detective Sam Spade, who's been having an affair with his partner's wife. The partner is killed while tailing a man for the firm's newest client—a beautiful and desperate young woman who calls herself Miss Wonderly—and suspicion falls on Spade himself. Spade soon discovers that Miss Wonderly is not who she claims to be—and is, in fact, mixed up in an international hunt for a million dollar artifact known as the Maltese Falcon.

Humphrey Bogart (left) was private eye Sam Spade in John Huston's 1941 *The Maltese Falcon*, the third version of the novel. With him are Peter Lorre, Mary Astor and Sydney Greenstreet (Warner Bros.)

Until Sam Spade came along, the general reading public in America didn't have a distinctly American-style detective hero outside the pulp magazines, where Hammett and others had been experimenting with "hard-boiled" detectives. The first thing readers of the book noticed was that Spade wasn't just another American imitation of the popular British aristocrat-sleuths of the era. Unlike S.S. Van Dine's Philo Vance and the other Yank copies of Lord Peter Wimsey and Sherlock Holmes, Spade was down and dirty. He rolled his own smokes, had no valet and talked tough to cops and hoods alike. He was the new gumshoe—and Hollywood wasn't quite ready for him.

I believe they made three serious mistakes when first bringing Hammett's new concept to the screen. The first was putting *The Maltese Falcon* in the hands of Roy Del Ruth, a young director who never really distinguished himself by putting his own brand on a film. Had they given the job to somebody else on the lot, say William Wellman who did *The Public Enemy*, the film would have sizzled and crackled. Del Ruth's film seems uncommonly slow today. The people walk across the set slowly and they talk slowly. It lacks snap.

Del Ruth also seemed intimidated by the stodgy new techniques of the talkies while Wellman managed to turn out films literally brimming with noise. Wellman's actors rattled their dialogue off like machine-gun fire while Del Ruth's players took their time to enunciate clearly. Result: tedium.

The second mistake was casting Ricardo Cortez as Sam Spade. Cortez, whose real name was Jake Kranz, was groomed as a Latin lover type in the Valentino mold when he came into pictures in the silent era. He delivered his lines "big" and always appeared as if he were posing for the camera. There's too much the air of the gentleman about him—which is all wrong for Sam Spade. Spade's a rogue who looks at the odds on everything before making a choice. The Cortez Spade is just a sexist lout who *thinks* he's a Latin lover.

A third mistake was casting Bebe Daniels as the femme fatale. Daniels was a big name in 1931, but she gave the impression she'd never done anything wicked in her life. She looked like a society matron trying to flirt with the delivery boy and making a mess of it. The part calls for a dish who's been using her looks to get men to do her bidding for years—but is playing the part of an innocent girl in trouble in a transparent attempt to win Spade over.

The 1931 version often plays the cable network late shows under the title *Dangerous Female*, but its stilted staging and ponderous acting immediately give it away as an old film without special distinction. Oddly, it generally is credited with being more faithful to the book than the two later versions. It isn't. Here's one case in point: "Miss Wonderly" never gets around to revealing her real name, Brigid O'Shaughnessy.

The first *Maltese Falcon* wasn't a box office smash, but Warners thought it had a very workable plot that could be teased and coaxed into being one of the fast-paced contemporary comedies the studio also did so well. So, in 1936, the studio asked one of the screenwriters from the first picture, Brown Holmes, to change a few names and locales and turn *The Maltese Falcon* into a laugh riot. He got the riot part, but not many of the laughs.

His *Satan Met a Lady* has no Sam Spade or Brigid O'Shaughnessy. Instead, it had debonair Warren William as a private eye coming back to his old firm and taking it over after his partner is killed. He couldn't care less about the death of his partner, but he's quite taken by the mysterious young client (Bette Davis) who leads him into the hunt for a different artifact: a "trumpet" made from a horn that's supposed to be filled with priceless jewels.

Director William Dieterle clearly bears no responsibility for the wreckage of Hammett's classic novel that takes place in this dreadful movie. Actually, he deserves some credit for making it go by quickly and for letting Davis bat her eyes relentlessly at William. The famous Bette Davis eyes are about the only reason to watch this film today.

Ricardo Cortez was an unlikely Sam Spade in the first film version of *The Maltese Falcon* in 1931. Cortez was then regarded as a "Latin Lover" type (Warner Bros).

Warren William faces gun-toting Bette Davis in *Satan Met a Lady*, **the peculiar comic remake of** *The Maltese Falcon* **from 1936 (Warner Bros).**

William, who resembled John Barrymore, was all wrong for the Hammett detective character because he was the moustache-wearing leading man type that people associated with "gentleman" parts. He had, in fact, played effete sleuth Philo Vance on screen and starred as Perry Mason in Warners' miserable series of 1930s films about Erle Stanley Gardner's famous criminal lawyer. After *Satan Met a Lady*, he went on to play the thief-sleuth known as the Lone Wolf in a film series.

Among the many mammoth changes *Satan Met a Lady* makes in Hammett's story: The charmingly evil Casper Gutman is transformed into a woman, played without much charm by character actress Alison Skipworth, who's possibly best remembered for her many screen run-ins with W.C. Fields. The other giant "oops" is the casting of a very young Marie (*My Friend Irma*) Wilson as the secretary. Wilson plays her as such an airhead that it's a wonder she doesn't float to the ceiling.

If the casting of Hammett's characters in the first two film versions seems awesomely bad, I should concede that both films had some casting gems. I would argue that Bette Davis could have played Brigid in all three films and held her own with the other actresses. Those who know Davis only as the grotesque old witch of *What Ever Happened to Baby Jane?* might be surprised to see how cute and sexy she could be back in the 1930s. She also was already one hell of an actress. She had already won her first Best Actress Oscar (in 1935's *Dangerous*) when she made *Satan Met a Lady* and was capable of playing any part with conviction.

And the minor casting in the 1931 version was very interesting, too. Sam's secretary Effie Perrine, for instance, was played by Una Merkel, who's probably remembered mostly today for playing comic moms in later movies and TV shows. It turns out she was a very attractive and offbeat girl in her youth. She has the sort of sassy attitude that was just right for Effie, the loyal secretary who puts up with Sam's affectionate pawing and continual come-ons while doing his dirty work without complaint.

The Fat Man's punk gunman, Wilmer, is also perfectly cast in the 1931 version. He's played by Dwight Frye, the bizarre little character actor who had his most famous role that same year: Renfield, the real estate agent who encounters vampire Bela Lugosi in *Dracula* and winds up as his insane disciple in a London lunatic asylum. Frye, who lived only to age 44, was the perfect Wilmer, a role that needs to be played slightly off-center, but with the true look of murder in his eyes. Frye had that nailed. Sadly, he ended his career as a supporting actor in horror movies.

The man who really understood what Dashiell Hammett was trying to create in *The Maltese Falcon* was writer-director John Huston, who was assigned to direct the 1941 version of *The Maltese Falcon*. Huston's film is not only the most faithful of the three to the spirit of Hammett's story, but it also remains a classic of American cinema more than 75 years later.

The best thing that happened to Huston was actor George Raft's decision to turn down the role of Sam Spade. That opened the door to casting Humphrey Bogart, the gesture that guaranteed the film would coalesce all the notions that Hammett and Huston had about the character.

Bogart was too small and too homely to play Spade. That was the conventional wisdom. (He also was too small and too homely to play Raymond Chandler's Philip Marlowe in *The Big Sleep* in 1946, but can you now imagine anyone else playing that part?) Bogart brought the air of weary cynicism to the part that the earlier actors weren't capable of playing—and that was what made him fit the role no matter how short or homely he was.

Bogart brought something else to the role that even improved upon Hammett's concept. He brought nobility to the gumshoe character. If you read the novel, you're left wondering if Spade isn't just a selfish man—unwilling to "play the sap" for the sexy Brigid because it's not a good career move for him. Bogart plays the part as if Spade is doing the right thing in "sending her over," not just for himself, but for his fellow man as well.

Bogart's Spade isn't the sexist lout of the earlier films, though he still calls his secretary "sweetheart" and touches her "inappropriately" from time to time. He doesn't sleep with Brigid, though he does in the book and in the 1931 film, and he's much more respectful to her when she first shows up as a client without portfolio.

What he is, though, is much tougher. He's the only Spade that we actually see rolling his own smokes. And when he starts picking on poor Wilmer (Elisha Cook, Jr.), you can really tell Wilmer is never going to get the drop on Spade, not on his best day. (The bit, taken from the book, where Spade slips behind Wilmer and pulls his overcoat down over his arms, is perfectly executed by Bogart.) And when he kisses Brigid off, you suspect he's had her number all along.

Huston's supporting cast is also near flawless. Peter Lorre is the definitive Joel Cairo, a man whose sexual orientation might be called "gardenia" after the scent he favors. Still, Lorre's Cairo is a gutsy little guy who keeps ticking after he takes a licking.

Sydney Greenstreet made his film debut in the 1941 *Falcon* and was an instant smash hit. His good-natured, effete but sinister Casper Gutman is now so legendary that literally scores of characters have been modeled on him. Hammett created every atom of that character, but Greenstreet made him come to life so vividly that he seems to hog most of the credit anyway.

Elisha Cook's Wilmer is also masterful and it now seems likely that poor Elisha was so unnerved by the way Sam Spade handled him in 1941 that he spent the rest of his career as a nervous little twit, expecting the worst from every leading man—and usually getting it.

Then there's Mary Astor, who won an Oscar that same year for her supporting role in Bette Davis' *The Great Lie*. In real life, Astor had the reputation of being a "hot number," especially after her "secret diary" was made public in a scandalous trial, revealing her to be much less the lady than she usually appeared on screen. In other words, she was born to play Brigid O'Shaughnessy

Huston fused all these marvelous elements into a fast-paced, exciting film in which the bizarre characters all seemed perfectly natural speaking the lines that mostly were from Hammett's original dialogue. By giving the film a much darker, more stylish look, Huston made *The Maltese Falcon* into a film worthy of comparison to the famous book.

None of the films featured Casper Gutman's young daughter, who (in the book) Spade finds doped-up in a hotel room. After she comes to, she skips out in the book and is never heard from again. I'm haunted by the notion of what it must have been like to be Gutman's kid. Did he drag her around the world with him on his hunt for the black bird, involving her with all the murders, thefts and other intrigue?

If Warners still wants to get the most out of its investment in the film rights to Hammett's book, isn't it time for *Maltese Falcon II: Revenge of the Fat Man's Daughter*?

Dashiell Hammett

The Thin Man

The 1933 novel and the 1934 movie

You could make a pretty good case for the notion that *The Thin Man* was Dashiell Hammett's most successful literary concoction, even though *The Maltese Falcon*—a much better book—was filmed a number of times, and led to a radio series built around its detective character, Sam Spade.

But *The Thin Man* was a popular book that's still widely read, was turned into an immensely popular series of six MGM feature films and, ultimately, a fondly remembered TV series starring Peter Lawford and Phyllis Kirk.

A new generation of Hammett fans also reveres *The Thin Man* because its leading characters, Nick and Nora Charles, are now almost universally believed to be Hammett's attempt to portray himself and his long-time love, Lillian Hellman, as characters on the printed page.

Moreover, the actors who played Nick and Nora in the films, William Powell and Myrna Loy, today are best remembered for those roles, even though both had long screen careers and played a wide assortment of other characters.

My opinion is that Hammett created four milestone characters in the mystery genre (the Continental Op, Sam Spade and Nick and Nora Charles), but that Nick and Nora are the ones we'll remember the longest because of their hilariously witty badinage and their wacky lifestyle.

For originality, I suppose the nameless agency detective the Continental Op should get the nod because Hammett was, with him, really creating the blueprint for what came to be known as the American hard-boiled private eye character. Sam Spade was the refinement of that burst of creativity, but after all the private eyes who followed Spade it's sometimes hard to remember which one he was.

Nick and Nora weren't so innovative. Agatha Christie really created the sassy husband-and-wife detective team a decade earlier with her second novel, *The Secret Adversary*, which introduced Tuppence and Tommy Beresford, the upper class British pair who enjoyed a racy lifestyle and also interacted like a TV sitcom team. They also went on to several other novels, became the first Christie characters to ever appear on screen (in the silent era) and finally turned up in the stylish BBC series *Partners in Crime*.

But Nick and Nora are so much more memorable, especially for Americans, because they came to embody the carefree 1930s urban lifestyle so perfectly—and that lifestyle still looks so awfully appealing today.

First published in 1933, *The Thin Man* introduces Nick as a former detective who has pretty much "retired" from the game in order to "manage" the assets of his new wife Nora, who's rolling in inherited wealth. With their dog Asta, they have come from their home in San Francisco to New York City to enjoy the Christmas holidays, mainly by shopping, partying, sleeping

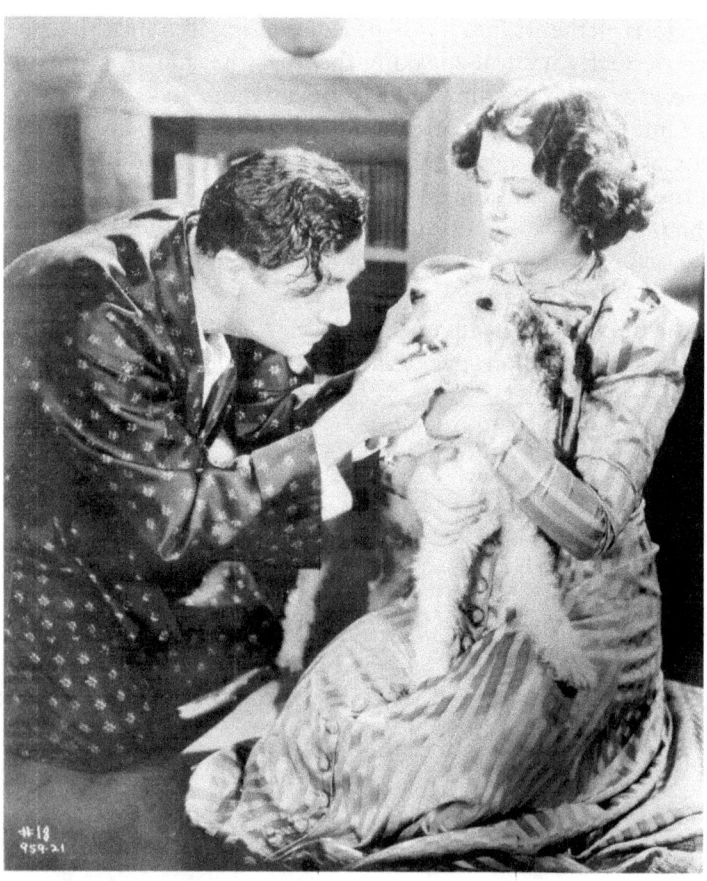

William Powell was Nick Charles, Myrna Loy was his wife Nora, and that's their dog, Asta, in *The Thin Man* (1934), the first of many films and TV episodes featuring the detective team dreamed up by Dashiell Hammett (MGM and the James Bawden Collection).

late and drinking as much bootleg hootch as they can. (In the book, the story takes place before the 1933 repeal of Prohibition.)

Their first adventure begins in a 52nd Street speakeasy when beautiful, wealthy young Dorothy Wynant recognizes Nick as the romantic sleuth who once worked with her father, inventor Clyde Wynant. Nick hasn't seen her since she was a little girl, but she tells him the Wynants divorced some time back and she would now like to visit her father, if she can find him.

Hammett's plot is complex and twisted. Nick is slowly but surely drawn into the search for Clyde Wynant, who seems to be missing. When people connected with Wynant start popping up as dead bodies, the police also take an interest. Wynant is described as a very tall, exceedingly thin man. That's where the title comes from, though nobody ever refers to anybody in the book as "the thin man."

There's nothing in Hammett's plot that would make you think this would ever become a book people still would be reading more than 80 years later. But the characters make it worthwhile. Nick seems to be perpetually half-loaded. He's also rather lazy and has to be prodded into action more often than not. When somebody asks him what he's discovered so far, he's likely to reply with a wisecrack, no doubt because he hasn't yet discovered much of anything. He sounds a good bit like Hammett himself in that same period, his early Hollywood years with would-be playwright Lillian Hellman.

In contrast, Nora seems pretty energetic and quite forgiving. She's amused by all the intimations that her new husband has partied down with what may be a regiment of loose women. She also is fascinated by the hoods and lowlifes that Nick encounters as he meanders his way through the task of finding Clyde Wynant. In fact, you can get the impression that Nora's somewhat open marriage to Nick is just a grand example of a society girl who's "slumming."

You'll discover from the book that "Charles" really isn't the name on their marriage license. After Nora has tossed several zingers at Nick, referring to him as "an old Greek fool," we learn that his family name really was Charalambides, but Nick's dad shortened it to Charles when he arrived at Ellis Island as an immigrant.

If there's one thing in the book that pointed *The Thin Man* toward a new life on the movie screen, it was surely Hammett's marvelously crisp dialogue and the bantering but loving relationship between Nick and Nora. She tells him things like, "I wish you were sober enough to talk to," while he reminds her he's busy "trying to see you don't lose any of the money I married you for" and so on.

In 1934, *The Thin Man* came to the screen in a snappy version directed by W.S. Van Dyke. Screenwriters Albert Hackett and Frances Goodrich turned the book inside out, starting out with the disappearance of Clyde Wynant (Edward Ellis), a murder and the setting-up of the principal suspects and all their likely motives before coming to the first scene of the book: Dorothy Wynant approaching Nick at the speakeasy.

Hackett and Goodrich wisely decided to drop Nick Charles' first-person narration and put us into a suspenseful situation before ever introducing the film's hero. That introductory scene is masterful: The camera shows a crowd of people at a bar, their backs turned to us, and we hear Nick's voice saying, "The important thing is the rhythm!" as he demonstrates the proper way to shake a batch of martinis.

When we finally see Nick, we discover he's a very well-dressed man about town who obviously isn't shaking the evening's first batch of martinis. He's so glib you'd think he was a standup comic. Ask him what he knows about something and he'll tell you, "I don't know anything. I've been in California for the past four years."

By 1934, William Powell was already a famous movie star. Though he'd played bad guys in silent films, he was known in the early 1930s as a romantic leading man, but also had already played a well-dressed, upper class private eye on screen several times: S.S. Van Dine's Philo Vance. (He even had a dog sidekick in *The Kennel Murder Case*.) But the Nick Charles character fit him like no other role had.

Myrna Loy also was well-known by 1934, but primarily as slinky types, like Dr. Fu Manchu's diabolical daughter in MGM's *The Mask of Fu Manchu*. Her entrance in *The Thin Man*—she's pulled into a crowded room by her dog Asta and falls flat on her face—was a signal that Loy was about to start using her flair for comedy repartee like she'd never done before.

The movie made the police a little dumber than Hammett did—Nat Pendleton, whose specialty was lunkheads, played the main police detective—and they gave poor Asta a sex change from female (the book) to male. By casting the young, beautiful Maureen O'Sullivan as Dorothy Wynant, they also made the character considerably more appealing than Hammett did. (She's a rather silly, heavy-drinking girl in the book.) O'Sullivan was then one of MGM's brightest young prospects and already angling to get out of her regular role as Tarzan's mate, Jane, in that series of films. The film also made Dorothy's brother Gilbert into a comic nerd character. In the book, he's more a weirdo.

But the biggest and most worthwhile change from book to film is the way the movie wraps up the mystery plot. Hammett had Nick kind of half-heartedly solve the mystery without any particular suspense or action. In the movie, Nick arranges a roundup of suspects at a dinner table and does one of those "one of you is the killer" speeches. It was a cliché even in 1934, but it gave the film a brisk finale and an excuse for some action.

Most diehard Hammett fans acknowledge that the movie is superior to the book, which certainly accounts for the fact that Hammett really did nothing more with Nick and Nora Charles after *The Thin Man*, his last full-length novel, while MGM filmed five sequels: *After the Thin Man* (1936), *Another Thin Man* (1939), *Shadow of the Thin Man* (1941), *The Thin Man Goes Home* (1944) and *Song of the Thin Man* (1947). Hammett supplied the original storyline for two of the sequels.

Though Hammett may have been inspired by Agatha Christie's Tuppence and Tommy, it's clear that his Nick and Nora Charles inspired many, many subsequent husband-wife sleuth duos from *Mr. and Mrs. North* through TV's *Hart to Hart*. The book is worth reading today just to see how that all got started, but also for Hammett's great sense of fun and his lively dialogue.

And even if the movie seems dated today, the 1934 *Thin Man* remains a treasure chest of 1930s styles, attitudes and mores—and contains those magical performances by Powell and Loy. I pull out the DVD and watch it every now and then just to remind myself how much fun Hollywood movies used to be.

A.P. Herbert
The House by the River

The 1921 novel and the 1950 movie

The early beginnings of the literary movement the French critics called *roman noir* usually are traced back to the late 1920s and early 1930s with the publication of the first so-called "inverted" mysteries. This new genre of mystery reflected the growing interest in criminal psychology among mystery writers and the result was the creation of murder stories often told from the viewpoint of the killer, which necessarily made them much darker in tone than conventional mysteries of the period.

Among those early classics are C.S. Forester's *Payment Deferred* and Francis Iles' *Malice Aforethought*. Readers knew from the start who the killer was and the suspense came from watching their reactions as the authorities tracked them down.

But there is a much earlier example of the "inverted" mystery, English author A. P. Herbert's very dark *The House by the River* (1921). It falls neatly into that genre with its tale of noted poet Stephen Byrne's cold-blooded murder of Emily Gaunt, the sexy young housemaid in his home, and his effort to involve his best friend in covering up the crime while eventually shifting suspicion onto him.

Nearly 30 years later, the novel was brought to the screen by one of the greatest of all film noir directors, Fritz Lang. Released by Republic Pictures, a Poverty Row studio devoted to low-budget commercial fare like Westerns and serials, *House by the River* was a commercial failure, but has now been rediscovered as one of the better films noir to come out of the late 1940s and early 1950s.

While creating this work of film art, Lang and screenwriter Mel Dinelli took great liberties with Herbert's original storyline, turning *House by the River* into something quite different from the original. In the novel, Byrne is a poet on the verge of greatness. He lives in an old house on the banks of the Thames River in what was the Hammersmith section of London. While his wife Margery is away, he makes advances to Emily, the new maid. When she resists him, he attempts to silence her and accidentally strangles her. Shortly after he discovers he's actually killed her, Stephen panics when someone knocks at his door. It turns out to be his close friend John Egerton, a shy, retiring civil servant.

Stephen can't hide from John, who knows he's at home, so he brings him in and reveals what he's done. He begs John to help him dispose of the body. He says he must conceal this crime because Margery is expecting a child and is in very delicate health. If she learned he had murdered Emily, the shock might cause her to miscarry, might even kill her.

John reluctantly accedes and they put the corpse in a large canvas bag, row out onto the river in the dead of night and dump it, hoping it will be carried out to sea by the tides. But we already know that the river is notorious for carrying logs, animal remains and other detritus back and forth for weeks until it finally washes up somewhere, often not far from where it started.

That's indeed what happens: The body is found and identified and police come to Stephen because the bag is marked with his name. Stephen informs the police that his friend John had borrowed the bag and never returned it, so suspicion shifts to John.

Louis Hayward, usually a swashbuckling hero in his movies, played a killer in Fritz Lang's *The House by the River*, the 1950 thriller from A.P. Herbert's 1921 novel (Republic Pictures).

The bulk of Herbert's novel deals with the suspicion aroused about John, though the circumstantial evidence against him never results in charges. The friendship between Stephen and John deteriorates, especially after Margery bears her child and Stephen begins a sordid affair with an attractive young single woman named Muriel. John has been hoping to woo and eventually marry Muriel.

Ultimately, Stephen, still haunted by his crime, writes a long poem that takes place in historical England, but closely mirrors his crime and his betrayal of his best friend. Margery accidentally finds the manuscript, reads it and begins to suspect that Stephen is the murderer. Stephen finally decides to kill himself by drowning in his beloved river, but instead ends up in a physical struggle with the angry John, falls overboard and drowns.

Herbert's novel adds an ironic twist to this fate-directed finale by having a statue in Stephen's honor erected on the river in memory of his contributions as a great poet. But the relentless river waters undercuts the base of the statue and it tumbles into the same turbulent waters where Emily's body was dumped at the beginning of this tragic saga.

Lang and Dinelli turned the story inside out, striving for more dramatic conflict. Dinelli was the inventive screenwriter who added the deaf-mute angle to Ethel Lina White's story *Some Must Watch* when Robert Siodmak filmed it as *The Spiral Staircase*. He came up with some equally inventive new twists for *The House by the River*, transforming it into a Cain and Abel story by changing neighbor John Egerton into John Byrne, Stephen's brooding, crippled brother, who has long envied Stephen because of his charm, his success and his lovely wife. John has been getting Stephen out of scrapes all his life, but this time he does so only to spare the feelings and health of sickly Marjorie (he changed the spelling of her name, too). John's deep love for Marjorie sets up yet another source of conflict.

Lang's casting of this grim film was most unusual. For the leading role of Stephen, he chose swashbuckling English leading man Louis Hayward, most famous for his heroic roles in *Anthony Adverse*, *The Man in the Iron Mask*, *The Son of Monte Cristo* and *The Saint in New York* (1938), in which he was the first actor to portray Leslie Charteris' famous sleuth Simon Templar, aka "The Saint."

As John, Lang cast American light leading man Lee Bowman. Marjorie was played by Jane Wyatt, then best known for her 1937 role as Ronald Colman's leading lady in *Lost Horizon*. Wyatt later won three Emmys as the definitive sitcom mom, Margaret Anderson, opposite Robert Young in TV's *Father Knows Best*.

Hayward is alternatively sinister and charming, proving he was more than capable of weightier roles. Wyatt, then about 38, was quite lovely and gave a strong performance as the troubled wife who discovers she's married to a killer. Bowman, who brings a depth to John that wasn't in the book, strikes just the right note as the film's ultimate hero.

The decision to make the two key male characters brothers was clever. We learn that Stephen has been living a more luxurious life than his bookkeeper brother principally because John gave him his share of their family inheritance. Rather than a poet, Stephen is now a novelist, but not a very successful one. Only the notoriety of Emily's murder makes him a commercially viable author. Dinelli's script gives Stephen a self-delusional sense of his own importance that reminds one of Raskolnikov in Dostoyevsky's *Crime and Punishment*. It becomes quite obvious when Stephen asks John, "Which one of us would the world miss the most?" He obviously has been busy rationalizing his willingness to put the blame for Emily's murder on John with his twisted "end justifies the means" sort of reasoning.

The movie also reverses the flow of evidence. It is now Stephen who borrowed the canvas bag from John, and John's name is inked on the bag, a clue that points suspicion directly at him. The Muriel subplot was dropped when Dinelli adapted the novel and it isn't missed. Instead, we have John's growing love for Marjorie and her fading loyalty to her increasingly rude and hot-tempered husband.

In the film's climax, Stephen attacks John with a length of chain, knocks him out and dumps him into the swift-flowing river, hoping people will assume he drowned himself because he was tormented by his guilt over murdering Emily. Then Stephen attempts to strangle Marjorie when he finds her reading the manuscript of his new novel, a thinly disguised account of the murder and his role in it.

In Herbert's book, Stephen accidentally drowns while trying to kill John. But the movie has John survive his ordeal in the river and return to the house, dripping with water, in time to thwart Stephen's strangulation of Marjorie. The panicked Stephen then imagines Emily's ghost is after him and becomes entangled in a curtain, which causes him to fall off the staircase to his death. It's not very convincing, but it does wrap things up quite neatly, allowing us to see John and Marjorie embrace as the end credits run.

The original novel is a more plausible, less exciting tale of a man's efforts to conceal his part in a murder. It's a very early preview of the dark turns that mystery would take at mid-century.

Lang's movie is an under-appreciated gem, spoiled only by the hurried and implausible ending. The haunting George Anthiel musical score, the artfully composed cinematography of Edward Cronjager and the film's oppressively dark mood help make it one of Lang's great noir classics, well worth seeing today.

Patricia Highsmith
Strangers on a Train

The 1949 novel and the 1951 movie; the 1969 movie *Once You Kiss a Stranger...*; and the 1996 TV movie *Once You Meet a Stranger*

I don't believe it's possible to remember Alfred Hitchcock's celebrated 1951 movie thriller *Strangers on a Train* without also recalling these unforgettable cinematic moments:

- Hundreds of people are in the grandstand, watching a tennis match, their heads shifting back and forth in unison as they follow the ball from one side of the court to the other. But the camera singles out one sinister man in the center of the crowd, staring straight ahead. He's Bruno, the villain, stalking his quarry: tennis player Guy Haines.
- The eyeglasses of Guy Haines' wife Miriam are dislodged when Bruno grabs her throat—and we watch her being strangled to death as reflected in the shattered lens of her spectacles.
- The film's exciting climax, with Bruno and Guy locked in a desperate struggle aboard a carnival merry-go-round that speeds out of control and finally self-destructs in a horrendous crash.

Here's an interesting point to consider: None of those immortal motion picture scenes occurs in the revered source novel by Patricia Highsmith. In fact, Highsmith's Guy Haines is an architect who never goes near a tennis court, her Miriam doesn't wear eyeglasses and nothing the least bit exciting happens on that merry-go-round in her story.

Hitchcock's *Strangers on a Train* isn't another example of the movies trashing a classic novel for the sake of a few "visual" thrills the book didn't have. In fact, the film is one of the masterworks of perhaps the greatest film *auteur* of the 20th century. It is by far my favorite among Hitchcock's films—and I've seen all but one, an early silent film that no longer exists.

On the other hand, the changes Hitchcock found it necessary to make in Highsmith's story don't mean Highsmith's novel was lacking in any way. The book, first published in 1949, was a bestseller and established Highsmith's reputation, paving the way for all the books that followed, including *The Talented Mr. Ripley* and its many sequels.

Strangers on a Train really is that uncommon phenomenon, a great book that was overhauled radically by a filmmaker, yet still served as the foundation for what turned out to be a classic American film.

The reason why the Highsmith and Hitchcock works turned out so different is simple: They were telling different stories within the same general plot framework. Highsmith was communicating a volatile, controversial notion: that each of us is capable of committing an unthinkable crime, even murder, given the proper circumstances. This theme

Robert Walker (right) is the homicidal Bruno in Alfred Hitchcock's *Strangers on a Train* (1951), from Patricia Highsmith's novel. With Walker are Leo G. Carroll and Ruth Roman (Warner Bros).

would be repeated time and time again in her subsequent novels and stories. In contrast, Hitchcock wasn't trying to make any sort of moral judgment. He simply wanted to take us on a roller coaster ride of suspense, living in the skin of a man caught up in a situation totally out of his control.

For Highsmith, *Strangers on a Train* was the opening round in what would become a lifelong fascination with the concept that seemingly normal people can, in some situations, commit anti-social acts. Her story also neatly dovetailed with what Hitchcock had made his *oeuvre*—innocent people "caught up" in suspenseful situations—so it's obvious why he wanted to make a film of it.

In the book, young architect Guy Haines accidentally meets Charles Anthony Bruno, a dissolute, alcoholic playboy, when they are seated together on a cross-country train journey. Bruno is fascinated by Guy because he's a handsome, rising star in the medium of architecture—a celebrity. He's also everything Bruno isn't: a successful young man who actually does something worthwhile.

A dissolute character, Bruno lives with his doting mother. She indulges his drinking and doles out his spending money over the objections of Bruno's father, a ruthless businessman. Bruno hates his father so much that he wishes the old man were dead.

Guy is a much better balanced human being, although he has one nagging problem:

his estranged wife Miriam, a sluttish woman who's pregnant with another man's child. Guy hopes to divorce her so he can marry Anne, a woman from a wealthy and powerful family. But Miriam is dragging her feet, perhaps anxious to cash in on the big contract Guy has just landed to design a multi-million dollar country club.

Once Bruno learns about Guy's "problem," he proposes a bizarre though highly creative solution: He should murder Guy's wife and Guy, in return, should murder Bruno's father. According to Bruno, the police would never suspect either of them because neither man would seem to have a motive. Each man would have killed a complete stranger.

Hitchcock was enthralled by this concept, but he knew he couldn't take it in the direction Highsmith did in the book. She wanted to demonstrate that the seeds of murder are in all of us. In the book, Guy at first resists Bruno's idea as the concoction of a madman. Then, when Bruno actually murders Miriam, Guy realizes that the madman has taken control of his life because Bruno now can threaten to tell the police Guy was his willing accomplice if Guy should turn him in. So, in the book, Guy murders Bruno's father, then lives in terror that he'll forever be in bondage to this demented man. (The movie also changes the character's name to Bruno Anthony.)

Highsmith now is regarded as much more than a mystery writer by literary critics. The detailed examination of the undercurrents of human life in her many novels has earned her the admiration and respect she never really achieved within her lifetime. (She died in 1995, after living a reclusive life in Europe.) Her Bruno rather obviously is a latent homosexual who wants to be the most important person in Guy's life, and so he uses Guy's growing guilty conscience to make a place for himself in Guy's much more desirable world.

This might have been the foundation for a truly important film, but probably not a very popular one. Highsmith's protagonist is too much like Raskolnikov, a "hero" so unsavory that he's never really been successfully adapted to stage or screen. If Hitchcock had stayed with her story, it would have required an audience to identify with Guy, a man who actually becomes a murderer, then spends the rest of his life trying to privately atone for it while also covering his tracks, so the police don't catch him. That's a hard sell for a filmmaker.

To help him find ways to make Highsmith's core story filmable, Hitchcock played a bold card: He hired America's most respected mystery writer, Raymond Chandler, to help write the screenplay. Chandler's *The Big Sleep*, *Farewell, My Lovely* and the other Philip Marlowe novels redefined the American detective genre in the 1940s.

Though it's said that Hitch and Chandler didn't get along very well over the course of the project, it's clear that Chandler brought his special *noir* sensibility to the film and livened up the dialogue. But the bulk of the screenplay was written by Chandler's co-author, novelist Czenzi Ormonde.

Working with Chandler and Ormonde from the initial adaptation by Whitfield Cook, Hitchcock found an ideal solution to the problem of having a guilt-ridden murderer as their hero: They would have Guy seem to be going through with the murder, but instead have him plan to warn Bruno's father that his son was a murderer. By redeeming the character of Guy, they made him the legitimate hero of the movie because thereafter it becomes a duel between Guy and Bruno or, if you will, good and evil. (Bruno, suspicious of Guy, hides in his father's bed on the night of the proposed murder and thwarts Guy's plan.)

Hitchcock also knew that Guy's architecture background was cinematically dull, so the movie turns him into one of the nation's top amateur tennis players, a well-liked celebrity-in-the-making whose eventual goal is to enter politics, perhaps with the aid of his future wife's father, a Senator.

That also gave Hitch the opportunity to create one of the most exciting last reels of his movie career. In the film, Guy learns that Bruno intends to plant Guy's monogrammed cigarette lighter at the scene of Miriam's murder. He plans to do this the same day that Guy is playing the most important match of his career in front of a huge crowd at Forest Hills. That enabled Hitchcock to create an amazing sequence in which Guy attempts to defeat his opponent in just three sets, so he can rush to the murder scene and stop Bruno.

By intercutting the scenes of Guy's desperate tennis match with Bruno's trip to the murder scene, Hitchcock builds tremendous tension. Both men face terrible obstacles. Guy's opponent rises to the challenge and turns the match into a battle that brings the crowd to its feet. Meanwhile, Bruno accidentally drops Guy's lighter down a storm drain, then attracts an unwelcome crowd as he struggles to retrieve it.

The sequence ends with Guy and Bruno savagely fighting each other for the lighter aboard a runaway merry-go-round. (A policeman fires a shot at Guy, but hits the operator of the ride instead, causing him to collapse on the lever that controls the merry-go-round's speed.)

Nobody but Hitchcock could come up with the stunning sequence that follows: Children holding on for dear life as the merry-go-round turns into a killing machine, whirling at faster and faster speeds, the painted horses bobbing up and down, their carved hooves striking down at the two fighting men while a toothless old maintenance man risks his life to crawl under the careening machine to reach the control switch.

The way the movie alters the basic story can serve as a primer for the differences between literary and cinematic storytelling. Film stories must be simple in order to move. The movie audience decides early that Guy is good and Bruno evil. It makes Miriam a much nastier character, so that our sympathy shifts more quickly to Guy.

Hitchcock also added a character not in the book—the precocious sister of Guy's fiancée—to serve as a sort of Greek chorus, letting everybody know what might happen to Guy as a suspect in his wife's murder. Hitchcock also gave the part of the sister to his own daughter Patricia. It's her best-ever performance on film.

After all the changes made to Highsmith's story, the material perfectly suited the director's style. In the book and the movie, Bruno is a frequently amusing character, which seems to add to his menace. Hitch knew that territory well and he gives the film a special air of whimsy that seems to temper some of the horrifying things that go on. For example, he uses cinematic shorthand to introduce the characters at the movie's start by showing us the feet of Bruno and Guy before he ever shows their faces. Guy is wearing dark, conservative shoes and Bruno is wearing flamboyant two-toned shoes. We watch as the two pair of feet make their way through the crowded railway station, into the same railroad car to the same table where their feet accidentally touch, giving them an excuse to speak to each other. By then, though, we already know these two fellows pretty well just by sizing up their footwear. It's an amusing way to get the dark storyline going.

Later, when an irritating child carrying a balloon appears beside Bruno in the amusement park where he is stalking Miriam, Bruno pops the kid's balloon with his lighted cigarette. It's something many of us might have wanted to do, but wouldn't because it would be considered mean-spirited. Bruno, who's sort of a big kid anyway, has no such restraints.

Yet Hitch is very cold-blooded in other parts of the film. Bruno seems to be flirting with Miriam as he stalks her and she glows from the attention. Yet, when she finds herself alone in a dark place with Bruno, Hitch shows us just her face as Bruno asks, off camera, "Is your name Miriam?" She answers, "Why, yes..." Then her expression changes as his hands close around her throat and her glasses fall away. Hitch plays the murder without any extraneous noise except the distant carnival sounds. As we watch a distorted view of the strangling through Miriam's shattered eyeglasses, we feel our blood starting to run cold.

Hitchcock loved the gimmick of the eyeglasses, though Miriam didn't wear any in the book. For one thing, it makes her seem more vulnerable, even though he's gone to lots of trouble to make sure we get the fact that she's a slut. They're rather tasteless and unattractive glasses, too, which helps further define Miriam's character as considerably less sophisticated than Guy's new love, Anne. The glasses also are so distinctively ugly that we readily associate them with the rather plain Miriam.

Later in the film, Hitch uses the glasses again for a special purpose: Bruno brings them to Guy as evidence that he's not kidding about murdering Miriam. When Guy sees the familiar glasses, the look on his face tells us he knows the nightmare is for real.

Still later, Hitch again calls on the glasses by putting a very similar pair on Barbara, Anne's suspicious sister. When Bruno sees them, he has a mental flashback to Miriam and the murder. It's a chilling moment as Barbara prattles on, unaware that Bruno is seeing her as the reincarnation of the hateful slut he already has killed once.

Hitchcock really has a ball with the climactic amusement park sequence, giving Bruno a series of near-comic mishaps as he blunders his way into planting the evidence that might convict Guy of Miriam's murder.

And the merry-go-round finale is quintessential Hitchcock. Highsmith put Bruno and Miriam on a merry-go-round in her stalking-murder chapter, but there is no carnival finale in her book. Hitch saw it as a whimsical yet breathtakingly suspenseful way to resolve everything. The merry-go-round might be seen as a symbolic reference to Guy's normal world, suddenly running out of control because of Bruno. Hitch even reminds us who the good guy is in that sequence by showing a little boy about to be flung off the machine by its whirling momentum—until Guy pauses long enough in his struggle with Bruno to lift the kid to safety. Hitch even makes the normally placid faces of the wooden horses look as if they're panicky real-life steeds. At times, the distorted horse faces even look like the ones in Picasso's immortal painting *Guernica*.

Farley Granger was an inspired choice for the role of Guy. He's handsome, but has that slight off-center look in his eyes that makes you believe he'd be vulnerable to someone like Bruno. But the film belongs to Robert Walker, whose slightly sissified, part-goofy Bruno is one of the screen's most memorable villains. It was beyond doubt the best performance Walker ever gave and it's the heart of this great film.

It's also fascinating to speculate on the possible pleasure Hitchcock might have derived from casting Walker in a career-making role. Hitchcock had just completed his long exclusive contract under the producer who brought him to America in 1939, David O. Selznick, a hands-on filmmaker and *not* the easiest man in the world to work under. Selznick was known to have a low opinion of Walker, no doubt because Selznick's wife, actress Jennifer Jones, had been previously married to Walker and divorced him to marry Selznick.

Farley Granger hangs on for dear life as Robert Walker kicks at him in the stirring conclusion of Alfred Hitchcock's *Strangers on a Train*, which takes place on a runaway merry-go-round. That doesn't happen in the Patricia Highsmith novel (Warner Bros. and the James Bawden Collection).

What did Patricia Highsmith think of the major changes Hitchcock made to her first big novel? In Andrew Wilson's Highsmith biography *Beautiful Shadow* (2003), he suggests she liked the film at first, especially Walker's portrayal of Bruno, but didn't care for the casting of Ruth Roman as Guy's future wife Anne. Later, though, he reports that she "bitched" a lot about what Hitchcock had done to her story and how little she'd been paid for it—the sum of just $6000 for all future rights.

One can only imagine what she thought when Warner Bros. used the *Strangers on a Train* screenplay as the basis for a putrescent remake 18 years later, *Once You Kiss a Stranger*... Filmed in bright colors with a "B" level cast by undistinguished director Robert Sparr, the remake was bereft of any suspense and it further scrambled the storyline.

The Bruno character is changed into a woman named Diana, played by Carol Lynley. We learn from the outset that she's mentally ill and is about to be institutionalized on the recommendation of her psychiatrist (Whit Bissell), who has concluded that she's homicidal. We have an early hint of that when she's displeased with her cat and decides to lock it in the refrigerator. (Fortunately, it claws her and escapes such a fate!)

There's also an early homage to the Hitchcock film when we see Diana emerge from the ocean after doing some spear-fishing and, irritated that a little girl is playing with a beach ball on the sand in front of her beach house, uses the spear gun to pop the beach ball. It's an echo of Bruno's balloon-popping stunt in the Hitchcock film.

Diana is stalking Jerry (Paul Burke), a professional golfer who always seems to lose the big matches to his No. 1 rival (Philip Carey). In the midst of their latest match, Diana seduces a drunken Jerry and offers to kill his rival golfer if Jerry will murder the psychiatrist who's about to send her to an asylum. Jerry thinks she's a bit fruity, but is stunned when Diana goes through with the murder, running over the rival several times with a golf cart, then braining him with a golf club.

There is no wind-up to compare with Hitchcock's runaway merry-go-round, but Diana does try to shoot Jerry's wife (Martha Hyer) with her spear gun and, that failing, run her down with a dune buggy.

Carol Lynley plants a kiss on Paul Burke in *Once You Kiss a Stranger...* This 1969 remake of *Strangers on a Train* features a gender switch of the original film's male villain to Lynley's sexy but sinister female (Warner Bros.–Seven Arts).

Equally sappy was a CBS-TV version called *Once You Meet a Stranger* (1996). This keeps the original meeting on a train, but switches the sexes of both Bruno and Guy to female and gives the Guy character, now called Sheila Gaines, yet another career scramble. She's now a former child star whose first husband won't give her a divorce. Margo Anthony, the screwy girl she meets on the train, kills the husband and expects her to fulfill her part of the deal by killing Margo's mother. Two of the more interesting actresses of the period played the parts—Jacqueline Bisset as Sheila and Theresa Russell as Margo—but the film retained none of the thrills of the original.

Hitchcock's *Strangers on a Train* is still thoroughly enjoyable more than half a century after it became a major box office hit. It's a film that young cinema fans should study for all it can tell them about the essentials of manipulative filmmaking. The two remakes should be avoided.

Fans of the Hitchcock movie will be richly rewarded if they search out Highsmith's novel. The book has grown in stature over the years and its message seems even more relevant today when it seems there are hordes of Brunos out there, doing nothing but dreaming up nasty things to do to normal folks like us.

Patricia Highsmith
The Talented Mr. Ripley

The 1955 novel, the 1960 movie *Purple Noon* and the 1999 movie

Originally published in 1955, Patricia Highsmith's *The Talented Mr. Ripley* has grown in stature over the years as a classic noir novel and now threatens to eclipse in popularity her first huge American bestseller, *Strangers on a Train*.

Anthony Minghella's 1999 film version starring Matt Damon, Gwyneth Paltrow, Jude Law and Cate Blanchett drew massive attention to Highsmith's novel, which was reissued with a movie tie-in cover. Now all five novels in the bizarre Ripley series are back in print and being read by millions of new Highsmith fans.

This is great news because *The Talented Mr. Ripley* is one of the most absorbing and interesting novels of the past century—a literary masterpiece that transcends the boundaries of the mystery genre and even its special corner for the darkest themes—the one labeled noir.

Most new Highsmith fans may not be aware that *The Talented Mr. Ripley* was filmed first by the great French director of thrillers, René Clément, in 1960, just five years after Highsmith published it—and still within the postwar era that the novel so accurately depicts. Clément called the film *Plein Soleil*; its American title was *Purple Noon*.

Neither Minghella nor Clément stuck closely to Highsmith's story, but most critics consider both films to be exceptionally good. I would agree. This is a unique situation in the age-old story of books into film. In this case, both films take significant liberties with the source material, but the riffs each filmmaker gives the book produce artistically and thematically dazzling results.

In Highsmith's original, Tom Ripley is a young man in New York, circa the mid-1950s, who's already on his way

Alain Delon is the treacherous Ripley in René Clément's 1960 *Purple Noon*, the first screen version of Patricia Highsmith's *The Talented Mr. Ripley* (Times Films and Janus TV).

to a life as a swindler of sorts. He's approached by a wealthy manufacturer who has been told that Tom was a college friend of the manufacturer's playboy son, Dickie Greenleaf. Dickie has gone off to Italy to become an artist rather than stay home to prepare for taking over his dad's business. Put simply, the father wants to pay Tom's way over to Italy in the hope that he can persuade Dickie to come home.

Though Tom barely knows Dickie, the idea of vacationing in Italy on the father's money is appealing. He makes the trip, ingratiates himself with Dickie and worms his way into the young man's inner circle, becoming his sidekick in virtually everything, much to the displeasure of Dickie's girlfriend Marge, an American writer.

At the heart of Highsmith's story is the notion that Tom is a lonely, twisted young man who envies the life he sees Dickie enjoying—and starts planning to enjoy it himself, no matter what it takes. He has the special "talents" for the job, too: an uncanny ability to impersonate people, a great knack for forging handwriting and a mastery of the art of telling lies.

Tom murders Dickie, who was starting to tire of his company, and begins to assume his identity and cash his checks from back home. Freddy, one of Dickie's playboy pals, puts two and two together, so Tom murders him too.

Highsmith was fascinated with sociopathic personalities all through her career—witness the demented Bruno in her first novel, *Strangers on a Train*—and she created the best of them all in Tom Ripley, who manages to dodge every bullet in *The Talented Mr. Ripley*, so he might go on to all those other novels.

When René Clément filmed *Purple Noon*, Highsmith had not published the first sequel, *Ripley Under Ground*, so it's obvious he thought moviegoers would not buy the idea of a murderer going free at the end. So the Italian police show up to arrest Tom (Alain Delon) just before the end credits roll.

That surely would have been a letdown to Highsmith fans, who relish the idea that Ripley always eludes the punishment he deserves, if Clément hadn't come up with an absolutely socko finale for the film that makes you want to forgive him for everything else. More about that later.

Clément also changed Dickie's name to Philippe, moved his family to San Francisco and omitted his obsession with painting, making him just a playboy with no particular career interests. He also had Tom kill Philippe with a knife aboard his own sailboat rather than club him to death with an oar on a small rented boat in San Remo.

In the original, Ripley forges a will, leaving the income from Dickie's estate to him. Clément's idea seems a little more intriguing: Tom forges a will and has Philippe leave his estate to Marge. As Clément saw it, it would make more sense for Tom to divert suspicion away from himself by having Marge wind up with the money. He wanted Tom to complete his takeover of his friend's life by taking his girl, too—because she has the money he wants.

But Highsmith always had Tom think of Marge as an irritating and unpleasant bore. She would never have her hero covet Marge. In fact, there's an undercurrent of homosexuality in Tom's persona. It's clear that he's drawn to Dickie and it's equally clear that he gets no special thrill from women. (No surprise since Highsmith herself preferred her own sex.)

Highsmith's version of Marge was rejected by both filmmakers since they both cast highly attractive women in the role: Marie Laforet in *Purple Noon* and Gwyneth Paltrow in *The Talented Mr. Ripley*.

The three principal players in the 1999 version of *The Talented Mr. Ripley*: from left, Gwyneth Paltrow and Jude Law, who were deceived by Matt Damon's Tom Ripley (photo by Phil Bray, Paramount Pictures).

Clément's ending for *Purple Noon* is by far the better finish in terms of impact. In fact, it's one that Hitchcock might have used if he'd decided to do *Ripley* as a follow-up to his hit *Strangers on a Train*. With Philippe now dead, his sailboat is being sold and the new owner wants it hauled out of the water so he can examine the hull. But, as the winches drag the boat out of the harbor, we see that a line has become entwined in its propeller. Attached to the line is the canvas bag containing Philippe's corpse, one skeletal hand conveniently dangling out for all to see.

Result: Game's end for Ripley.

Minghella's 1999 version is more respectful, letting us see Ripley go free, but ending with him in repose, visibly haunted by the things he's done along the way. Paltrow's Marge is the only one who strongly suspects that Tom has murdered Dickie, and she vilifies him in a powerful scene in the film's final moments.

Minghella's significant riffs on Highsmith's original all seem intended to flesh out the characters, to add nuance and depth to the story, which they do. His script begins in New York where the Greenleafs mistakenly assume he went to college with Dickie because he's wearing a jacket from Dickie's college while serving as a piano accompanist to a singer at a concert. As we learn later, the jacket was borrowed, as is nearly everything Tom ever wears.

Matt Damon's Tom is nerdish compared to Delon's in *Purple Noon*. That's why it's more fun to watch him take on Dickie's persona because it vividly alters his own look and mannerisms.

Minghella also leaps deeply into the homosexual sub-theme, making it clear that Tom is attracted to handsome Dickie (Jude Law) while unmoved by the beauty and grace of Marge. In the windup, Tom actually takes up with another man in an obvious gay relationship. This is an appealing twist because it's probably something Highsmith might have done if gay themes were more readily accepted by publishers in 1955. Anyway, Minghella uses Tom's homosexual appetites as yet another way of showing us that Tom Ripley is the way he is because he's a deeply alienated young man, far from the mainstream of his time.

Minghella also creates the new character of Meredith (Cate Blanchett), a wealthy young woman attracted to Tom (thinking he's Dickie), in order to suggest that Tom is creating a mirror image of Dickie's life, which also includes a doting girlfriend.

Like Clément, Minghella also ditches painting as Dickie's "occupation" (Highsmith made it clear Dickie was a dreadful painter) and makes him instead a jazz fan and would-be saxophone player. This was an inspired change because it allowed Minghella to fill his soundtrack with late 1950s jazz (especially Chet Baker's "My Funny Valentine," which Damon sang, Baker-style, in a music video to promote the film). It also sets up a great scene in an Italian café where Dickie and Tom perform with an Italian jazz combo. It's a super sequence.

(Clément had a similar sequence, also invented for his film, in which Tom and Philippe talk a blind man into selling them his white cane, so they can use it to pretend they're blind, fooling a pretty girl they encounter on the street.)

Both films are beautifully photographed in color on location in Italy and both also have incredible musical scores. Nino Rota (*La Dolce Vita*, *The Godfather*) composed the *Purple Noon* score and Gabriel Yared did *The Talented Mr. Ripley*.

Though the Ripley of *Purple Noon* is closer to the sociopath Highsmith created, Minghella's Matt Damon version makes us understand his Tom more completely—and perhaps feel for him a bit, despite what he does.

Both films are exceptionally good, but if you're looking for a thriller, *Purple Noon* fills that bill better. *The Talented Mr. Ripley* is a more artistic, more intellectual film. You'll enjoy them both more, though, if you've read the book first.

Tony Hillerman
The Dark Wind

The 1982 novel and the 1991 movie

In his 1980 novel *People of Darkness*, mystery writer Tony Hillerman introduced his second series detective, Jim Chee. Chee works for the Navajo Tribal Police, just like Hillerman's original sleuth, Joe Leaphorn, who's a generation older and several ranks higher. The second Chee novel, 1982's *The Dark Wind*, is one of the best among Hillerman's long series of novels about mystery on the Navajo reservation in America's sprawling Southwest. It was the first Hillerman story to become a movie.

Actor Robert Redford, a great admirer of Native American culture, made the deal with Hillerman and, with his partners, produced *The Dark Wind*, starring Lou Diamond

Phillips as Jim Chee. It was eagerly awaited by Hillerman's enormous following of mystery readers, who seemed delighted that Phillips would play Chee. The actor was still "hot" from his much praised performance as doomed rock star Ritchie Valens in the hit 1987 film *La Bamba* and he also seemed acceptable to Native Americans because he's part Cherokee.

What was not to like? The film would be directed by Errol Morris, one of America's most acclaimed documentary filmmakers (*Gates of Heaven*; *Vernon, Florida*; *The Thin Blue Line*), who was trying his first fiction film, and it would be filmed on authentic locations with a largely Native American cast.

Yet *The Dark Wind* was a conspicuous failure. It never received a conventional release and went straight to video. It pretty much dashed the hopes of Hillerman fans for screen versions of his stories—until PBS and Redford teamed a decade later to make three Hillerman films for the *Mystery!* television series.

In retrospect, it's easy to understand why *The Dark Wind* stalled in the starting gate. Much

The DVD cover from *The Dark Wind*, the 1994 film based on Tony Hillerman's novel, starring Lou Diamond Phillips as Navajo Indian sleuth Jim Chee (Studio Canal and Artisan Home Video).

of the novel follows Jim Chee's lonely investigation of a mysterious plane crash on the reservation and the drug smuggling deal that somehow went awry. That meant that the screenwriters were either going to write in a partner for Chee or else he'd be on screen, talking to himself via off-camera narration. They chose the latter course. That means that more than half the film plays with voice-over narration, which is fine for a nature documentary, but deadly dull for a feature film with a human storyline. As a result, the story, which is complex, trudges along in a confusing fashion, leaving the audience panting for action.

The filmmakers also decided to insult Hillerman fans by eliminating the character of Tribal Police Captain Largo, Chee's boss, and substituting Hillerman's other detective hero, Lt. Joe Leaphorn, played by Fred Ward, the character actor best remembered for his role as astronaut Gus Grissom in *The Right Stuff* (1983). Ultimately, Hillerman did bring Leaphorn and Chee together in his novels, starting with *Skinwalkers* (1987), but it was jarring to readers of the book to find the more experienced, savvy Leaphorn playing second banana to a young detective new to the job.

Another reason why *The Dark Wind* wasn't a commercial success was its lack of a romantic love interest for Chee. The only female character even near his own age is the grieving widow of one of the dope smugglers and Chee seems more interested in studying footprints in the sand than checking her out.

The book and the movie open with a very strong hook: A group of Hopi Indians find the body of a man whose hands and feet have been skinned and his boot left in the road, possibly so that passersby will find the body. Chee quickly realizes that the murder may be linked to the plane crash, drug smuggling and the case he is working on—a series of vandalistic attacks on a water well in Hopi jurisdiction.

Though *The Dark Wind* was a financial disaster, it's not without merit. The desert location footage is compelling at times and Michael Columbier's Native American–themed musical score is good. Phillips doesn't have much opportunity to do any acting, but he has the right look, attitude and feel for Jim Chee. Unfortunately, he often seems only borderline competent at what he's doing.

The real problem is the Neal Jimenez–Eric Bergren screenplay. They should have uncluttered the storyline a bit and perhaps concentrated more on the tension between Hopi and Navajo cultures as Chee struggles to gather evidence under difficult circumstances. They also might have built up the role of the widow and maybe had her tag along with Chee, so he'd have someone to talk with besides himself.

Whatever went wrong, the first movie based on a Hillerman novel certainly didn't inspire many people to try his novels. They're hardly ever dull, but the movie crawls like a desert tortoise in the noonday sun and today serves only as a curiosity item for diehard Hillerman fans.

Tony Hillerman
A Thief of Time

The 1988 novel and the 2004 TV movie

Tony Hillerman's 1988 bestseller *A Thief of Time* is one of my favorites among the many mystery novels he wrote about Lt. Joe Leaphorn and Officer Jim Chee of the Navajo Tribal Police. The suspense is unrelenting and Hillerman makes splendid use of the exotic southwestern backdrop for his story and the special emotional stuff that's going on in the minds of his two heroes.

Hillerman's novels about Leaphorn and Chee, who sometimes worked alone in their separate books, represent a modern trend in the mystery genre toward so-called "ethnic" mysteries because we learn so much about the Navajo way of doing things as they go about their police business.

At the same time, Hillerman often is credited with merging the once mighty genre of the frontier western novel with the contemporary police procedural, which may account for the widespread popularity of the books. Male and female readers each could find something appealing in the Leaphorn-Chee mysteries and almost all have made the bestseller lists.

Hollywood interest in the books wasn't high, though, no doubt because both the traditional western and mystery genres were pretty much being phased out by the studios in the 1990s because they didn't appeal to young moviegoers. But actor-filmmaker Robert Redford, who loved the books, determined to start bringing them to the screen. The first was *The Dark Wind*, starring Lou Diamond Phillips as Jim Chee and Fred Ward as Joe Leaphorn. Filmed in 1991 by Errol Morris, the acclaimed documentary-maker, it was a financial disaster. It didn't go into even limited release until 1994.

Redford got a second chance nearly a decade later when the PBS *Mystery!* series, under pressure to develop American-made mysteries to replace the mostly British programs on its schedule, made a deal with Redford for a series of adaptations of the novels.

The first, *Skinwalkers*, wasn't very good, but it became one of PBS's most popular shows of the year, and more Hillerman films were ordered. *A Thief of Time* followed *Coyote Waits* as the third in the series and was quite clearly the best, even though it wasn't awfully faithful to the original novel.

Hillerman's book follows Lt. Leaphorn (Wes Studi) as he attempts to find a missing archeologist whose research involved her with criminal elements responsible for thefts of ancient pottery from sacred native burial sites. The suspense mounts as bodies start turning up, all of them connected to the illegal pottery trade.

Officer Jim Chee (Adam Beach) is stuck with a much more banal assignment: trying to track down the men who stole a backhoe from a locked maintenance yard. But his tracks begin to cross those of Leaphorn, and they both realize they're really working the same case.

Adam Beach as Navajo detective Jim Chee in the TV movie version of Tony Hillerman's *A Thief of Time* (PBS).

There's a major difference between the Leaphorn-Chee relationship in the books and the way it's depicted in the TV version of *A Thief of Time*. In the books, the men aren't real tight. They don't normally work as partners and, in fact, work different territories. They are also quite different in temperament and focus. At times, Hillerman even lets us know they don't quite like each other, though they always show each other respect.

In the TV films, they work for the same boss and Chee shows Leaphorn a good deal of reverence. It's not exactly Holmes and Watson, though. Chee has to do what Leaphorn tells him because Leaphorn outranks him, which often leaves the impression that Chee is Leaphorn's assistant. At one point in *A Thief of Time*, Chee even strokes Leaphorn a bit, suggesting that the older policeman can get results because, "You're Joe Leaphorn—the legendary Joe Leaphorn!"

Leaphorn replies, rather cynically, "You're roadkill when they start calling you 'legendary.'"

In the novel, Leaphorn is under great stress. Emma, his wife of many years, has just died of cancer and he takes a leave of absence from his tribal police duties. He has, in fact, decided to retire and has already submitted his letter of resignation. He's asked to come back on duty during his final week to execute a search warrant of the lodgings of archeologist Eleanor Friedman-Bernal, who's suspected of taking pottery from sacred Anasazi burial sites.

Once Leaphorn drags himself into the hunt for the missing archeologist, he's distracted from his grief. His interest in the detecting work that has been his life is renewed.

At the same time, Chee is coming off the end of a romantic relationship. His former girlfriend had left the reservation and wanted him to leave, too. But Chee decided to stay in the only world he knows intimately. He's now seeing pretty lawyer Janet Pete, whose last relationship broke up for much the same reasons.

In the Alice Arlen teleplay, both these strong character elements are either eliminated or altered. Emma(Sheila Tousey) is ailing, but not dead, so Leaphorn's days on the force aren't numbered. In fact, Emma has several scenes and plays a meaningful role in the solving of the mystery.

Arlen also changed the relationship between Chee and Janet. She is given some of the characteristics of the ex-girlfriend and is working on Chee to leave the reservation to start a new life with her. The dynamic of their relationship is completely different. In the book, Chee is beginning to realize this smart, attractive Native American is a better match for him. In the movie, he already knows this and, in fact, is sleeping with her.

The teleplay also radically changes the character of Maxie Davis, a young researcher working on the reservation. Played by comely Dawn Lewis, she's now a redheaded sexpot who even attempts to seduce Leaphorn. In the book, she behaves herself and doesn't even flutter her eyelids at the old police veteran.

Arlen claims they wanted to keep Emma alive "because [Tousey] is a brilliant actress." When I asked Arlen to confirm my theory that they combined the Janet character with that of Chee's former girlfriend to create more romantic tension, Arlen simply said, "Sure."

As for the much-sexier Maxie character, Arlen explained she wasn't that much more sexy in the script and suggested that actress Dawn Lewis turned her into an "over-the-top vixen" with her performance. "We were attempting to cleverly divert your attention," Arlen said.

The TV version makes some other changes that are bewildering, but don't really impact the story. For example, park ranger Bob Luna gets a gender switch and is now *Mildred* Luna, played by Beth Grant. (Arlen said that was done "for fun.") Scenes in the book where Leaphorn travels to the East Coast are eliminated.

Janet decides to buy a used Buick in the book version of the story and cons Jim Chee into giving it a tryout while she's away on a short trip. Chee reluctantly does so, then gets into a wild chase after the backhoe thieves and wrecks the car. In the TV version, the car he wrecks is upgraded to a fancy BMW convertible. The Jim Chee known to readers could barely afford to repair a used Buick. Trying to imagine him finding the money to repair a BMW is totally absurd. (Arlen didn't explain that change.)

The three *Mystery!* versions of Hillerman's novels all suffered from the same basic problem: lackluster direction that gives the films a plodding pace. One good example: In *A Thief of Time*, a key character is a hermit who lives in the wilderness. He's a mentally disturbed murderer the police believe was killed in a shootout, his body swept away when he fell into a river. The background information we need to know could have been supplied in dialogue between Leaphorn and the boy's father, a powerful Mormon rancher played by Peter Fonda. Instead, the pace of the movie is stopped while we get a confusing flashback sequence that seems out of place.

Two of the best action sequences in the book also were squandered by director Chris Eyre. One finds Fonda's character desperately attempting to hide from someone who has come to kill him; the other is the climactic scene where Leaphorn comes face to face with the killer in a remote Anasazi burial ground. Both sequences fall flat in the film.

Still, much of the careful sleuthing by Leaphorn and Chee is retained in the film. There also are some very nice cameo performances, especially by Graham Greene, who plays Christian evangelist Slick Nakai. Greene, who was Oscar-nominated for his supporting role in *Dances with Wolves* (1990), had put on a lot of weight since 1990 and was barely recognizable, but he really brings that character to life. The revival meeting sequence is one of director Eyre's better moments in *A Thief of Time*.

If you haven't read the Hillerman novels, these TV adaptations probably play a lot better. I've talked with several TV mystery fans who loved the PBS films and never realized how many liberties were taken with Hillerman's plots. One thing they definitely have going for them: beautifully photographed American Southwest vistas.

Dorothy B. Hughes

In a Lonely Place

The 1947 novel and the 1950 movie

Why buys the movie rights to a distinguished mystery novel like Dorothy B. Hughes' *In a Lonely Place*, then tosses key elements of the novel out with the garbage?

That's always the big question from readers when they discover the book they love has been changed into something radically different when the movie version comes out. The only acceptable answer: because a movie isn't a book.

Alfred Hitchcock turned Patricia Highsmith's *Strangers on a Train* inside out when he made the famous movie version. Highsmith's debut novel was a bestseller in 1949 and remains her most famous literary work. But Hitchcock's movie is also a classic, considered by some to be his finest film. Yet it's not the book.

The same argument might be made for Hughes' 1947 novel *In a Lonely Place*, which director Nicholas Ray filmed in 1950. The book is still revered—and the movie is now considered a classic of noir cinema. Yet the film turned the novel inside out.

Hughes, like Highsmith, had a peculiar sensibility about the leading characters in many of her dark novels. They often do unsavory things. Highsmith's Tom Ripley, for instance, is the protagonist of five novels, beginning with *The Talented Mr. Ripley* (1955), but is also a murderer and thief. Hughes' Dix Steele, the protagonist of *In a Lonely Place*, is a rapist and murderer.

What the book gives us is a direct view into the heart of such a person, although we don't realize that until the plot finally resolves itself in the final chapters. We might not want to stay with Mr. Steele if we knew from the beginning that he's guilty of the crime that the police suspect him of committing.

Once you get with the thrust of the novel, you recognize that Steele is a certain kind of man with a depressingly sick view of the woman's role in the world. Hughes never gives us insight into Steele's childhood, but she does provide this much information: He's a recently returned World War II veteran who can't seem to get his life together after the exhilarating highs of his wartime experiences. In the end, we learn that his first murder victim was a girl in Europe—and he keeps wanting to re-live that moment.

Dix Steele lives on the periphery of the movie business, claiming he's writing a mystery novel that's mostly myth. His best friend Brub is a Beverly Hills police detective who just happens to be working on a murder case that comes uncomfortably close to involving Steele as a suspect. Meanwhile, Steele becomes entranced by sexy Laurel Gray, who lives in the same apartment court where he's staying, in the "borrowed" apartment of a friend who's supposedly on a trip to Latin America.

Like Tom Ripley, who would come along later when Patricia Highsmith felt the world was ready for a villain-as-protagonist, Dix Steele is living in an elaborate structure of lies, which is probably his greatest contribution to fiction.

Two of Hughes' novels already had been filmed. The first film was *The Fallen Sparrow* (1943), in which anti-hero John Garfield returns from fighting for freedom in the Spanish Civil War and finds himself hunted by undercover Nazis. Then came *Ride the Pink Horse* (1947), in which Robert Montgomery attempts to blackmail a gangster during a fiesta in a small New Mexico town—and gets into a peck of trouble.

Both are strongly unconventional films in the dark noir tradition. The movie rights to *In a Lonely Place* went to Santana Productions, the independent production company set up by Humphrey Bogart and Lauren Bacall after Bogart ended his long contract with Warner Bros. Though Bogart was firmly established as American film's No. 1 anti-hero, it's likely he didn't relish playing a serial rapist and killer, so changes were called for in the screen adaptation of Hughes' novel.

Director Ray and screenwriter Andrew Solt turned the story into a metaphor for McCarthy Era Hollywood, making Dix Steele innocent of the murder charges, but "guilty" because of his past activities and his associations. Steele (Bogart) is now a Hollywood screenwriter who hasn't had a hit in some time. He's resigned to the fact that he can't express his own ideas freely, but must turn mediocre novels into movies in return for large sums of money. Though he compromises his ideals, he still does what he can by severely altering the plots of the books he adapts, putting in his own point of view wherever he can.

Assigned to adapt an awful bestseller, he pays a hat check girl who has read it to come home with him and tell him the plot, rather than read it himself. When she turns up murdered the following morning, he's the natural suspect because of his history with the police—a long series of violent fights with people and his abuse of women.

In the movie, Dix is not guilty of the murder, but guilty of everything else. He's a violent hothead who's on a collision course with his destiny. Though he's still entranced by sexy Laurel Gray (Gloria Grahame), he comes close to beating her to death when he realizes she's finally going to leave him because of his violent nature.

The role was a challenging one for Bogart, who seems so credibly cruel and mean-spirited that you begin to believe he's actually revealing his true nature on screen. Ray's film therefore becomes an entirely different sort of artistic expression—a serious portrait of a deeply flawed man who grinds down nearly everyone within his orbit.

Ray does a lot to make *In a Lonely Place* a most personal sort of film. The real-life apartment court where Dix and Laurel live in the movie is the place where Ray lived in the same period. What's more, Ray was then married to Gloria Grahame. They separated during the making of the film and later divorced. It's interesting to speculate on how much the odd dynamics of this story, very misogynistic, even for its time, had on their relationship.

Humphrey Bogart is a troubled screenwriter in the 1950 noir thriller *In a Lonely Place*, based on the Dorothy Hughes novel (Columbia Pictures).

Both the novel and the film, though remarkably different in point of view, now seem way ahead of their time in terms of their insight into human behavior. The book seems to warn women against the hidden dangers in certain men, whose anti-female attitudes still were largely acceptable in the late 1940s. The film seems to suggest that its protagonist is an evil man, completely capable of murder, even though he's actually innocent of the murder in the foreground of the storyline.

Both book and movie deserve to be celebrated by new generations. They represent yet another example of how a book and a film can be radically different, yet both remain classics of their medium.

Francis Iles
Before the Fact

The 1932 novel and the 1941 movie *Suspicion*

In the early 1930s, English mystery novelist Francis Iles began to re-define the mystery genre with his so-called "inverted" mysteries, starting with *Malice Aforethought* (1931) and *Before the Fact* (1932). Those books earned that new nickname because the author completely reverses the familiar "whodunnit" process in both novels by letting you know who the killer is right from the start.

Iles, the pen name for popular mystery writer Anthony Berkeley Cox, now usually gets credit for revolutionizing the mystery genre with those two novels. Though there had been similar approaches taken before that—such as A.P. Herbert's *The House by the River* (1921)—the two Iles novels, coming back to back as they did, really launched the "inverted" mystery trend that eventually brought us hundreds of "psychological" mysteries; mysteries told from the killer's perspective; and those mysteries like the *Columbo* television series in which we know what the detective is trying to find out and the fun comes in watching him fumble his way toward the solution.

Before the Fact was extremely popular, no doubt because its criminal anti-hero is a charming playboy named Johnny Aysgarth, who's liked by everyone, especially the ladies. You have to root for him once he meets Lina, the heroine, a shy spinster-in-the-making who really deserves her one chance at love—and finds it with the irresistible Johnny.

From the start, though, we know that Lina marries Johnny and has gradually discovered he's a thief, a con man and a murderer who's planning to make her his next victim in order to inherit her family fortune. In the final chapter, Lina has concluded that Johnny might well wind up in prison for what he's already done, so she'd rather die than face life without the charming man she loves. For that reason, she calmly downs the poisoned drink he brings her, accepting her fate though she'd much rather have gone on living with her rogue of a husband.

The film world's No. 1 purveyor of suspense thrillers, England's Alfred Hitchcock, read *Before the Fact* in the early 1930s and was enthralled with the notion of bringing it to the screen. He imagined handsome Cary Grant as the ideal casting for Johnny and was intrigued with the idea of having such a charmer be the villain of a thriller.

In 1941, Hitchcock finally got his chance to do *Before the Fact*. He had been brought to America in 1939 by producer David O. Selznick and had firmly established himself in Hollywood with the romantic mystery *Rebecca* (1940), which had won the Academy Award as Best Picture, and the action-packed thriller *Foreign Correspondent* (1940).

Cary Grant brings a glass of milk that may be poisoned to leery wife Joan Fontaine in Alfred Hitchcock's 1941 *Suspicion*, based on the Francis Iles novel *Before the Fact*. Fontaine won the Best Actress Oscar for her performance (AMC).

At RKO, Hitchcock developed the script with the help of his wife Alma Reville and his assistant, Joan Harrison. In their rough draft, Lina writes a letter to her mother in which she reveals her suspicion that her husband is trying to kill her. Hitchcock's twisted sense of humor inspired him to end the picture with Lina asking Johnny to mail a letter for her, then drinking the poison. In the last scene, Johnny cheerfully mails the letter that will incriminate him.

But before screenwriter Samson Raphaelson completed the script, RKO notified Hitchcock that the film couldn't end that way because the Breen Office, Hollywood's censorship agency, had ruled that no criminal could be shown getting away with his crime, even if there was a chance he'd be prosecuted later.

Hitchcock was furious, but could do nothing about it. The script was changed to have Lina tear up the letter she's just written to her mother. Then she discovers that Johnny had planned to drink the poison himself because he could see no way out of a likely prison term for embezzlement of funds from his former employer. She even learns he had no role in the death of a friend that she was sure he'd murdered.

Still, Hitchcock couldn't help leading moviegoers to the brink of a cliff anyway—literally. With Lina's suspicions in full flower, he has Johnny decide to leave her after he drives her to her mother's house in her open-topped LaGonda roadster. Naturally, he drives way too fast, right alongside a cliff with a precipitous drop to the ocean below, and the door on her side of the car opens as they round a curve. When he grabs for her, Lina is sure he's trying to shove her out the door, but it turns out he's trying to keep her from falling.

Suspicion ends happily with them driving back home together, Johnny's arm around her, promising to take his medicine for his crimes and start their life over on a decent path. But up until then, the audience is thoroughly convinced that Johnny is still trying to kill Lina.

Hitchcock never got over the feeling he'd compromised *Before the Fact* because of that ruling by the censors. He also was not a fan of the name change to *Suspicion*, which he felt was a tacky and sensational title.

Film critics were much kinder. By and large, they loved *Suspicion* and felt that Hitchcock was better served by the new ending. Hitch succeeded in landing Cary Grant for the role of Johnny and critics also believed filmgoers would have felt cheated if one of their favorite stars had turned out to be such a dark character as the Johnny of the book. It was a great beginning for the Hitchcock-Grant team and they wound up making three more fabulously successful films together: *Notorious* (1946), *To Catch a Thief* (1955) and *North by Northwest* (1959).

Joan Fontaine, who deserved the Best Actress Oscar in 1940 for her heartfelt performance as the second Mrs. de Winter in *Rebecca*, but lost out to Ginger Rogers in *Kitty Foyle*, was cast in the similar role of Lina. This time she won the Oscar.

In retrospect, *Suspicion* ranks among Hitchcock's all-time best films and contains one of his most memorable scenes: Cary Grant carrying the "poisoned" glass of milk up the stairs to Lina's room. You can't take your eyes off that glass because Hitchcock put a light source in it and it actually glows in the dark.

Before the Fact remains a very good read all these years later and it's a special treat to read it and wonder if *Suspicion* would have flopped if the censors had let Hitchcock follow the book more closely.

Carolyn Keene
The Hidden Staircase

The 1930 novel and the 1939 movie
Nancy Drew and the Hidden Staircase

In the early part of the 20th century, an industrious marketing genius named Edward Stratemeyer created what was nothing less than a factory for the manufacture of books aimed at young readers. He outlined a number of book series built around characters he dreamed up: the Hardy Boys, Tom Swift, the Bobbsey Twins and, among others, the first teenage girl sleuth, plucky Nancy Drew.

Starting with *The Secret of the Old Clock* in 1930, the Nancy Drew mysteries became a publishing phenomenon and gave American girls one of their very first literary role models. What was there not to like? Nancy was independent, drove her own convertible roadster, dressed fashionably and behaved like a free-spirited young adult most of the time.

Perhaps the most popular of all the original books was the second in the series, *The Hidden Staircase*. Like all the others, it was authored by "Carolyn Keene," a fictional person whose byline was used by all the nameless writers who wrote for the series. The most influential of them all was Mildred Wirt, who wrote the first three, including *The Hidden Staircase*.

In 1938, Warner Bros. began to film a series of *Nancy Drew* mystery movies under a special arrangement with the Stratemeyer Syndicate. Altogether, four were quickly filmed as low-budget "B" pictures in 1938 and 1939. Only one film was based on an actual Nancy Drew mystery novel—the last one in the series, *Nancy Drew and the Hidden Staircase*.

To play Nancy Drew, the studio chose talented, precocious teenager Bonita Granville, who already had earned a 1936 Best Supporting Actress Oscar nomination as the nasty girl who spreads malicious rumors about two female teachers at an all-girls school in William Wyler's *These Three*, adapted by Lillian Hellman from her play *The Children's Hour*. Until she played Nancy, Granville had spent most of her screen time playing obnoxious brats. In the four Nancy Drew films, she was kind-hearted and very pro-social in her attitudes, but so irrepressible that she often seemed wired. Though 15 when she started the series, Granville seemed much more a kid than the Nancy of the books, who was stylish and clever and probably would have been considered "cool" by girls her own age, if they'd had such a word back then.

In the original novel, Nancy is threatened by a "miser" named Nathan Gombet, who forces his way into her house while her father, attorney Carson Drew, is out of town. Gombet claims that lawyer Drew cheated him on a deal to acquire his property and wants to tear up the papers he signed.

Later, Nancy volunteers to help the aged Turnbull sisters, who live alone in an old house in the country and are being frightened by mysterious intruders who enter their spooky old mansion during the night. After Nancy agrees to spend a few nights there, she begins to suspect the Turnbulls' sinister neighbor, Nathan Gombet, of trying to frighten them into selling their property to him. The thrills start piling up when Nancy discovers a secret staircase that leads to tunnels built during the Civil War era that link the Turnbull and Gombet mansions.

Screenwriter Kenneth Gamet made wholesale changes in the original story. Gone is "miser" Gombet and his evil black housekeeper, along with one of the more absurd subplots of the book—the kidnapping of Nancy's father by Gombet, who holds him hostage while demanding he sign a new, much-richer contract to purchase Gombet's land. Nancy's pal Ted Nickerson (Frankie Thomas) is also written into the story, along with lots of so-called comic relief featuring dim-witted police official Captain Tweedy (Frank Orth), who doesn't appear in the book.

In the movie, there's a murder (or is it suicide?) that doesn't happen in the bloodless original and the bad guys are all "race track people" who want to scare the Turnbulls off their land, so they can build a race track there. Instead of being a victim that

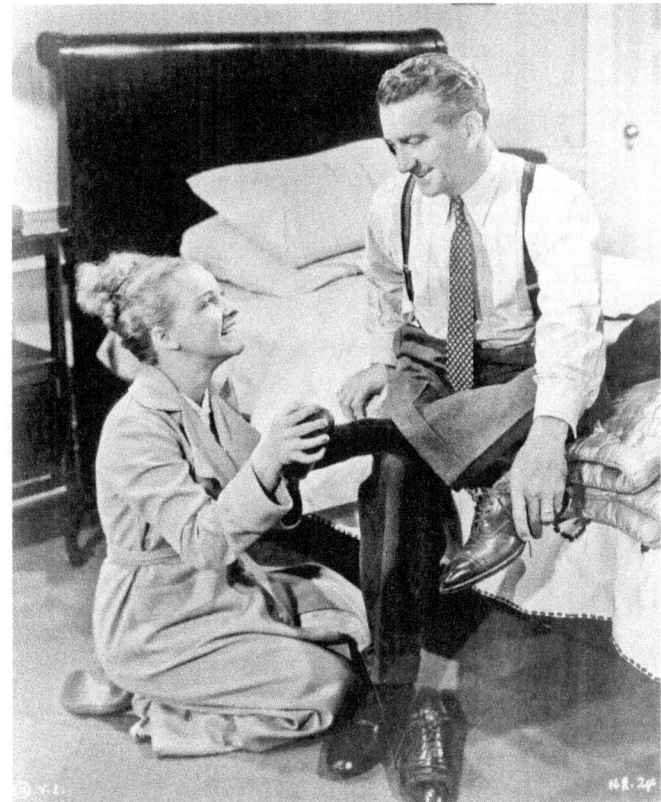

Bonita Granville, the first actress to portray teen detective Nancy Drew on the screen, relaxes on the set with actor John Litel, who played her father in the four Nancy Drew films she made in 1938 and '39 (Warner Bros. and the James Bawden Collection).

Nancy has to rescue, her dad (John Litel) is one of the rescuers in the movie, which ends with the underground tunnels flooding and both Nancy and Ted in danger of drowning.

Though dozens of today's female mystery writers claim they were inspired by reading the original Nancy Drew mysteries, you aren't likely to hear many claim the Nancy Drew movies as inspiration. The first screen Nancy is too hyper, too likely to scream at the slightest provocation and way too likely to need the help of the opposite sex, even when all there is to represent the male gender is her dorky teenage boy friend Ted.

Possibly that's why the Nancy Drew mysteries never really caught on in the movies: They somehow missed the special appeal the books had for young American girls, who longed to be like the literary Nancy, not the perky reformed brat that Bonita Granville played on screen.

In later years, all the original Nancy Drew books were revised or rewritten to eliminate racist characters and "update" Nancy to contemporary status. In some cases, the plots were even overhauled. To read the originals, it's necessary to track down the now extremely valuable original editions—or the marvelous series of exact facsimile editions published by Applewood Books.

Nancy Drew has had a series of second chances on screen, including the 1977–78 ABC-TV series *The Nancy Drew Mysteries* with Pamela Sue Martin and the 1995–96 syndicated TV series *Nancy Drew* with Tracy Ryan. The film *Nancy Drew* (2007) with Emma Roberts as Nancy tried to update the concept to the present day, but was not a box office success. Meanwhile, the books continue to sell to juvenile readers.

As for Bonita Granville, she didn't suffer from the failure of the Nancy Drew movie series. After her adult screen career began to wane, she married oil millionaire Jack Wrather, who purchased the rights to a pair of long-running franchises, *The Lone Ranger* and *Lassie*. She played small roles in Wrather's *Lone Ranger* movies and was for years the supervising producer of the *Lassie* TV series. One of her last duties was working as a spokesperson for the Queen Mary ocean liner attraction in Long Beach, California. She died in 1988 at age 65.

Gypsy Rose Lee
The G-String Murders

The 1941 novel and the 1944 movie *Lady of Burlesque*

One of the strangest of all best-selling mystery novels was Simon & Schuster's *The G-String Murders* (1941), written by Gypsy Rose Lee, perhaps the most famous of all 20th century American strip tease artists.

Lee, whose real name was Louise Hovick, is best known today as the central character of the hit musical show *Gypsy*, which tells the story of her emergence as a burlesque star at the urging of her infamous stage mother, Rose Hovick. What Gypsy lacked in pulchritude, she made up for with her wit and humor. Her trademark act was stripping while doing a running commentary, usually delivered in a brassy, humorous style.

She was one of the most colorful of all characters of her time. Famed Broadway columnist Walter Winchell had her substitute for him as a columnist when he went on vacation in the 1930s. As the legend goes, she got the idea to write a murder mystery once she gained a little experience writing for Winchell.

Truth be told, Gypsy didn't write *The G-String Murders* herself. It's now widely known that the real author was Craig Rice, a female screenwriter and novelist who used a man's name. (Her real name was Georgianna Rice.) Rice wrote her own mystery novels, most of them done in a light, humorous style. One was the popular *Home Sweet Homicide*, which was turned into a movie in 1946.

But it's all too evident that Craig Rice must have sat down with Gypsy Rose Lee and tapped the famous stripper for all her knowledge of backstage life in the world of 1930s burlesque. The book, which became a bestseller and went through several editions, has Gypsy as its main character and takes place at an old opera house now occupied by a burlesque troupe. There's a series of backstage murders of showgirls, and Gypsy winds up as a potential victim herself.

So convincingly did Lee and Rice convey the burlesque house setting that *Time* magazine's reviewer wrote that it was not only a competent mystery thriller, "but almost a social document."

In 1944, producer Hunt Stromberg—long affiliated with MGM, where he had made such immortal films as *The Thin Man*, *Northwest Passage* and the Oscar-winning *The Great Ziegfeld*—decided to go independent. Turning to United Artists as his distributor, he produced a movie version of *The G-String Murders* called *Lady of Burlesque*. It was extremely popular, earning more than $2 million at the box office, an impressive amount for 1944.

For his leading lady, Stromberg might well have considered the real Gypsy Rose Lee, who was only 32 and at the peak of her fame. Lee had been featured in several films by then, some under her real name. Now it seems likely that her booming value as an actress may have cost her the leading role in her own autobiographical mystery story. As it turns out, Lee was getting the biggest break of her acting career that same year, playing the title role in *Belle of the Yukon*, a Technicolor musical, at rival studio RKO, co-starring with action hero Randolph Scott and pop singer Dinah Shore.

Barbara Stanwyck plays a strip tease dancer involved in a backstage murder mystery in *Lady of Burlesque*, **based on the novel** *The G-String Murders* **by real-life stripper Gypsy Rose Lee. (United Artists).**

Stromberg turned to one of Hollywood's most popular stars, Barbara Stanwyck, to play Gypsy Rose Lee. Stanwyck had started out as a Broadway showgirl under her real name, Ruby Stevens, and had even very successfully played a burlesque star in the hit 1941 comedy *Ball of Fire* opposite Gary Cooper.

Still, trying to imagine Stanwyck as Gypsy wasn't easy. Stanwyck was small, petite-figured and far from voluptuous in build while Lee was statuesque and shapely. Probably to avoid any unfavorable comparisons, *Lady of Burlesque* screenwriter James Gunn wrote Gypsy out of the movie and replaced her with the new character Dixie Daisy.

In the movie, Dixie (Stanwyck) is the headliner of the burlesque troupe working at the Old Opera House. She's romantically involved with house comedian "Biff" Brannigan (Michael O'Shea, making his film debut). One of the other girls in the show is involved with a gangster (Gerald Mohr), who occasionally beats her up. In fact, there are lots of petty jealousies and grudges between some of the girls.

When one of the showgirls is found dead backstage, apparently strangled with her own g-string, the police conclude there's a killer amongst them. Dixie certainly believes that because somebody tried to choke her while she was passing through a dark corner of the basement during a raid by police.

The movie sticks fairly closely to the novel's plot, but it changes some characters radically and eliminates others. H.I. Moss, the show's producer, for instance, is renamed S.B. Foss for no apparent reason. A suspiciously weird stagehand who virtually lives in the high reaches of the theater is virtually eliminated from the story. Meanwhile, the warm relationship between Gypsy and "Biff" in the book cools down considerably when Dixie replaces the Gypsy character.

There's another amusing change that certainly must have to do with strict movie censorship rules of the period. In the book, the girls are delighted when they get a new toilet in their wing to replace the leaky one that keeps breaking down. Though the movie retains the new toilet sequence, the toilet somehow is turned into a bathroom sink. Apparently toilets were banned from the screen in 1944, even when not being used by anyone.

Also due to censorship rules of the day, there is no real stripping shown in the movie. That was a break for Stanwyck, who might not have looked so much like a headliner if forced to show her "goods," which were considerably less prominent than the physical gifts of sister strippers Marion Martin, Victoria Faust and gum-popping Iris Adrian.

Still, Stanwyck is given one big song-and-dance number, "Take It Off the E-String, Lay It On the G-String," which gives her the chance to show she could bump and grind with the best of them. She also gets to dance with frisky young Pinky Lee, a real-life burlesque comic who later became a children's TV star. Their silly number is the highlight of the film.

Stanwyck considered *Lady of Burlesque* one of her worst movies. Why did she agree to do it? Most likely because it was directed by the accomplished William Wellman (*Wings*, *A Star Is Born*, *Nothing Sacred*, *Beau Geste*), who had directed her in several films already, including *The Great Man's Lady* (1942).

Though the title and main character of *The G-String Murders* were junked when it came to the screen, the rest of the film was reasonably faithful to the book—and its box office success suggests that readers of the bestseller probably flocked to the film and didn't bad-mouth it so much that they kept other moviegoers away.

Jeff Lindsay
Darkly Dreaming Dexter

The 2004 novel and the 2006–13 Showtime TV series *Dexter*

One of the most unusual new fictional detective heroes of the 21st century has to be Dexter Morgan, the blood splatter analyst who works for the Miami Police Department's forensics lab by day, but spends most of his nights as Florida's most successful serial killer.

In 2007, *Dexter*, starring Michael C. Hall in the title role, was ranked as the most popular series on the Showtime pay-TV network, which had completed two seasons of the hit show that year. Then, in early 2008, *Dexter* made his commercial broadcast network prime time debut on CBS, helping the network replace programs lost to the 2007–08 strike by the Writers Guild of America. The entire first season of *Dexter* was then telecast on CBS. The series continued on Showtime until 2013, leaving its hero alive and kicking, but living a new life under a new identity far from the world of post mortems and blood splatter analysis.

Because *Dexter* played originally on a pay cable network, it was not subject to the sort of censorship other contemporary thrillers have faced when adapted for TV. (The commercial network version was toned down considerably, though.) Still, fans who read the Jeff Lindsay novel that launched the *Dexter* phenomenon must have noticed that lots of changes had been made in the original storyline, even for the Showtime version.

During the full TV run of *Dexter*, the screen credits claimed the source for the series was Lindsay's first Dexter novel, *Darkly Dreaming Dexter*, even though Lindsay has published several additional novels about the character, carrying the story in a definitely different arc from the one followed by the TV writers.

Michael C. Hall played a well-intentioned serial killer who worked as a Miami Police blood-splatter analyst in TV's *Dexter*, based on Jeff Lindsay's novel *Darkly Dreaming Dexter*. From the DVD cover for Season One (Showtime and CBS).

For instance, in the books, Dexter is "accompanied" on his night prowls by the Dark Passenger, an amorphous entity that talks to Dexter and counsels him on when it's time to pay a visit to an intended victim. Dexter doesn't exactly "see" the Dark Passenger, but senses its presence like a sort of disembodied conscience of some kind.

The TV show turned the Dark Passenger into the ghost of Dexter's adoptive father, Police Detective Harry Morgan (James Remar). He is seen only by Dexter, of course, and turns up in every episode to counsel Dexter on his serial killer activities.

Readers and viewers alike know that Dexter was "inspired" to become a killer who enjoys dismembering people because of a childhood trauma: He was present when a murderer violently killed Dexter's mother right in front of him. He was saved from total damnation when Harry, the Miami police detective, adopted him and recognized Dexter's fascination with murder while he was still a child.

Harry didn't try to rehabilitate the boy once he noticed he was mutilating animals. Instead, he set Dexter on his current path by turning him into an instrument of justice in a society too often denied real justice. Before he died, Harry managed to channel Dexter's desire to kill and focus it on the really bad guys. Harry created a system of "rules" that Dexter now follows as an adult. The paramount rule is to kill only those who really deserve it. That's why Dexter doesn't prey on pretty girls or hookers, but instead tracks down and kills the serial killers the police aren't able to nail within the law.

In the novels, Lindsay promulgates the notion that the sort of horrifying experiences Dexter had as a child often can ignite homicidal sparks in children, which may blossom as they grow older. Lindsay's books have made it clear that Astor and Cody, the small daughter and son of Dexter's girlfriend Rita, are little Dexters in the making, thanks to the brutality they witnessed when their father, a drug dealer, used to abuse their mother in front of them.

In the third novel, Astor and Cody pester Dexter to take them along with him on his night prowls for victims. Cody seems to have some psychic connection to Dexter and recognizes him as a soul mate. The TV series avoided that dark corridor and kept the children reasonably pure. Now the series has left them behind after killing off Rita and having Dexter move on to different women for relationships. Along the way, he even becomes the doting father of his own little boy.

One of the major characters in the books is Dexter's sister Deborah Morgan, played by Jennifer Carpenter in the TV series. A uniformed Miami cop in the first novel, she was later promoted to detective, which means she's sometimes involved in the investigation of Dexter's murders. (In real life, actors Hall and Carpenter were married between seasons three and four. They subsequently divorced.)

In the books, Deborah knows about Dexter's after hours "hobby." In the TV series, she doesn't discover it until the final episode of the sixth season. (Her name is spelled Debra in the TV version.)

In the novels, Dexter constantly thinks of himself as not really a human being. He considers himself almost a different species of creature, but one of Harry's "rules" was to try to always seem as "normal" as other people. That's a tough assignment for a man who lusts to kill.

In the closing chapters of *Darkly Dreaming Dexter*, Dexter's police supervisor, Lt. LaGuerta, dies. But she lived on in the TV show before finally meeting her end in a very dramatic fashion that involved Dexter's sister. One of the second TV season's major developments was the surveillance of Dexter by Sgt. Doakes (Erik King), a mean-spirited Miami police colleague who suspects Dexter is a killer. Doakes meets a violent end in the second season of the TV show, but it's nothing like the horrifying finish for him at the end of the second book in the series. He's technically alive, but his hands, feet and tongue have been removed by a serial killer.

Another major plot thrust of the second TV season was the romance between Debra and Special Agent Frank Lundy of the FBI, played by guest star Keith Carradine. It was a tense relationship because Lundy headed a special task force with the mission to find the serial killer who, in reality, was Deb's own brother Dexter. This romance takes place in the second novel, *Dearly Devoted Dexter*; the Lundy character is named Kyle Chutsky in the book. The Chutsky-Lundy character was overhauled for the TV show and is eventually murdered. In the novel, a serial killer amputates one of Chutsky's legs and one arm.

Showtime also sexed up the relationship between Dexter and Rita for the TV screen before she was written out of the show. Dexter isn't supposed to be interested in sex because he really gets turned on by his serial killer activities, not sex acts with women. With Rita, he was faking it at first in order to appear more like a normal guy. Rita, who was sexually abused by her former husband, was fine with Dexter's gentler approach. She had no idea he was "gentle" because he isn't really into lovemaking at all.

However, the TV show seemed to suggest that Dexter was beginning to enjoy it just a bit more than he did initially. That probably helped his credibility as a TV character, especially since Rita was played by actress Julie Benz, who is drop-dead gorgeous.

A crucial character in the cliffhanger-like storyline of Season Two of the TV show was Lila (Jaime Murray), an Englishwoman whom Dexter meets at an AA–type meeting. (Rita thought Dexter might be a drug addict, rather than a murder addict, so she had pressed him to seek help through a rehab program.) Lila becomes Dexter's mentor, then his lover, and ultimately she itches for a chance to join him on his night prowls. She touches off the dramatic events that closed the second season.

Lila does not appear in any of the novels. Nor do lots of other characters, including Rita's mother Gail (played by guest star JoBeth Williams), who comes to visit her daughter and takes an instant dislike to Dexter in the TV series.

After seeing every episode of the TV series, I'd say more than half the story developments were original to the series and not Lindsay's source novel. The TV *Dexter* has done a very good job of maintaining the integrity of the character, even though you will find lots of differences in him and his fellow characters in Lindsay's novels.

The phenomenal success of *Dexter* as a TV series reflects on the darker nature of American television in the new century. It would have been unthinkable a decade earlier to present a TV "hero" who kills people at least part of the time because he enjoys it. It seems to be a natural outgrowth of progressively darker characters in suspense and thriller fiction, most especially Thomas Harris' Hannibal Lecter of *Red Dragon* and *The Silence of the Lambs*. Perhaps because of the success of *Dexter*, Lecter eventually ended up as the main character of his own NBC series, *Hannibal*.

From the outside it may seem as if *Dexter* is a sort of nice and friendly Jack the Ripper. That's not quite the case. Because the TV show has a very whimsical approach to the Dexter character and Michael C. Hall is such a handsome, charming player, it's possible to view Dexter as the latest in a long line of "outside the law" heroes like Zorro, who punishes only the bad guys.

Of course, Dexter doesn't just slash a "Z" in the bad guy's shirt with his sword and let it go at that. Instead, he uses a bone saw and a fine set of surgical scalpels and has all kinds of witty and amusing things to say while slicing and dicing the bad guys into kibble. That's the 21st century for you.

John D. MacDonald

The Executioners

The 1958 novel and the 1962 and 1991 movies *Cape Fear*

In 1958, John D. MacDonald was the king of paperback thriller authors. He had not yet created his series character, Florida shamus Travis McGee, the central character in 21 novels, but he had written more than three dozen other popular novels, including a new one called *The Executioners*.

The Executioners was a spellbinder with an evil character called Max Cady driving the lean storyline. Cady has just been released from prison and is hell-bent on revenge against the man who testified against him in court, leading to his conviction for raping and savagely beating a teenage girl.

Gregory Peck (right) faces sadistic, vengeance-driven killer Robert Mitchum in *Cape Fear*, based on the thriller *The Executioners* by John D. MacDonald (Universal-International and MCA-TV).

He comes to the rural village of Harper, near the larger community of New Essex, where he finds his man, Sam Bowden, working as a lawyer and living comfortably with his wife and three children. His mission is to make Bowden know how it feels to lose everything.

Taut and fast-moving, *The Executioners* is loaded with suspense, but has much more going for it, including MacDonald's shocking exposure of how ineffective the law can be when it comes to protecting innocent people from a stalker like Cady, who carefully avoids breaking any laws, the whole time he's moving in for the kill.

Ultimately, MacDonald forces his successful "civilized" family to set aside all its notions of right and wrong in order to defend itself against this vengeful force of nature gone mad. It is, in essence, an endorsement of vigilantism as a last resort.

A few years later, while playing the lead role in *The Guns of Navarone*, actor Gregory Peck read *The Executioners* and thought it had excellent screen possibilities. He was then producing many of his own films, so he took it to his *Navarone* director, J. Lee Thompson, and asked his opinion about its viability as a film. By the time Thompson read the book, it was clear they wanted to do the film together, so they took the project to Universal.

Right away they began to re-conceive the novel for the screen, starting with its title, which they thought might give moviegoers the wrong idea about what they were going to see on the screen. Peck liked what he called "geographical titles" so he pulled out a map of the U.S., ran his finger up the eastern seaboard in the vicinity of North Carolina, the general locale of MacDonald's story, and stopped when he found a spot called Cape Fear.

Now called *Cape Fear*, the project was almost certain to face censorship problems, even though Hollywood was in the midst of shedding a generation of rules about the content and language of films. For one thing, Cady's plot for vengeance included his planned rape of Bowden's teenage daughter, a major no-no for movies in the early 1960s. Then there was the problem that Bowden starts planning to murder Cady once he realizes the law wasn't going to protect his family.

In the book, the trouble between Cady and Bowden begins in the final days of World War II when both men were in the Navy. Bowden was then a lawyer with the Judge Advocate General's department, what we now know as a JAG assignment. While off-duty in Melbourne, Australia, Bowden comes upon the drunken Cady and realizes the man is raping and beating a 14-year-old girl in a dark alley. Summoning help, Bowden sees Cady arrested and charged. Then he's required to appear in court as the key witness.

Mainly because of Bowden's testimony, Cady is sentenced to a prison term of life at hard labor. Cady was a battle-hardened veteran with the rank of staff sergeant and had been in the service seven years. He had just come off 200 days of combat and had a bad case of nerves. Because of that mitigating factor, his life was spared.

After the war, his sentence was reviewed and Cady was released after completing 13 years of his life sentence. He emerged a bitter man whose own wife had left him and remarried. Before starting his life over again, though, Cady is determined to destroy Bowden and his family.

The screenplay by James R. Webb made some fundamental changes. First, Bowden's family was whittled down in size. His two sons were eliminated, leaving only 14-year-old Nancy at home with her parents (Peck and Polly Bergen). The wartime confrontation between the two antagonists is dropped and, instead, we learn that Bowden witnessed the rape incident in Baltimore, not Melbourne. Cady's (Robert Mitchum) time in prison was changed to eight years. This un-complicates the film's narrative because it reduces the amount of background information we need and tends to focus our attention on the teenage girl.

Webb kept the incident where Cady poisons the Bowden family dog, but there's no longer the attempt to shoot one of Bowden's sons because the sons are no longer in the story.

In his youth, director Thompson, who was British, had worked with Alfred Hitchcock when Hitch still was making films in his native England. He had adopted Hitchcock's approach to complex stories, which was to pare them down to the bone. He also had picked up lots of technique from Hitchcock, which clearly shows in *Cape Fear*. Hitchcock's favorite composer, Bernard Herrmann, was hired to score *Cape Fear*.

The other fundamental change from the book is the decision to move the Bowden-Cady showdown to the Cape Fear river, putting everyone on board a houseboat. Once they decided to call the movie *Cape Fear*, I suppose they had to go there somehow. It was a big improvement over MacDonald's showdown, which takes place in the Bowdens' home.

In some interviews conducted during the film's initial release, Peck suggested that he wanted to hire a powerful actor to play Cady, knowing full well the part was the juicier one and whoever played it might steal the picture. He was right. It seems clear to me that they wanted Mitchum for Cady because they remembered how nasty he was as the child-chasing killer in *The Night of the Hunter* (1955). Mitchum fit the Cady role perfectly and did indeed steal the picture.

In the DVD version of the first *Cape Fear*, director Thompson refers to Mitchum as "explosive" and says that was just what he needed to make Cady come to life—the feeling that he was teetering on the edge and might erupt with violence at any time.

Thompson had hoped to hire Hayley Mills to play 14-year-old Nancy, but she was busy with back-to-back Disney films. In her place, he cast young Lori Martin, who plays the part beautifully, but seems more child than blooming teenager. His other casting was flawless: warm, cozy Polly Bergen as Carol Bowden; Martin Balsam as the police chief; Telly Savalas, in his pre–*Kojak* period, with hair, as a private eye who helps Bowden; Jack Kruschen as the defense counsel Cady hires, and dancer Barrie Chase as Diane, a new character Webb created to replace the barfly that Cady rapes and beats up in the book.

Herrmann's intense score is one of the best he ever did. It was so good, in fact, that Martin Scorsese decided not to change it when he remade the film. Scorsese hired composer Elmer Bernstein to conduct Herrmann's score and used it for the new film.

The first *Cape Fear* movie was a big hit and was acclaimed by critics. Looking at it with the perspective of the years, the film was a strong upgrade from the novel and, considering the censorship it faced, is still one of the grimmest, edgiest films of its era. It does make one giant concession, though: It lets Max Cady survive the showdown with Bowden, which he doesn't do in either the book or the 1991 remake.

The Scorsese version originally was something Steven Spielberg wanted to direct. Both Spielberg and Scorsese were great admirers of the 1962 film, but Spielberg had too many other irons in the fire and Scorsese, who was then making *Goodfellas*, didn't think he was the right person to remake a classic thriller, generally not the genre of film he prefers.

But Robert De Niro wanted to tackle Max Cady, a character with some resemblance to his classic Travis Bickle character in Scorsese's *Taxi Driver* (1976). His passion for it was one of the factors that influenced Scorsese to take a serious look at directing the picture.

Ultimately, Scorsese began to believe it might be interesting to try and do a classic thriller, respecting all the conventions of the genre, but also adding depth and dramatic texture. Once he began working with screenwriter Wesley Strick, his vision for the new *Cape Fear* began to form.

The essential change for the 1991 *Cape Fear* is the insight it gives us into the family Cady is trying to destroy. It's not the same family we met in the book—happy husband, wife, three kids and a dog—nor even the streamlined version of the 1962 film. This time, for example, Sam Bowden is carrying a small load of guilt over his original involvement with Cady. He's now the former defense attorney for Cady and we learn that he withheld evidence about the victim that might have brought a lighter sentence for Cady. He withheld it because he couldn't get over the explosive violence Cady had used to hammer the woman he raped. He wanted the man put away for a long time, which is not the attitude a defendant wants from his lawyer.

Bowden's marriage is also drawing near the rocks. His wife, whose name is now Leigh, is played by the volatile Jessica Lange, not the comfy Polly Bergen. Leigh suspects Sam of cheating on her, which he may be doing with his legal clerk (Illeana Douglas). The new version cleverly uses this new character of the clerk to replace the barfly character

Ex-convict Robert De Niro (left) seeks revenge on lawyer Nick Nolte in Martin Scorsese's 1991 remake of *Cape Fear* (Universal City Studio and Amblin Entertainment).

Barrie Chase played in the original. By making her an intimate of Bowden, her rape and beating serves as another shot Cady fires across Bowden's bow.

The Bowdens' daughter is a little older (15, going on 16) and is played by the quirky Juliette Lewis, who makes her predecessor in the role, Lori Martin, look like a cloistered nun in comparison. The daughter, renamed Danielle, smokes grass and reads porn novels (both supplied by Max Cady) and, in one sizzling scene with De Niro, seems about ready to do him, if he'll only be so kind as to show her how.

Replacing Gregory Peck as Sam is a slimmed-down and bookish Nick Nolte, who wears rimless spectacles and shows no signs of his usual scruffy-tough screen persona. He plays Sam as a man unsure of his own capacities and unable to control his own family, shortcomings his archenemy, Cady, uses against him throughout the film.

Scorsese's film is much darker as it probes the human souls of the central characters. Lange's Mrs. Bowden seems so incurably hot that we never know for sure if she isn't a bit attracted by the heat emanating from Max Cady. At one point, she even thinks out loud, telling Sam that she wants to see how strong he is—or how weak.

Again, though, it's Max who steals the show. De Niro gobbles the screen as he ups the psycho-potential of this man, blends in a little Bible belt Pentecostal snake handler style and gives us an intensely physical performance—from his opening scene in prison, where we first see he's covered with crazy tattoos, to his climactic struggle with Bowden aboard a runaway houseboat during a tempestuous storm. (De Niro and Juliette Lewis were Oscar-nominated for their performances.)

If the original censors freaked over the 1962 *Cape Fear*, they would have needed serious time in rehab after seeing the 1991 version. The scene where Max runs his thumb over the lower lip of the trembling Danielle and she begins to suck on it, tells you more about this girl-woman than you probably want to know. Likewise, the violence is cranked way up until De Niro's Max seems some kind of indestructible monster after surviving beatings with chains, hot soup tossed in his face and various other forms of stylized screen crucifixion.

Scorsese has acknowledged there was an attempt to pay homage to the original film, aside from the use of Herrmann's powerful score. For one thing, he cast Gregory Peck, Robert Mitchum and Martin Balsam in cameo roles so they could play scenes with the actors who now had their old parts. It's a wonderful little gimmick and it works in all kinds of ways.

Scorsese's version goes back to the original MacDonald showdown in the Bowden house, but then adds a second showdown aboard the houseboat in the Cape Fear river. Armed with the much more impressive digital special effects of today's films, Scorsese turns the finale into something truly awesome to behold.

To write this assessment, I re-read the original novel and re-screened both films, all within three days. That way, the changes are readily apparent. They all seem to work for me, too. The book is as good as it was 60 years later. But now I can truly appreciate how well-served MacDonald was by the filmmakers who brought his work to the screen. Both films are classics. Who could ask for more?

Ross Macdonald
The Moving Target

The 1949 novel and the 1966 movie *Harper*

Fans of Ross Macdonald must have been extremely enthused in 1966 when they learned that Lew Archer, his private eye character in a long string of best-selling novels, was going to be played in a movie by Paul Newman, one of Hollywood's most adored leading men, in a big-budget, all-star version of the first Archer novel, *The Moving Target*.

Looking back on Macdonald's stature in the mystery genre, this was an extremely important development. It told the fans that Hollywood perceived Macdonald's Archer as an A-picture property. You don't see the studio hotshots rounding up the biggest stars for a major studio version of a mystery novel very often.

What's more, they had hired the hottest writer in 1960s Hollywood, William Goldman, to adapt Macdonald's novel for the screen. Clearly, they really wanted to make a classy picture. That was another reason why the first Ross Macdonald screen project seemed to have nothing but promising signs.

But some rude shocks were in store. In fact, the movie turned out to be a celluloid calamity for hardcore Macdonald fans, despite the hearty box office returns and all the good reviews from critics who had never read a Lew Archer mystery.

No doubt the greatest shock came when Newman, apparently acting on a superstitious whim, insisted that they change the name of Macdonald's detective hero from Lew Archer to Lew Harper. Why spit in the eye of Macdonald's legion of readers? As legend

He was Lew Archer, private eye, in the Ross Macdonald novel *The Moving Target*, but Paul Newman wanted his name changed to Lew Harper in the 1966 movie version called *Harper* (Warner Bros.–Seven Arts and WB-TV Worldwide).

has it, Newman had such success with his 1963 film *Hud* that he thought there was some kind of magic in having a single-word title that began with "H." (His film the following year was another "H" picture, *Hombre*, from an Elmore Leonard novel.)

As a result, *The Moving Target* became *Harper* and the name on Lew Archer's office door was repainted to say "Lew Harper."

For the truly reverent fans, this was sacrilegious. They liked to think of Macdonald as being America's foremost author of the hard-boiled private eye school and his gumshoe, Lew Archer, in a direct line of succession from Dashiell Hammett's Sam Spade and Raymond Chandler's Philip Marlowe. Archer's name, legend has it, was inspired by Miles Archer, the murdered private eye partner of Sam Spade in *The Maltese Falcon*.

In fact, within the mystery world, *The Moving Target* is considered a seminal work. It now seems to be the book in which the baton as most respected mystery writer in America was passed from the ailing king, Raymond Chandler, to the heir apparent, Ross Macdonald.

(Archer remained Archer when television got around to him a few years later, but the actors who played him in separate projects, Peter Graves and Brian Keith, were as different from Paul Newman as you could possibly get.)

Macdonald (real name: Ross Millar) was born in Los Gatos, California, and raised in the Canadian province of British Columbia. Attracted to the mystery genre as a young man, he was especially fond of Raymond Chandler's novels. Married in his youth to a writer who later became the popular mystery novelist Margaret Millar, Macdonald published his first mystery novels after serving in World War II. He gradually began developing a detective hero clearly modeled on Chandler's Philip Marlowe.

In *The Moving Target*, Lew Archer has already left his Long Beach, California, police job and begun working as a private detective, mostly doing the routine work of evidence-gathering for divorce cases and the like. He operates in the same Los Angeles–Southern California milieu as Chandler's Marlowe. He has the same cynical view of his turf, seeing it as a boom town environment for profit-driven urban sprawl.

Through his first-person narration, Archer lets us know that the L.A. area of the late 1940s, the period of *The Moving Target*, is mostly run by corrupt rich people and the racketeers and crooked cops they manipulate. These power brokers usually live a decadent lifestyle in grotesquely large homes in suburbs like Santa Teresa—the community most readers recognized as Santa Barbara in Macdonald's books. In all this, Macdonald was following the lead of Chandler, whose Marlowe saw the same sort of postwar Babylon being built in the smoggy valleys and sun-drenched beach towns of Southern California by all the wrong people.

In *The Moving Target*, Archer's personal life is pretty much a ruin. His wife has dumped him and his business barely supports him, let alone the once-mandatory sexy secretary private eyes were supposed to have (for example, Sam Spade's Effie Perrine and Mike Hammer's Velda). So, like Marlowe, Archer frequently winds up helping people he really doesn't like or respect because he doesn't have much choice.

In *The Moving Target*'s opening chapter, an offbeat case comes Archer's way. He's hired to find the wealthy missing husband of Mrs. Sampson, a handsome woman of middle years who's an invalid due to a fall from a horse. Mr. Sampson has been gone only a few days and the police haven't been called. Mrs. Sampson suspects her husband is on a bender and probably shacked up with one of his lady friends. She wants Archer to find him, bring him home and do it quietly—before he starts giving money away to the religious crackpots who litter the L.A. landscape.

This opening is uncannily like the opening of Chandler's first Philip Marlowe novel, *The Big Sleep*. Marlowe goes to the manorial estate of an invalid man who also has a missing person for him to find. His client also has a young, beautiful daughter who's hot to trot. So does Macdonald's Mr. Sampson. And so on.

Ultimately, Archer learns that Sampson has been snatched and is being held for ransom by a motley crew of gangster wannabes and typical Southern California low-life flakes. The wider his investigation goes, the more corruption he finds among Sampson's cronies, family members and friends. Even Mrs. Sampson is sort of hoping the old boy is found dead because that will un-complicate her life a great deal and leave her richer than she'd ever hoped to be.

In short, it's one of those cases that make a noble private eye want to throw up—if he could find time to do it while chasing down all the potential bad guys and gals.

Harper, the movie version, starts out well enough with a nice bit of behind-the-credits character building. We see Newman's Lew Harper wake up in his small, cluttered L.A. apartment, badly needing a cup of coffee, but finding he has no alternative but to fish yesterday's coffee grounds out of the garbage can and recycle them with fresh hot water. This is not a very successful private eye.

But there's a problem: Newman is so handsome, so well-groomed and so lean and fit that we don't believe it for a minute. This looks like a man who spent the previous day posing for the cover of *GQ* magazine, holding a tennis racket with a sweater knotted around his neck and all decked out in spotless, well-pressed whites.

Then we follow Harper's Porsche convertible up the freeway to the Santa Theresa turnoff (they couldn't even spell Archer's town without adding a lucky "h" to Teresa!) and eventually to the Sampson mansion. He drives through the huge iron gate, up the long winding driveway and across the palatial grounds, where he stops briefly to make a clucking noise as he sees the Olympic-size pool, braced by rich tropical landscaping, and the sexy girl diving into the water way off in the distance.

They keep giving us these little hints that Harper is a borderline economic failure, like the door on the driver's side of his Porsche that has just a primer coat of paint on it. (Lew Archer arrived at the Sampson place in a taxi cab, but Newman probably insisted that Harper have his own wheels. Newman, after all, was a racing fan and later an actual competitive driver.)

It's charming to find that Mrs. Sampson is played by Lauren Bacall, who played the trouble-prone older daughter of the invalid client in *The Big Sleep* in 1946. By 1966, Bacall had solid gold credentials as a mystery player, having married and worked often with her late husband Humphrey Bogart in various noir projects for film, radio and television. By 1966, Bacall was so good at playing twisted but sexy matrons that no one could have played Mrs. Sampson any better.

For most of *Harper*, screenwriter Goldman followed the complex Macdonald plot pretty closely, making understandable changes needed to update the 1948–49 period of the novel. For one thing, he changed has-been silent movie star Fay Estabrook into a failed 1950s starlet who "got fat" and saw her acting career go to blazes. This worked very well once they cast Shelley Winters in the role. Winters *was* a former starlet who "got fat," but she also got to be one hell of a dramatic actress—and she steals every scene she's in with Newman.

But then Goldman threw something at us that was really off the wall—and seems to serve no purpose but to antagonize Lew Archer fans. He writes in the detective's ex-wife, who can't stand Harper any more, but still sleeps with him when he's really in a jam. Though Janet Leigh does her best with this part, it has no place in the story unless somebody decided a romantic leading man like Newman couldn't possibly go through a whole movie without making out with somebody.

If you're a fan of a detective hero like Sherlock Holmes, you don't want some screenwriter giving him a sex life he isn't supposed to have. That's the way the Janet Leigh scenes play in *Harper*. They're extraneous nonsense.

Director Jack Smight had some nice casting ideas for *Harper* that helped make the movie a box office hit, like putting former teen idol Robert Wagner in the role of the double-dealing playboy who hangs around the Sampson estate, supposedly to keep Sampson's hot-pants daughter Miranda (Pamela Tiffin) from bothering the gardeners and pool boys. But then Goldman wrote in some tacky "sidekick" gags for Wagner to play while accompanying Harper here and there. It messes up the character and makes him too likable for the way he turns out in the final reel.

Another offbeat casting choice was picking Julie Harris to play a nightclub blues singer wrapped up in the sinister goings-on. Anybody who remembered Harris from *I Am a Camera* in 1955, playing the same character Liza Minnelli won an Oscar playing in *Cabaret* nearly 20 years later, certainly wasn't surprised that she could play a singer—and, fortunately, we didn't have to hear much of her singing in *Harper*. The result was a really interesting performance, even though Goldman also reshaped her character, moving away from Macdonald's original concept.

Goldman's final touch was to leave us in doubt about whether or not Harper was going to turn in the ultimate villain to the police. Macdonald had the bad guy turn himself in, but that wouldn't have played quite as cynically as moviegoers wanted their stories in the 1960s when we were involved in the Vietnam war and nobody seemed to want to 'fess up to anything bad they'd done lately.

If there's one overwhelming bad thing about *Harper*, I'm sure most true Ross Macdonald fans will say it's the casting of Newman. His performance is all charm, smart-ass remarks and Hollywood charisma. He either hadn't yet come to understand what he could do in the area of dramatic nuance, or else he didn't think *Harper* needed his best effort. He might have been right from a purely commercial point of view since *Harper* was a big hit and prompted a sequel, *The Drowning Pool*, a decade later.

When I first saw *Harper*, I loved it. But I hadn't read Macdonald yet and I didn't know how important Lew Archer is to the American detective genre. Like Philip Marlowe, Archer is a philosopher-poet of crime. His insights into the human condition lift the Archer novels out of the mystery genre and into the realm of serious contemporary fiction. And, like Chandler, Macdonald was close to being right about everything, now that we have the perspective of the years.

There are still lots of good reasons to see *Harper*. Johnny Mandel's jazz score is marvelous and Conrad Hall's camerawork is superb, especially whenever Pamela Tiffin shows up in a bikini to do the Froug on a diving board, reminding us how well spectacular young women and the dance crazes of the 1960s went together.

But a real mystery fan will get a lot more out of reading *The Moving Target*, an important book in the history of mystery that helped launch the long, brilliant career of Lew Archer. And the name is Archer, damn it!

John P. Marquand
Think Fast, Mr. Moto

The 1937 novel and the 1937 movie

I.A. Moto occupies an unusual place in the history of the mystery. He's the only popular "detective" character created by a Pulitzer Prize winning novelist, who later disowned him as "a disgrace." Moreover, he was never really a detective, but more properly a secret agent working for the Empire of Japan—a nation the U.S. went to war against shortly after Mr. Moto was featured in a popular series of American-made mystery-action movies.

Moto first appears in John P. Marquand's 1935 novel *No Hero*. He was not the main character in that novel, which gives him something in common with Charlie Chan, another famous Asian sleuth, who made his debut ten years earlier as a subordinate character in *The House Without A Key*.

But Chan moved up to the leading role in the other five novels that Earl Derr Biggers wrote about him. Strangely, though, Moto never did become the central character in any of the six Marquand novels. Instead, he almost always was a peripheral character in stories mostly about young American protagonists, who crossed his path in the course of events and found Mr. Moto ready to step in to play some crucial role.

In *Think Fast, Mr. Moto*, the third in Marquand's series, the hero is young Wilson Hitchings, who's sent to the Shanghai branch of the family firm, Hitchings Brothers, a huge banking and investment company with vast holdings in the Far East. Hitchings is being taught the workings of the firm he someday may inherit, but the family first wants to test his mettle by giving him a difficult task his elders haven't been able to handle: To journey to Hawaii and buy out, then shut down a gambling casino operated by a distant cousin who calls her quasi-legal operation The Hitchings Plantation. The family is afraid some scandal will develop there and damage the reputation of Hitchings Brothers at a time when competition in the Far East is fierce and any kind of problem might scare away investors.

Along the way, young Hitchings meets Mr. Moto, who believes the gambling house is being used as a secret front for efforts to smuggle funds to rebels in Manchuria, where his government has colonial ambitions. Moto turns out to be right. Hitchings discovers that sinister foreign forces have taken over the gambling house and are forcing the pretty Hitchings cousin, Eva, to serve their needs with her operation. Wilson falls in love with her and decides to help her out—with the vital assistance of Mr. Moto.

In 1937, 20th Century–Fox decided to start a new series of mysteries as a companion to their highly successful Charlie Chan series. To play the part of Moto, the studio followed the example of the Chan films and avoided casting a real Japanese. Instead they made a very odd choice: Hungarian émigré Peter Lorre, who had his hair slicked back and his teeth enhanced a bit in size, but otherwise wore little makeup to aid his transformation into an Asian. He spoke some very trite "Japan-esy" dialogue, but did nothing to conceal his rather obvious Hungarian accent.

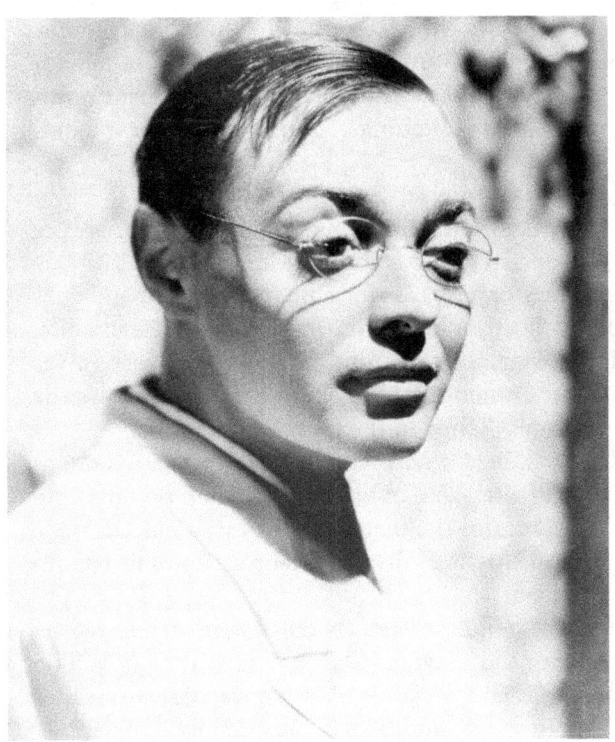

Hungarian-born Peter Lorre passed himself off as Japanese crime-fighter Mr. Moto in a series of mystery thrillers that ended when Japan attacked the U.S. on December 7, 1941 (20th Century–Fox).

The diminutive Lorre seemed to relish this rare chance to play an action hero instead of the criminals and nutcases he usually played. He took on the Moto role aggressively, with a great deal of humor and even a little swagger.

Rather than start filming the Moto books from the start—the first one, *No Hero*, features an alcoholic as its dubious protagonist and gives Moto little to do—the studio picked *Think Fast, Mr. Moto*, which has a much more intriguing storyline and more action for Moto.

However, the movie version, scripted by director Norman Foster and Wyllis Cooper, saved very little of the original Marquand concept. They changed Wilson Hitchings to Robert Hitchings (Thomas Beck) and he never gets to Hawaii. The girl he meets and falls in love with is not Eva Hitchings but international adventuress Gloria Danton (Virginia Field). Hitchings is not the heir to a vast investment empire, but rather the son of a shipping line owner. Most of the action takes place on shipboard or in Shanghai and its environs. They also gave Mr. Moto a new first name: Kentaro.

Moto gets much closer to co-equal focus in the movie. It starts with him on an undercover gambit in San Francisco that's not in the book: Moto, disguised as a bearded peddler, attempts to sell an antiquity to a Chinatown dealer while really investigating a murder. When his cover is blown, he immediately tackles a gang of armed thugs and overpowers them with the use of his jiu-jitsu technique. Knowing he's now a marked man, he escapes on the same boat to Shanghai where young Hitchings is getting a spirited sendoff from his rowdy pals in the cabin across the hall from Moto's.

When the half-soused party pals of Hitchings try to drag Moto over to their party, he politely resists. Irked, they try to jostle him and Moto responds by throwing a couple of them over his shoulder and across the room. (Stuntman Harvey Parry doubles for Lorre.) He makes quite an impression on Hitchings, who befriends him, despite this embarrassing line, "Now I know who you are," says Hitchings. "You're the Japanese Sandman!"

Moto shrugs that one off, saying, "Strange things is Americans!"

The writers further the bond between the men by making them both graduates of Stanford University. (No doubt a major surprise to the Stanford Alumni Office.)

Gloria, the new female attraction of the story, boards the ship in Honolulu and goes on with the voyage to Shanghai. Hitchings is attracted to her immediately. Meanwhile, Moto discovers the ship's steward trying to steal a letter from his stateroom, recognizes him as the murderer he was seeking in San Francisco and, believe it or not, throws the man overboard. (Moto definitely isn't soft on villains, in the books or the films.)

In Shanghai, Hitchings is greeted by Wilkie (Murray Kinnell), his company's rep in China, who warns him about treacherous White Russian women who will do anything to get Americans to marry them and take them to the States. Yes, it turns out Gloria is one of those, but not a treacherous one. All this is Hollywood fabrication and has no connection to the novel.

Though the film does involve sinister foreign powers (Nicolas Marloff, played by Sig Ruman, is the Russian-sounding name of the movie's villain), company man Wilkie also turns out to be scheming against Hitchings and his family. Moto miraculously escapes his ordered execution and saves the day. Hitchings and Gloria presumably live happily ever after.

Think Fast, Mr. Moto is a very entertaining action picture with a core of mystery. Though Lorre's caricature of a Japanese would seem offensive to a majority of viewers today—he even says "Ah so!" half a dozen or more times—he's really an engaging character and most vividly a "good guy," even though the real Japanese Secret Service clearly was up to no good in the days when Moto was supposedly working for them in the Far East.

Fox made eight Mr. Moto films between 1937 and 1939, but Japan's growing militarism and hostility toward America made it much harder to sell Moto as a movie hero in the States. Marquand continued to write Mr. Moto novels, which he always claimed he did just for the money, but the December 7, 1941, sneak attack on Pearl Harbor finished Moto as a character. Marquand had written *Last Laugh, Mr. Moto* before the attack and it was published in 1942. It was his final novel about the mysterious little secret agent—but he gave Moto a cameo appearance in his 1957 novel *Stopover Tokyo*, playing a helpful aide to a pair of American agents trying to stop a Communist takeover of postwar Japan. Fox filmed *Stopover Tokyo* that same year, leaving out the Moto character.

In 1965, Fox tried to revive Moto as a player in the international spy movie craze led by the James Bond movies. Henry Silva played Moto in *The Return of Mr. Moto*, which received devastating reviews, did poor business and seemingly ended forever the presence of Mr. Moto on movie screens.

Ed McBain
Cop Hater

The 1956 novel and the 1958 movie

Many mystery experts date the beginning of the "police procedural" genre from the 1948 release of Jules Dassin's documentary-style action film *The Naked City*, NBC Radio's 1949 launching of Jack Webb's *Dragnet* and, finally, the 1956 publication of Ed McBain's *Cop Hater*, the first in his long series of 87th Precinct novels.

The 87th Precinct novels were fundamental building blocks in the creation of the subgenre that deals with the authentic procedures that police departments follow in solving mysteries and bringing criminals to justice, employing teams of investigators rather than the detectives who worked alone in thousands of mystery stories dating back to the time of Sherlock Holmes.

A milestone novel, *Cop Hater* shows how the detectives of one precinct in a large, fictional, New York–like metropolis track down a man who has shot three police officers execution-style. Its pioneering inclusion of modern forensic evidence-gathering techniques would lead to the popular entertainments of today, from the novels of Patricia Cornwell and Kathy Reichs to the various *CSI* television series and spinoffs.

The murders of the first two detectives, partners Reardon and Foster, with the same .45 caliber handgun lead investigators to believe that someone had a grudge against them, but they keep hitting dead ends trying to follow that line. Detective Hank Bush becomes Victim #3, but the killer takes a bullet from Bush in the process and starts leaving a trail of bloody clues all over the city.

Published in 1956, *Cop Hater* was turned into a movie by producer-director William Berke. Berke had been an actor in silent pictures before starting to write, produce and direct "B" Westerns and jungle movies (he directed the Johnny Weissmuller *Jungle Jim* in 1948). He turned mostly to television in the late 1940s.

Robert Loggia is Detective Steve Carella, defending his wife Teddy (Ellen Parker) against an assailant in *Cop Hater*, the 1958 film version of Ed McBain's first novel in the 87th Precinct series (United Artists).

Berke acquired the rights to the first two 87th Precinct novels—the other was *The Mugger*—and produced two low-budget films with casts of mostly TV actors. Both films were independently produced and released by United Artists in 1958. Berke made one last film, also released in 1958, *The Lost Missile*, which featured several actors from the *Cop Hater* cast, before he died at age 54 in February 1958. At the time he died, none of the three films had yet gone into wide release.

Cop Hater was the first novel written under the name Ed McBain, which was one of several pen names used by author Salvatore Lombino. His best-known pen name was Evan Hunter and the period of the late 1950s and early 1960s was very profitable for him with two immense hit movies, *Blackboard Jungle* (1955) and *Strangers When We Meet* (1960), based on Evan Hunter bestsellers.

But the Ed McBain legacy would prove to be the longest and richest. NBC turned *87th Precinct* into a weekly 1961–62 TV series and several more novels in the series were adapted into movies either for theaters or for TV. Lombino churned out 87th Precinct novels until he died in 2008.

In *Cop Hater*, readers meet Steve Carella, a young detective of Italian extraction. He has fallen in love with a beautiful young lady named Teddy Franklin, who happens to be deaf. Carella would gradually emerge as the pivotal figure in the *87th Precinct* series and his subsequent marriage to Teddy gave the books a special romantic interest that attracted many female readers.

The screenplay by Henry Kane, another veteran of "B" movies and television, retained most of the McBain characters and plot developments, with a few very prominent exceptions. The most radical change was eliminating Detective Hank Bush and replacing him with Detective Mike Maguire. Maguire does everything Bush did in the book, so it just amounts to a name change for which there seems no apparent motive.

Maguire still has an exceptionally sexy wife named Alice (Shirley Ballard), whose dissatisfaction with her rather crude husband plays a crucial part in the solving of the mystery of the cop killings, just as it does in the book.

Another significant change is the re-naming of the tabloid newspaperman whose sensational reporting gets one officer shot and puts Carella and his girl in the cop killer's sights. His name is Savage in the book, Miller in the movie. Perhaps the fact that he's played by an actor named Gene Miller inspired the change.

The other changes made by screenwriter Kane make perfect sense. For instance, in the book, Teddy knows when Steve is at her door by a way he has of twisting the door latch back and forth as a signal to her that it's safe to open up. In the movie, Teddy (Ellen Parker) knows that someone's outside when a light flashes over the door, a signal that somebody is ringing her doorbell. This system used by many hearing impaired people. However, she can't tell who's at her door—and that's why the killer is able to gain admittance to her apartment for the climactic showdown with Carella.

The casting of *Cop Hater* is especially interesting. Carella is played by a very young Robert Loggia, who would not become a familiar face to moviegoers for another 27 years when he earned an Oscar nomination playing the "leg man" to criminal lawyer Glenn Close in 1985's *The Jagged Edge*. Detective Maguire was played by another face soon familiar to most: Gerald O'Loughlin, who would become a TV regular as Lt. Eddie Ryker, nursemaid to the young cops in ABC-TV's *The Rookies* (1972–76).

Two other members of the *Cop Hater* ensemble would also become very familiar faces to both moviegoers and TV watchers: Vincent Gardenia, who played a police informer known as "Danny Gimp," and Jerry Orbach, who played Joe "Mumzer" Sanchez, spokesman for the teenage street gang initially suspected of involvement with the cop killings. Gardenia went on to win a Tony on Broadway for Neil Simon's *The Prisoner of Second Avenue* and an Emmy for *Age-Old Friends* (1989). He was Oscar-nominated for his performances as the baseball manager in *Bang the Drum Slowly* (1973) and as Cher's father in *Moonstruck* (1987). He also had recurring roles in the hit TV series *All in the Family* and *L.A. Law*. Orbach, also was a Tony winner (*The Fantasticks*), was best known for his long-running role as Detective Lennie Briscoe on NBC's *Law & Order*.

Berke's *Cop Hater* is not a very powerful film and surely would have been much better if made by a younger, more creative director with a bigger budget. It might have led to a long series of movies that echoed the success of the McBain novels, which still remain quite readable in the 21st century.

Ed McBain

Fuzz

The 1965 novel and the 1972 movie

In his 1965 novel *Fuzz*, Ed McBain turned more toward the comical side of life in the 87th precinct, even though the *bête noire* of the story is the Deaf Man, the most diabolical villain in the precinct's long history. McBain was pretty successful in balancing humor with mystery, but the 1972 film version tipped much more sharply toward the comic. The novel was adapted for the screen by McBain himself, writing under his other pen name, Evan Hunter. (His real name was Salvatore Lombino.) Somebody must have convinced the author that the movie would be much more profitable if they upped the quotient of fun, sex and action.

They were right—it was a big hit.

In the book, McBain's usual protagonist, police detective Steve Carella, stays in the background more than usual. They couldn't have that for the movie since they'd hired one of Hollywood's big box office stars of the 1970s to play Carella: Burt Reynolds. They also beefed up the minuscule part that cop Eileen Burke played in the book because Raquel Welch, then very hot, was cast as Eileen (whose surname is changed to McHenry for the movie). Though the ads showed Reynolds and Welch getting real close to each other, they had almost no scenes together and, according to widely reported rumors, Welch took such a strong dislike to Reynolds that she insisted they spend as little time together as possible while making the picture.

The central plot of the book involves an extortion plot by the Deaf Man, who threatens to kill city officials one by one if his demands aren't met. At first the police don't realize it's their old nemesis, so they don't take

Cops Burt Reynolds (top) and Jack Weston dress up as nuns to catch the bad guy in a comic scene from the 1972 movie *Fuzz*, based on the Ed McBain novel (United Artists Television).

his threats seriously. But then he kills two city officials, and youngsters paid to deliver his messages to the precinct headquarters report that the man who hired them had "a thing in his ear." The police realize that must be a hearing aid and that the Deaf Man is back to torment them again.

The 87th Precinct officers are having enough trouble without the Deaf Man trying to humiliate them. Their offices are in the midst of a "redecorating" phase: A crew of painters from Public Works are draping drop cloths everywhere and getting green apple-colored paint all over virtually everything. Carella, who has been posing as a derelict in order to catch whoever's drenching the city's bums with gasoline and setting them on fire, is in the hospital, recovering from serious burns. Meyer Meyer is consulting a lawyer because a new book is coming out with a character named after him and he fears this will be the ultimate embarrassment. And so on.

In the movie, the painters set the comic tone of things right away, dripping green paint on the heads of nearly all the bald guys in the precinct. Carella (Reynolds) recovers from his burns in record time and is back on the job with barely a blip in the storyline. Meyer Meyer (Jack Weston) has no legal problems in the movie and, in fact, hasn't much to do except look befuddled, which is pretty much the general look of his fellow officers for much of the movie.

In fact, there are times during the movie when you may wonder if the Deaf Man has the right take on things. He has this long-time grudge against the 87th Precinct, so Carella & Co. eventually assume he's staging his latest crime wave just to make them look inept. Actually, he needn't have bothered. They look inept before the crime wave starts.

Here's a prime example: The signature sequence of the movie re-envisions a section of the book in which the officers have staked out a public park, hoping to snag someone connected to the murder-extortion case when they come to pick up the payoff money. Everyone's in disguise. Carella and Meyer are dressed as nuns, even though Reynolds hasn't shaved his moustache. Eileen (Welch) and Detective Bert Kling (Tom Skerritt) are bundled up together in a sleeping bag, posing as lovers, with Kling doing the best he can to fondle her realistically. Officer Genero, who hates dogs, is posing as a blind man, with a K-9 attack dog on a leash. Others are scattered around the park.

When the pickup guy bolts, it's Keystone Cops time. Carella and Meyer look like drag queens trying to sprint. Kling and Eileen struggle to get out of their twisted sleeping bag. (In the book, it's Detective Willis, not Kling, in the sack with Eileen.) The attack dog refuses to attack and Genero accidentally shoots himself in the foot! The suspect is finally cut off by long-legged Eileen, who holds him at gunpoint. She easily out-ran the pack of them, no doubt happy to leave the horny Kling in the dust.

In the movie, the nebulous role of the Deaf Man is played by Oscar-winning actor Yul Brynner, who does the character in a stoic style. The movie offers no back story on the Deaf Man, but the book didn't either. We really don't know why the precinct detectives fear him so nor do we understand why he has a vendetta against them. Readers of the entire 87th Precinct series of novels understand him a little better, but not much. McBain always guarded his background closely.

In the final pages of the novel, after the Deaf Man's attempt to kill the mayor has been thwarted, the master criminal, shot and bleeding badly, climbs to the roof of a building. He's almost mistaken for a derelict and torched by two teenagers, the ones who set Carella on fire. The teenagers are stopped by Genero while the Deaf Man gets away. All they find later is a trail of blood drops leading to the edge of the roof.

The movie does a more satisfying number on the Deaf Man, allowing the kids to set him on fire. He jumps into the river and presumably drowns. But as the final credits roll, we see his hand reach up from the depths and we know he's going to survive once more. As that scene plays, we hear the wistful old standard "I'll Be Seeing You" on the soundtrack and realize it's being sung, in the film's ultimate Hollywood in-joke, by Dinah Shore, Burt Reynolds' girlfriend at the time.

Ed McBain
King's Ransom

The 1959 novel and the 1963 film
Tengoku to jigoku (*High and Low*)

The prolific author Salvatore Lombino saw films and TV shows made from many of the bestsellers he wrote under his most popular pen names, Evan Hunter and Ed McBain. In an interview with me, he conceded that the most unusual of them all was the film made from his Ed McBain novel *King's Ransom* by the legendary Japanese director Akira Kurosawa.

Kurosawa is best remembered for the feudal samurai movies he made under the influence of the American Westerns he saw as a youngster in Japan. He readily admitted that his classic *The Seven Samurai* was full of cinematic style he picked up from watching all those American Westerns. So, naturally, it was remade in America as a Western—*The Magnificent Seven*. A big moneymaker, it spawned three sequels, a TV series and a 2016 remake.

But *King's Ransom* was something entirely different for Kurosawa to consider bringing to the screen.

It was the tenth in McBain's series of police procedurals about the mythical 87th Precinct—and one of his all-time best because its characters and theme were almost Shakespearean in stature. Its protagonist Doug King is an executive of the Granger Shoe company, a major manufacturer of women's shoes, known for its high standards for durability and quality design. A self-made man, King rose from the ranks at Granger Shoe, a company that has been his life for most of his adult years. He knows the company inside and out and expects to run it once the Old Man either dies or retires.

But, as the novel opens, King is being pressed by a core group of junior executives to join them in a stock coup that will unseat the Old Man and bring in a new management team. They want to reverse the current trend of lagging sales by downgrading the product, making it cheaper and more appealing to the contemporary female shopper.

Their plans disgust King and he has no intention of going along with them. What they don't know is that he has been secretly buying up company shares and is about to close a major private stock purchase that will give him the clout to oust the Old Man and take over Granger Shoe himself, without their help.

It's a huge gamble by King, who has mortgaged his home and put everything he has into his secret maneuver. He has drawn a check for the secret stock purchase and asks his right hand man, Pete Cameron, to take it to the buyer so the deal can be closed before the others attempt their coup.

That's when something stunning happens: King gets a phone call from a man who claims he has kidnapped little Bobby, King's only son. Even though he knows paying the ransom will bankrupt him, blow his chances of taking over the company and possibly even cost him his present job, King knows he has no choice.

As the detectives of the 87th Precinct arrive to handle the situation, King learns that the kidnapper has made a huge mistake: He has mistakenly taken his son's best friend Jeff, the son of King's chauffeur, because the boy was wearing one of Bobby's outfits.

Toshiro Mifune and Kyoko Kagawa play parents who believe their son has been kidnapped in Akira Kurosawa's 1963 *High and Low*. The source novel, Ed McBain's 87th Precinct police thriller *King's Ransom*, took place in America, not Japan (Janus TV).

Suddenly King is faced with a totally different set of dilemmas: If he refuses to pay the ransom, they might kill Jeff, but King would still be able to take over Granger Shoe. Would the negative publicity about him letting another man's son die cause the public to boycott Granger Shoe's products?

King's wife Diane is sickened that he even considers letting Jeff die just to save his own career. She threatens to leave him, taking Bobby with her.

Meanwhile, a similar set of dilemmas is developing for kidnapper Sy and his sidekick Eddie. Sy learns he has the wrong boy, but vows to go ahead with the plan, counting on King to pay the ransom anyway. He intends to kill Jeff no matter what happens because he's afraid the boy will be able to identify them. Eddie is prepared to go along with Sy, but Eddie's wife Kathy, revolted by the scheme, is determined to force the men to abandon it, set the boy free and head for Mexico.

Given the psychological tides McBain stirs up, *King's Ransom* becomes less a police thriller than it is a high drama set against the backdrop of a heinous crime. As the plot races along like a ticking timer on a keg of dynamite, we're swept up in the emotional struggle of King to save his soul as well as his career and its future.

Clearly Kurosawa saw great appeal in King's dilemma and realized that *King's Ransom* could be adapted for the modern Japanese culture in a way that would put the focus on this man's struggle to preserve his honor as well as his career.

To play the King character (called Kingo Gondo in the movie), Kurosawa turned to his most reliable leading man, Toshiro Mifune. In this unaccustomed role, Mifune seems every bit as forceful a presence in a business suit as he always was in the robes of a feudal samurai.

Kurosawa's film begins exactly as the novel does, in a private meeting between Gondo and the executives who want him to join forces with them to bring off a coup at the company now called National Shoe. Mifune glares at the men, then takes one of their proposed new shoes in his huge hands and tears it to pieces, pointing out its inferior quality.

Though that scene is straight from the book, Mifune's destruction of the shoe is a vivid visual metaphor for the violence that is a crucial part of his personality. Kurosawa, even more potently than McBain, is telling us that the modern business world is the habitat of cutthroats in civvies.

Gondo's wife, called Keiko (Kyoko Kagawa) in the movie, is well aware of this aspect of his personality. When their son Jun runs through their house, shooting at his pal Shinichi with a toy gun, Keiko observes, "He takes after you. He likes violent games."

Kurosawa's version of the story closely follows the McBain novel, but only up to a point. Then it diverges radically. For instance, Gondo's wife never threatens to leave him. Apparently a Japanese woman of the 1960s wouldn't do such a thing. And we never see the kidnappers' side of the story, so there is no emotional tug of war going on among the criminals. In the book, King delivers fake ransom money to the kidnappers while Detective Steve Carella hides in the back seat, ready to arrest Sy. King himself chases Sy on foot, dodging gunshots, and brings him down, redeeming himself. Eddie and Kathy let Jeff go and escape, presumably to Mexico.

In the Japanese film, Gondo pays the ransom, loses his bid to take over National Shoe and has to start all over again running a small shoe company. The Eddie and Kathy characters, whom we never meet, are murdered by the kidnapper, who gives them an overdose of nearly pure heroin. The kidnapper is tracked down by the police, convicted and sentenced to death.

Though Kurosawa's film turns into a police thriller in its final half-hour, spinning out the story with lots of action that never occurs in the book, it's conclusion is respectful of the original: Gondo presumably benefits from his ordeal by learning to retain his humanity.

McBain's novel is more compact, more suspenseful and every bit as profound as the Japanese film, though Kurosawa's towering reputation has garnered *High and Low* much more respect than McBain's novel ever got from critics. McBain said he enjoyed seeing what Kurosawa did to translate his novel into a Japanese crime drama. That's the way to approach the film today, but read the book first, by all means.

Walter Mosley

Devil in a Blue Dress

The 1990 novel and the 1995 movie

Writer Walter Mosley's debut novel, *Devil in a Blue Dress*, was a landmark event for mystery fans. It introduced Ezekiel "Easy" Rawlins, a superb new detective hero in the first really great noir-style mystery with an African-American environment.

The movie version that followed, written and directed by black filmmaker Carl Franklin with Mosley on board as an associate producer, beautifully captured the book's mood and style, preserving its 1948 Los Angeles setting and making only a few major story changes that didn't negatively impact the final product.

The overall significance of both the book and movie is a grimly realistic view of post–World War II Los Angeles that reminds you of the gritty observations of Raymond

Denzel Washington played troubleshooter Easy Rawlins in the 1995 film version of Walter Mosley's detective novel *Devil in a Blue Dress* (Tri-Star Pictures).

Chandler if he had been able to look at his own L.A. with the eyes of a man of color, trying to get by in a very sordid world.

When we first meet Easy Rawlins, he's a worker at an L.A. area aircraft company who has just been laid off. Like many young black men discharged from military service in Southern California after the Second World War, Rawlins had found work in one of the many defense plants that had flourished during the war years and were now booming as the aviation industry began to expand dramatically.

Rawlins is originally from Texas and his pride and joy is the fact that he has earned enough money to buy his own home, which he treats like a castle, even though it's just one of those small claptrap houses thrown up in tracts to house the thousands of Americans who were leaving their rural home states and rushing to the fast-growing West Coast metropolis.

Facing overdue mortgage payments, property taxes and the other costs of home ownership, Rawlins is more than willing to listen when his pal Joppy, who runs a saloon over a meat market in L.A.'s black district, introduces him to a white man named Albright, who may have a job for him.

The job seems simple enough: The man is looking for a white girl named Daphne Monet, who was supposed to marry the man's employer, but instead ran out on him, taking $30,000 in cash that the jilted man wants back. Because Daphne has an affinity for black men and occasionally hangs out in clubs they frequent, the man thinks Rawlins might have an easier time drifting through the clubs, nosing around for clues to her current whereabouts.

Rawlins is no dummy. He realizes he's not being hired for his talent for sleuthing, which he's never tried doing before, but rather for his ethnic suitability. Easy knows white men nosing for clues in black nightclubs won't be given the time of day, but a well-liked, easy-going black man might do a lot better.

Easy soon finds himself involved with gangsters, political fixers, the corrupt race for mayor of Los Angeles, various hired guns and a couple of murders. Worse yet, a pair of L.A. police detectives think he's a prime suspect in those murders and are intent on rousting him just about every time he turns up anywhere.

Though Rawlins is an amateur detective who doesn't even own a gun, he does have "Mouse," a multi-gun-toting pal who comes in from Houston to lend Easy a hand. "Mouse" fears nothing, but he's also trigger-happy and Easy spends a lot of time trying to talk "Mouse" out of killing people.

From the perspective of 21st century America and the Black Lives Matter movement, Mosley's story goes a long way toward explaining why residents of L.A.'s black and Latino neighborhoods have a long history of distrusting the police. It also says a lot about the inner city tensions that led to major race riots yet to come in Watts and East L.A. It's obvious that black Americans might have been glad to leave the Jim Crow South in the late 1940s, but Mosley makes it clear that 1948 L.A. wasn't exactly Heaven for homeboys.

In turning the book into a movie, producers Jonathan Demme and Jesse Beaton wisely chose Carl Franklin to direct. The young African-American filmmaker had dazzled critics with his 1992 contemporary thriller *One False Move*, which proved he had instinctive cinematic skills that served this type of material very well. To play Easy Rawlins, they turned to the most exciting young black actor of the period, Denzel Washington, who had emerged from TV's *St. Elsewhere* series and scored in a series of major roles in important films, then collected his first of two Academy Awards for 1989's *Glory*.

Another major coup was hiring actor Don Cheadle, in one of his first real showcase movie roles, to play "Mouse" with the relish the character needs to really rise up out of the shadows in Mosley's story.

Yet another great choice was Jennifer Beals, fresh from her 1992 starring role in the surprise smash hit *Flashdance*, to play Daphne. Daphne has to project a genuine earthiness and the kind of appeal that might cause mayoral candidates, hired guns and would-be private eyes to fantasize about getting it on with her. Beals delivered all of that and more.

In adapting the Mosley book to film, Franklin made two major changes: the reworking of the Daphne character and the creation of a more action-filled ending. In the book, Daphne has stolen $30,000 from her rich suitor, a candidate for the mayor's office, but she isn't a thief in the movie. In the book she gets a lot closer to Easy Rawlins than she does in the movie and so we don't get to see any bedtime frolics on the screen. None of the Daphne changes are troublesome.

As for the ending, the book has a shootout, but it's a tame one that only occupies a few paragraphs. Franklin jives it up quite a bit and builds the suspense that Mosley didn't bother with in the book. The net result is about the same: The bad guys who are trying to torture some information out of Daphne get blown away quite efficiently by Easy and "Mouse."

Ultimately, the book has much deeper layers of detail about what black life in 1948 L.A. must have been like, but the movie does a marvelous job of recreating the look of that era and did it by filming on redecorated Los Angeles streets rather than on sound-

Don Cheadle (left) played the gun-happy "Mouse," trouble-prone helper of amateur sleuth Easy Rawlins (Denzel Washington), in *Devil in a Blue Dress* (Tri-Star Pictures).

stages. The result is a wildly creative use of mood and atmosphere to transport us bodily into the world of Easy Rawlins.

If there's any disappointment about *Devil in a Blue Dress*, it's the fact that nobody saw fit to bring Denzel Washington back to the role for film versions of Mosley's other Easy Rawlins novels.

Stuart Palmer

The Penguin Pool Murder

The 1931 novel and the 1933 movie

Back in 1931, just a year after Agatha Christie introduced Miss Jane Marple in *Murder at the Vicarage*, American mystery writer Stuart Palmer followed up with his own spin on the elderly spinster sleuth genre and created Miss Hildegarde Withers in *The Penguin Pool Murder*.

Right away, Hollywood saw a winner in that character and in 1932 RKO launched a series of Hildegarde Withers mystery movies with *Penguin Pool Murder*.

Though there are some fundamental differences between the popular book and the successful film, the movie really follows the book quite closely in terms of storyline and should not disappoint fans of the book.

Police Detective James Gleason (left) helps amateur sleuth Hildegarde Withers (Edna May Oliver) question a witness (Clarence H. Wilson) in *The Penguin Pool Murder*, first in a series of movies about Stuart Palmer's lady detective (RKO).

Unlike Miss Marple, who's pretty much a village busybody with no real career outside of her amateur detective work, Hildegarde Withers is fully employed as an elementary school teacher in *Penguin Pool Murder*, which takes place in busy New York City, in contrast to Jane Marple's quiet, slow-paced St. Mary Mead.

When *Penguin Pool Murder* begins, Miss Withers is taking her grammar school students on a tour of the city aquarium. When a student asks why the penguins seem to be upset, Miss Withers discovers they have good reason to be squawking: Someone has dumped a dead body into the aquarium tank.

Miss Withers calls the police and, in short order, meets for the first time a man who will become very important in her life: Inspector Oscar Piper. Together they begin to probe the death of Wall Street financier Gerald Lester, who was killed by someone who used the long, sharp hatpin that Miss Withers had lost during the classroom tour, plunging it through Lester's ear into his brain.

Suspicion quickly points to Philip Seymour, the former boyfriend of Lester's wife, beautiful Gwen Lester. The two had secretly met at the aquarium, but were surprised by Lester, who had been tipped that his wife was meeting another man there. Seymour and

Lester fought briefly; the younger, stronger Seymour knocked Lester out, then dragged him through the access door to the backstage area of the aquarium. The widow is also implicated in a possible plot when Miss Withers overhears her exclaim, "What have we done?" to Seymour upon learning her husband has died.

The film version follows the original plotline fairly closely, but first shows us the growing tension between Gwen and her husband, whose surname is unaccountably changed to Parker for the movie, and also gives us glimpses of the people who will become the other murder suspects before Miss Withers and her class finally appear on screen to discover the body.

In the novel, Palmer first describes his heroine as a 39-year-old Boston-born "spinster." He doesn't tell us if she's a pretty or homely woman, but makes sure we know she carries an umbrella and wears sensible shoes. In the casting of the movie version, the choice was obvious: Miss Withers is a rather stiff, old-fashioned looking lady with an overbearing manner. She is, in effect, the woman who plays her: the durable old character actress Edna May Oliver, who is best remembered for her many Dickensian characters in film versions of *David Copperfield*, *A Tale of Two Cities* and others.

Often uncharitably called "horse-faced" by critics, Oliver was nearly 50 when she first played Miss Withers and not considered an actress likely to be involved in romantic goings-on. Nonetheless, both the book and the film soon bring Withers together with Inspector Piper in a low-voltage romance that probably surprises them as much as it does us. The attraction certainly isn't physical, but seems rooted in their grudging respect for each other as detectives.

The casting of Oliver as Withers isn't a sharp contrast with Palmer's vision of her in the book, but the casting of character actor James Gleason as Piper definitely is. Here's how Palmer describes Piper when Miss Withers first sees him arrive at the crime scene: "a tall. gaunt man in a loose topcoat. He looked like a newspaper reporter grown gray in the harness, and Miss Withers took one look at his protruding lower lip and thought it was like a sulky little boy's."

Gleason, in contrast, was small, slight of build and not the least bit imposing. He looked ages older than Oliver, though he was about three years younger than his co-star. They made a ridiculous pair—the tall, stiff Oliver and the short, fidgety Gleason. But both were marvelous actors and the interplay between them is always amusing and works quite well, even though it's not the way Palmer wanted it.

The casting of other roles also has its ups and downs. Mr. Hemingway, the director of the museum, is played very broadly by Clarence H. Wilson, who skirts the fringes of outright comedy for a character we're supposed to take much more seriously.

On the other hand, the casting of Mae Clarke as the sexy Gwen couldn't be better. Sadly, the talented and gorgeous Ms. Clarke is now remembered almost exclusively as the woman who had a grapefruit shoved in her face by James Cagney in *The Public Enemy* in 1931, just the year before she made this film. We're supposed to wonder about Gwen's morals and motivations—and Clarke does a good job sustaining the suspense about her character.

When Gwen is charged with being an accessory to the murder and Seymour faces the homicide charge, a lawyer named Costello, who was standing by when the body was found at the aquarium, steps forward to represent her at her trial. This rather slick role is played by Robert Armstrong, who rarely got to play anybody slick in his long career. He's best remembered for the film he made right after this one: *King Kong* (1933), in which he's the rugged explorer Carl Denham who subdues the giant ape and brings him to Manhattan.

Seymour is played by Donald Cook, another veteran of *The Public Enemy*. He was later one of the actors to play Ellery Queen on the movie screen.

Another variation between book and film comes in the character of a pickpocket-murder suspect. In the book, the pickpocket pretends to be a deaf-mute so he won't have to answer police questions. In the movie, they make him a deaf-mute. Period. It serves to tighten up the story a bit.

Penguin Pool Murder is actually a very brisk and handsome-looking production. Willis Goldbeck's script keeps the mystery's secrets right up until the end and is generally quite respectful of Palmer's original concept. The film also has two other plusses: Atmospheric photography by John Alton, later a master of films noir, and a solid musical score by the great Max Steiner, who did some of Hollywood's most famous scores, including those for *King Kong* and *Gone with the Wind*.

RKO, pleased with the results it got from director George Archinbaud, ordered a series of Hildegarde Withers mystery movies. The Oliver-Gleason team returned in 1934 with *Murder on the Blackboard* and 1935 with *Murder on a Honeymoon*. When Oliver left the series, she was replaced by Helen Broderick (the mother of Oscar winner Broderick Crawford) in 1936's *Murder on a Bridle Path*. Later the same year, ZaSu Pitts was Miss Withers, still opposite James Gleason, in *The Plot Thickens*. Pitts and Gleason returned for the final film in the series, 1937's *Forty Naughty Girls*.

Though Hildegarde Withers remains a very interesting female sleuth in the Marple mold, there was, to my knowledge, only one other serious attempt to revive the character: a 1972 TV movie called *A Very Missing Person*, made for ABC by Universal, with Eve Arden as Miss Withers and James Gregory as Inspector Piper. It didn't makes any waves, so no further films were made.

Stuart Palmer continued to write Hildegarde Withers mysteries into the 1960s. His final Withers novel, *Hildegarde Withers Makes the Scene*, was published in 1969, the year after he died. Completed by Fletcher Flora, it was the basis for the Eve Arden TV movie.

Palmer worked on a lot of movies in the 1930s and 1940s and was one of the writers for RKO's *Falcon* mysteries. During that time, he often collaborated with Craig Rice on the scripts. Rice was a woman who used a man's name for her books. They struck up such a friendship that they actually merged their detectives for a series of stories featuring her John J. Malone, a boozed-up lawyer-sleuth, and Miss Withers. The stories were published in a 1963 book called *The People vs. Withers and Malone*.

There have been few instances of two mystery writers suddenly deciding to put their characters together in a series of mysteries. It may have worked for Palmer and Rice to keep their characters going after they seemed to have faded in popularity.

Robert B. Parker
Ceremony
The 1982 novel and the 1993 TV movie

By 1977, when Ross Macdonald had begun to suffer the debilitating effects of the disease that finally killed him and there were no more Lew Archer mysteries to come, it already was clear who would take his place as the next heir to Raymond Chandler: Robert B. Parker.

Parker already had published the first four novels about Spenser, the tough but sensitive private eye who knew the streets of Boston, Massachusetts, at least as well as Chandler's Philip Marlowe and Macdonald's Lew Archer knew the streets of L.A. and the sprawling suburban cities of Southern California. Parker almost seemed tailor-made for his role. He had been a college professor of literature, devoted to studying the gutsy works of Hammett and Chandler and, like Chandler, he wanted to tell us about the urban society he knew by making us look at it through the eyes of a late 20th century private eye.

Parker's affection for Chandler's stories ran so deep that it eventually led him to tackle a special mission of love: completing Chandler's unfinished Marlowe novel *Poodle Springs*, which was published in 1989 under both their names. Then, with the approval of the Chandler estate, he wrote *Perchance to Dream*, a sequel to Chandler's *The Big Sleep*.

So it was no accident that Parker's Spenser became the contemporary detective character most often compared to Chandler's Marlowe. Still, Spenser was unique in his own way from his first appearance in *The Godwulf Manuscript* (1973). He represented the new sort of American man who began to emerge in the 1960s: tough enough to handle the bad guys, but most definitely in touch with his feminine side when he wasn't knocking heads together.

Spenser was a gourmet cook, had an appreciation of fine art, good books and different philosophies. More important, he was sensitive to the feelings of others—women in search of independence, gays, racial minorities—and so sure of his own place in the scheme of things that he's never had a real feeling of angst in more than 30 years as perhaps America's most enduring contemporary P.I.

In 1985, the ABC television network responded to the growing popularity of Spenser by giving him a new and exciting venue: a weekly prime-time series, *Spenser: For Hire*. They filmed it on location in Boston, giving viewers a chance to watch a detective show that didn't take place on the same old streets of L.A. that everybody knew by heart since the days of *Dragnet*.

The critics loved *Spenser: For Hire* and raved about its marvelous cast: Tall, rugged and handsome Robert Urich, a protégé of Burt Reynolds, as Spenser; dark, mysterious and irresistibly cool Avery Brooks as Spenser's best friend, a professional ruffian known only as Hawk; chic and smart Barbara Stock as Spenser's lady, psychologist Susan Silverman, and affable Richard Jaeckel as Lt. Martin Quirk, Spenser's loyal friend on the Boston P.D. This was a smart, action-packed, often amusing, but basically realistic one-hour program that wanted to push the envelope of the TV detective genre and take it in the new directions bolder writers like Parker wanted to see it explore.

But the competition was stiff and viewers weren't quite ready to flock in big numbers to a show that asked them to junk so many of their well-entrenched concepts about

Avery Brooks (left) was "Hawk," the violence-prone assistant to Robert Urich, who played Spenser, the modern Boston private eye (ABC).

private eyes. *Spenser: For Hire* began to tank in the ratings and, despite some cast changes and several shifts to new nights, ABC cancelled it at the end of its third season.

The program had built a small but extremely loyal following, and these fans lobbied ABC to bring it back. That wasn't about to happen, but an interesting solution presented itself: What if ABC reunited most of the original cast and crew and filmed a few two-hour episodes based directly on the Parker novels?

Parker and his wife Joan warmed to the idea and agreed to become involved. They remembered that the pilot episode of the TV series was, in fact, an adaptation of Parker's fourth Spenser novel, *Promised Land*, and it received some of the best reviews in the show's history. Parker knew the presence of Spenser on TV meant more new readers and increased sales for the books. He even tried his hand at screenwriting by adapting his 1982 novel *Ceremony* for the screen. Joan came on board as a producer.

ABC saw it as a win-win proposition. The films should satisfy the rabid Spenser fans, who had been demanding more Spenser for years. And the financial risks could be spread out by showing the movies first on the Lifetime cable network, then repeated on ABC. So in 1993, *Ceremony* launched the comeback of Spenser as a TV sleuth.

The storyline is one of Parker's best in the long series. Susan asks Spenser to find 16-year-old runaway April Kyle, a girl she had counseled while working with troubled youngsters from a suburban high school district. They suspect that she has drifted into Boston's tawdry "combat zone" to work as a prostitute. The girl's mother desperately wants the girl back, but her father, a stubborn man with political ambitions, never wants to see her again.

The father's loveless attitude and rudeness puts Spenser in a volcanic mood. Though he'd like to punch the man out, he settles on telling him he'd rather spend the rest of his life at a Barry Manilow concert than work for him. But, after all that, Spenser winds up searching for April anyway—without payment, strictly as a favor to Susan.

Urich and Brooks reprised their series roles in the movie, but Barbara Williams was the new Susan Silverman. The film opens with Spenser chasing a thug through a deserted old factory building, a sequence that doesn't take place in the book. The thug has a young woman in his clutches, so Spenser beats him up and prevents the girl from falling from a high catwalk. Presumably, the gratuitous sequence is there to remind us Spenser can get physical when necessary.

Once we get into the main story, there's also an immediate detour from the original: It's now Mrs. Kyle (Lynne Cormack) who's most adamant about not having Spenser search for her missing daughter. She blames Susan for failing to counsel April properly. Her husband Harry (Dave Nichols) is less forceful, but it's clear he fears that a search would stir up bad publicity that might hurt his planned campaign for Massachusetts governor. After hearing this, Spenser is as disgusted with the father as he was in the book.

"Work for you?" he tells Harry Kyle. "I'd rather talk philosophy with Madonna!" (Perhaps Parker figured nobody in the 1990s would remember Barry Manilow, so he updated Spenser's wisecrack to include a newer pop star.)

Spenser agrees to search anyway and starts by contacting her former best friend, Amy Gurwitz. For reasons not apparent, the girl becomes Patty Gurwitz in the movie. Patty (Alexa Gilmour) isn't very helpful, so Spenser gets a lead on April's whereabouts by hassling her pimp, an unpleasant character called "Red" (William Colgate), and recruits Hawk to "watch his back."

In one of the movie's best sequences, "Red" looks on as Spenser and Hawk disarm and humiliate several pimp types in a tavern. "Red" is impressed, but they don't scare him. Without warning, Spenser punches the pimp in the throat, leaving him gasping for air. When he finally catches his breath, "Red" tells them April is now working at a "sheep ranch" in Providence, Rhode Island. As they leave him, "Red" is still sucking air big time.

"He should have been afraid of us," Hawk observes.

Spenser and Hawk learn that a "sheep ranch" is a special brothel for men with extremely kinky tastes. There Spenser finds April (Tanya Allen), dressed in a little girl's outfit, no doubt as bait for pedophiles. He hustles her out, even though she tells him she doesn't want to go home. When she begs Spenser to stop the car alongside the road and let her go to the bathroom behind some trees, she runs away.

"The old 'whiz in the woods' trick," Spenser grumbles ruefully after he realizes he's been outfoxed by a 16-year-old girl.

Eventually, Spenser tracks April back to Boston, where she's staying with Patty and Patty's sugar daddy, an obese pervert (Mitchell Poitras in the novel, Mitchell Dietrich in the movie). Susan tells Spenser that this man is really an important state school official, responsible for the handling of troubled high school kids. The deeper Spenser digs, the worse the situation gets. It's now clear that Dietrich (Jefferson Mappin) is rounding up sexually promiscuous teenage girls, getting them to work in porno films filmed at his estate, then sending them over to Tony Marcus (Henry Gomez), kingpin of prostitution and other rackets in Boston's "combat zone."

The action finale finds Spenser and Hawk busting up a large private sex party at Dietrich's house while Susan spirits April out of the place. As Spenser leaves, the cops move in, raiding the joint and crushing Dietrich's racket. The raid, by the way, is led by McNeely, the vice division commander in both book and film. Between book and film, however, McNeely must have undergone a sex change operation because he's now a she—an African-American woman, played by Lili Francks in the film.

Clearly, ABC, Lifetime and Parker wrestled with how to end the movie. In the book, Susan reluctantly agrees with Spenser that April will only run away again if she's taken home. So Spenser places her in a high-class Manhattan brothel run by his friend, whorehouse madam Patricia Utley, a key character from earlier Spenser novels.

Surely that wouldn't fly with the network brass, so Parker had to come up with a new wrinkle. It turns out to be a pretty good one that also fills an information gap readers may have noticed in the book: There never was a reason given why April didn't want to go home. In the movie, we learn that April's clean and decent dad had been a customer at one of the kinkier brothels and that April knew about it. Worse yet, Kyle was being blackmailed over it by the Boston vice lords, who were happy to back his campaign for governor and were delighted to keep his hooker daughter as their ace in the hole.

As the movie closes, Susan has persuaded April to go into a rehab program and is preparing to pay Spenser his "fee" in some physical manner. From the look on his face as Susan plasters herself all over him, he seems pretty happy about the way everything turned out.

For the time being, so was ABC. The initial reaction to this Spenser movie was good, but the films performed better on the Lifetime network than they did on ABC and soon budgets were cut and economies were forced upon the Parkers and their producers, including a shift from filming in Boston to new, cheaper location shoots in Canada.

ABC withdrew from the deal after four films, but the A&E cable network struck a new arrangement with the Parkers for more Spenser movies. By then, Urich had been diagnosed with a rare form of cancer and already was committed to starring in the UPN network's new version of *The Love Boat*. Brooks was starring in the *Star Trek: Deep Space 9* series and had other projects.

Undaunted, A&E launched production on *Small Vices* and premiered it in 1999 with veteran character actor Joe Mantegna as the new Spenser and an unknown named Sheik Mahmud-Bey as Hawk. The new Susan Silverman was Marcia Gay Harden, who would go on to win a Best Supporting Actress Oscar the following year for *Pollock*.

Parker knew the hardcore fans of the TV Spensers would cry foul if Urich didn't play the part. He had hopes his loyal readers would believe Mantegna was the more authentic Spenser.

"The Joe Mantegna Spenser is as close as we've ever gotten to the book Spensers," Parker told me in a 1999 interview. "The complaints about Mantegna boil down to the fact he's Italian and doesn't weigh 200 pounds. The answer to the first complaint is 'I don't care' and the answer to the second is 'Neither was Bogart.'"

It turned out to be a moot point. While the new Spenser movies *Small Vices* and *Thin Air* were still playing on A&E, Urich was fighting for his life. He died on April 16, 2002, at age 55. For many viewers, their interest in seeing Spenser return to the screen died with Urich. The Mantegna Spenser films, though competently made, did not get anyone very excited, so A&E ordered no more.

Edgar Allan Poe
"Murders in the Rue Morgue"

The 1841 short story; the 1932 movie;
the 1954 movie *Phantom of the Rue Morgue;*
the 1971 movie; the 1986 TV movie

Edgar Allan Poe's famous short story "The Murders in the Rue Morgue" retains a hallowed place in the history of the mystery genre: It introduced the first detective character in literature, Auguste Dupin, along with several other conventions of the mystery story that would be adopted by generations of subsequent story-tellers.

Many believe Poe was inspired to write a detective story after reading the autobiographical writings of François Eugene Vidocq, the convict and killer who became a police informer and eventually founded the world's first police detective bureau, the French Sûreté. By 1841, when Poe wrote "Rue Morgue," Vidocq's fame was international and his *Memoires* had been dramatized on the English stage.

Poe even refers to Vidocq by name in his story, having Dupin criticize Vidocq's much-touted methods of catching criminals. Dupin feels that Vidocq's detectives concentrate too much on minute details and often miss the big picture.

For all its importance in literature, "Murders in the Rue Morgue" never has been brought to the screen exactly the way Poe told it. That's easy to understand: Poe's story is not exactly action-packed. At best, it displays Dupin's—and Poe's—cleverness. It begins with an extended treatise by the author on the analytical method, which he came to call *ratiocination.* Where Poe might have given readers action, he too often chooses to provide pontification.

Still, the modern reader certainly can see the basic elements of the detective story being laid out by Poe in this important tale. Dupin was clearly the model for all eccentric private detectives to come, especially Conan Doyle's Sherlock Holmes and Agatha Christie's Hercule Poirot. Dupin's nameless friend, the story's narrator, was the first Dr. Watson–type sidekick and Poe's bumbling French gendarmes obviously set the stage for the Inspector Lestrades and so many other incompetent policemen of the genre.

Dupin is a young man from a once illustrious family, reduced to poverty when the unnamed narrator—presumably Poe himself—meets and befriends him during a visit to Paris in the early 19th century. Together they share "a time-eaten and grotesque mansion" that has been deserted for years because of "superstitions into which we did not inquire." Dupin likes to stay home behind heavy drapes all day, reading and sleeping. At night, he roams the streets of Paris with his new friend, the narrator.

Dupin first learns of the terrible Rue Morgue murders by reading accounts in the newspapers. He and his friend are puzzled by the circumstances: Madame L'Espanaye and her daughter Camille were murdered in a loud, violent encounter with the killer or killers in the wee hours of the morning, yet when neighbors and gendarmes came to investigate they found Mme. L'Espanaye's fourth-story apartment locked from the inside with all windows nailed shut.

How did the killer escape? How did he manage to shove the daughter's body up the fireplace flue with such force that it took several men to extract it? And how did the

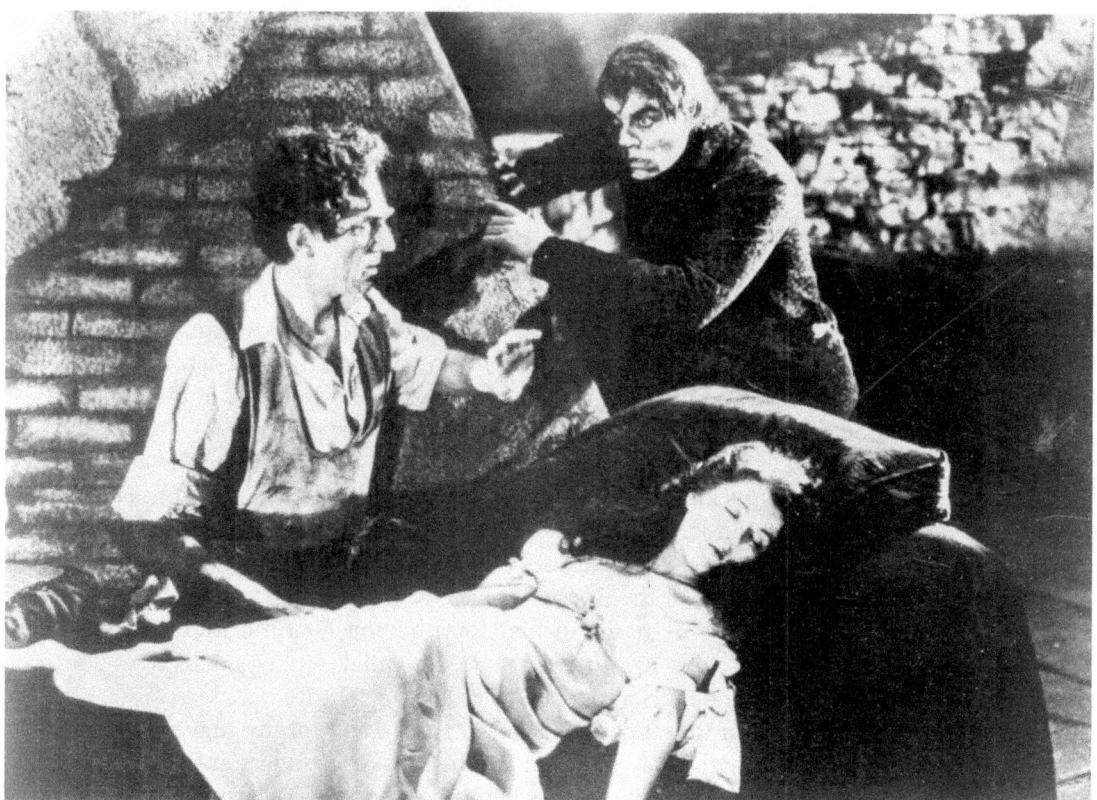

Bela Lugosi prepares to conduct an evil experiment on Sidney Fox while Noble Johnson looks on in the 1932 *Murders in the Rue Morgue*, which had little to do with Edgar Allan Poe's original story (Universal Pictures).

mother's body wind up in the yard, four floors down, with her head nearly severed by a razor?

Police also are baffled by the lack of motive. The killer left money and valuables behind, so robbery was not the issue. There's more confusion when witnesses report they heard two voices during the melee, one distinctly speaking French, the other speaking a foreign language. The witnesses all disagree on which foreign language was spoken.

But soon the case seems solved as the newspapers report the police have arrested Adolphe Le Bon, a bank clerk who had helped the women carry home 4000 francs in gold they had withdrawn from the bank on the day of the murders. He was the last to see them alive. Why did Le Bon leave the gold behind if greed was his motive? The newspaper articles don't speculate.

These perplexing contradictions arouse Dupin's curiosity, so he decides to visit the crime scene. He's permitted to do so, we learn, because he knows the prefect of police. Once in the apartment, Dupin finds some hairs on the chimney hearth, overlooked by police, which he's certain did not come from either victim's head. He also finds a scarf of a type worn by sailors from Malta. He examines the windows and discovers the nails in one frame are just the heads of nails set in place and don't really hamper the opening and closing of the window. Outside, he finds a lightning rod that might be scaled, giving access to shutters covering the windows of the murder apartment.

Operating on a hunch, Dupin runs an advertisement in *Le Monde,* a newspaper widely read by seagoing men, claiming that he has found in the large Parisian park, the Bois du Boulongne, a large specimen of *ourang-outang,* a kind of ape common to Borneo. (We would call it an orangutan today.) He offers to return the animal to its owner if that party will call at Dupin's place the following day.

When a sailor arrives, Dupin coaxes him into telling the whole horror story of how the caged animal had escaped and committed the murders with the sailor in close pursuit, the only witness to the ape's rampage with a razor. There's no dramatic finale, but we can assume that Dupin impressed the authorities with his solution to the crime because he appears twice more in stories by Poe, "The Mystery of Marie Roget" and "The Purloined Letter," each time as a "consulting detective" for the Paris police.

The first time *Murders in the Rue Morgue* came to the screen was in a silent film made circa 1914. The first major feature film drawn from the famous story came from Universal in 1932. That year, Universal was just beginning to realize what financial promise there was in becoming Hollywood's primary source for so-called "horror" movies. Starting with Lon Chaney's *The Phantom of the Opera* in 1925, then the spectacular back-to-back success of *Dracula* and *Frankenstein* in 1931, the studio had shown great skill in making and marketing such movies.

Hungarian actor Bela Lugosi was still a very hot property for Universal in 1932 after starring in *Dracula*. But Universal needed another established horror story like *Dracula* or *Frankenstein* to serve as a vehicle for Lugosi. They assigned writers Tom Reed and Dale Van Every to reshape Poe's "Rue Morgue" into a horror picture for Lugosi.

The changes they wrought in Poe's tale—with the help of future superstar director John Huston, who wrote some of the dialogue—are overwhelming. For instance, there was no character for Lugosi to play in the story, so they made one up: Dr. Mirakle, a mad scientist whose dream is to prove the theory of evolution by mixing the blood of apes with that of humans.

Dr. Mirakle does this under his cover as a carnival sideshow entertainer who exhibits a large ape he calls Erik. While he delights customers by engaging in spirited "conversations" with the ape in "Erik's language," he secretly goes about his real business: snatching prostitutes off the streets of Paris and performing experiments on them in his home near the Seine.

In Lugosi's first stirring scene, he appears before a captivated carnival audience, ranting about his genius and assuring everyone, "I'm not a sideshow charlatan!" Dressed all in black, his hair done up in a foppish pompadour style, he looks like a 19th century edition of Liberace by way of Transylvania. He promises the patrons who dare to buy tickets that they'll be witnessing "a milestone in the development of life."

In the crowd is medical student Pierre Dupin (Leon Ames) and his friend Paul (chubby comedian Bert Roach), who takes the place of Poe's nameless narrator. Dupin is no longer Poe's brilliant eccentric, but instead a rather drippy young man whose sole connection to the murders is his lovely sweetheart, Camille (Sidney Fox), who has attracted the attention of Dr. Mirakle and his ape. (In Poe's original, there is no such connection between Dupin and the Camille in his story.) If this movie Dupin is related at all to the Dupin of Poe's story, he's obviously a low-achieving cousin.

In Poe's story, the murders of Camille and her mother are clearly an accident caused by a jungle animal who's unused to human contact and has learned how to wield a razor by watching his master, a sailor, shave himself.

But in the 1932 film, the ape is a movie monster. Instead of a hapless sailor, the movie ape is owned by a mad doctor, who somehow believes that injecting ape blood into the veins of beautiful women will improve upon evolution. So far it hasn't worked very well because each "experiment" inevitably ends with the death of the girl who gets Erik's blood. Dr. Mirakle accepts no blame for this crackpot scheme and points his finger instead at the victims and their "tainted blood."

(By the way, the film shows us one hooker who screams incessantly under Lugosi's "treatments," then is unceremoniously dumped through a trap door into the river below. She was played by a young actress named Arlene Francis, who would later become one of early television's most charming and sophisticated personalities—best remembered as a panelist on the long-running quiz show *What's My Line?*)

Dr. Mirakle feels quite crushed by these repeated failures. After all, he explains, he has consecrated his life to this "great experiment" and look what he gets for all his hard work!

For all its silliness, the 1932 film does move right along quite briskly. Despite its great liberties with Poe, it retains the original story's most famous incident: the locked room murder and the corpse—not Camille this time—shoved up the flue. In this case, the insipid medical student Dupin is considered a suspect until he convinces the authorities that the clump of hair found in the victim's hand came from the real killer—an ape. He insists they check out Dr. Mirakle, a weirdo who just happens to have a ferocious ape handy.

The film ends with Dr. Mirakle meeting with a violent end and the ape carrying Camille over the Paris rooftops, Dupin and the gendarmes in pursuit. The monster is finally dispatched with a well-aimed gunshot and Camille survives without the indignity of being shoved up a flue, as she was in the original story. Presumably she'll marry Dupin and they'll live happily ever after.

Though the storyline of the 1932 movie is ludicrous, director Robert Florey gave it a very stylish neo–Germanic look. Florey, a European immigrant, began the American phase of his career by directing the four Marx Brothers in their first movie, *The Cocoanuts* (1929), so he must have been well-prepared for Bela Lugosi, whose outrageously florid acting style seems perfectly suited to this bizarre tale.

The film's Dupin, billed as Leon Waycoff, later changed his name to Leon Ames and became a popular TV character actor, playing likable TV dads in both *Life with Father* (CBS, 1953–55) and *Father of the Bride* (CBS, 1961–62), then as the nosy neighbor on *Mr. Ed* (CBS, 1963–65). Sidney Fox, the film's Camille, had a brief career as a leading lady and died in 1942 at age 31.

Though it barely resembles the Poe story, the 1932 *Murders in the Rue Morgue* has a special niche in the history of the horror film, mostly due to Lugosi's colorful, scenery-chewing performance and the film's certifiably creepy ambience.

Universal's "golden age of horror" pretty much ended along with World War II in 1945. But less than a decade later, Hollywood was gearing up for another big run at the genre as studios looked for any sort of attraction to help lure people away from their new television sets.

One of those was the 3-D movie, a gimmick that had been around since the 1930s, but hadn't really been perfected until the development of a process called Natural Vision, which created the illusion that viewers could actually see into the movie screen while objects appeared to fly off its surface and into the audience. The effect was created by filming two separate versions of each scene simultaneously, each one separated the same distance as two human eyes. When the viewer put on polarized spectacles, the two blurred images were fused into a single image with great depth.

The first really big hit movie in Natural Vision 3-D was Warners' *House of Wax*, a colorful remake of their 1933 film *Mystery of the Wax Museum*. That film's box office success naturally cued Warners to look for a follow-up project and the result was a new 3-D version of Poe's famous story, this time called *Phantom of the Rue Morgue*. Again, the original Poe story was deemed too uneventful for a modern detective mystery, so screenwriters Harold Medford and James R. Webb fashioned it into another horror movie.

The studio turned to the usually quite serious character actor Karl Malden to play the archvillain of the piece: Dr. Marais, who specializes in animal behavior and keeps his own private zoo in Paris. (Malden won a Best Supporting Actor Academy Award for 1951's *A Streetcar Named Desire* and later became president of the Academy of Motion Picture Arts & Sciences.) Marais has a vicious ape caged in his mansion and has trained it to be what might be called a "Pavlovian" monster. Marais gives his intended female victims bracelets with little bells. When the ape hears the bells jingle, it's programmed to kill whoever is wearing them. (His ape is played by Charles Gemora, who also was inside the ape suit in the 1932 Lugosi version!)

There is no Dr. Marais in Poe's story and no jingling bell bracelets. (Pavlov's famous experiments in the psychological conditioning of lab animals hadn't taken place when Poe published his story, but why quibble?) However, the movie does have a Dupin, although a markedly different one. This one is called Paul Dupin (Steve Forrest), a university professor who seems considerably less eccentric than Poe's Auguste Dupin. When we meet him, he's engaged to marry the lovely Jeanette (Patricia Medina) and has a loyal following of students, including a very young and boyish lad named Georges, played by future TV talk show host and game show millionaire Merv Griffin. (Forrest, the younger brother of movie star Dana Andrews, played his first hero role in *Phantom of the Rue Morgue*. He never became a major movie star like his brother and is best remembered today as the star of TV's 1970s police series *S.W.A.T.*).

When Dupin's razor is found at the scene of one of the ape's murders, he becomes a suspect, a radical turn away from Poe's story. Dupin's beloved Jeanette becomes the quarry of the ape when Marais gives her a jingling bracelets, claiming it's a "gift from Paul." Will Dupin be able to save his girl and prove his innocence? Not to worry.

In the action-packed climax, the ape comes after

Nasty Karl Malden attempts to woo Patricia Medina in *Phantom of the Rue Morgue*, a 1954 update of Poe's *Murders in the Rue Morgue*, filmed in 3-D (Warner Bros.).

Jeanette, is shot and, in its last act, leaps from a tree, lands on Marais and kills him. Dupin and Jeanette live happily ever after. None of this has anything to do with the Poe story.

Though seldom seen in its original 3-D format today, *Phantom* is replete with 3-D gimmicks that no longer make any sense. For instance, a knife-throwing sequence early in the picture seems to exist solely for the purpose of having knives come flying out into the audience. There's also a trampoline act that sends acrobats lunging out of the screen time after time. Seen without 3-D, as they invariably are today, these scenes seem especially extraneous.

The film was made by veteran Warner Bros. house director Roy Del Ruth, who began in silent movies as a gag writer for Mack Sennett. Always regarded as competent, but not especially inspired, he's best remembered today for directing the 1931 version of Hammett's *The Maltese Falcon* and for his spooky comedy *Topper Returns* (1941).

In the 1960s, a new wave of interest in Poe began in Hollywood, prompted by the success of American-International's *House of Usher* with Vincent Price as Poe's Roderick Usher. Price began a cycle of Poe movies for AIP that were, for the most part, highly profitable. In 1971, a new *Murders in the Rue Morgue* was filmed by AIP with Jason Robards as the star name.

Adapted for the screen by Christopher Wicking, this *Rue Morgue* has even less connection to Poe's story than the previous versions. For one thing, it completely eliminates Dupin. In his place is Inspector Vidocq (Adolfo Celi), which may have been Wicking's idea of a mystery in-joke. (As mentioned earlier, Vidocq was the real-life founder of France's first police detective bureau.)

There are times when Wicking seems to be adapting Gaston Leroux's *The Phantom of the Opera* instead of Poe's story. The setting for the story is a Paris theater where nightmarish grand guignol plays are performed, including one seemingly based on Poe's "Rue Morgue," featuring a killer ape named Erik (like the ape in the 1932 Lugosi movie!). The *Phantom* connection seems complete with the casting of Herbert Lom, who played the title role in Hammer Films' *The Phantom of the Opera* in 1961. In this one, Lom is the demented Rene Marot, who wears an ape suit while committing a series of murders in the theater.

None of the characters, including theater company boss Cesar Charron (Robards), makes any appearance in the original story and it's notably devoid of suspense. Director Gordon Hessler, who came to Hollywood from Germany via England, no doubt was hired because he had done several similar movies for AIP, including *The Oblong Box* (1969), *Scream and Scream Again* (1970) and *Cry of the Banshee* (1970), none of them very distinguished.

Robards, who was then one of America's most respected stage actors and had played a wide variety of character parts in films, clearly was slumming when he took this role. Five years later, he won his first Academy Award as *Washington Post* editor Ben Bradlee in *All the President's Men* (1976), then won a second Oscar in 1977 playing Dashiell Hammett in *Julia*.

On December 7, 1986, the CBS television network telecast *Murders in the Rue Morgue*, an all-new version of Poe's story, filmed on location in France with an "A" budget and Oscar-winner George C. Scott (*Patton*, 1970) as the star. Never mind that Scott, then a portly 59, was playing Poe's young detective Auguste Dupin. At least screenwriter David Epstein didn't write Dupin out of the script.

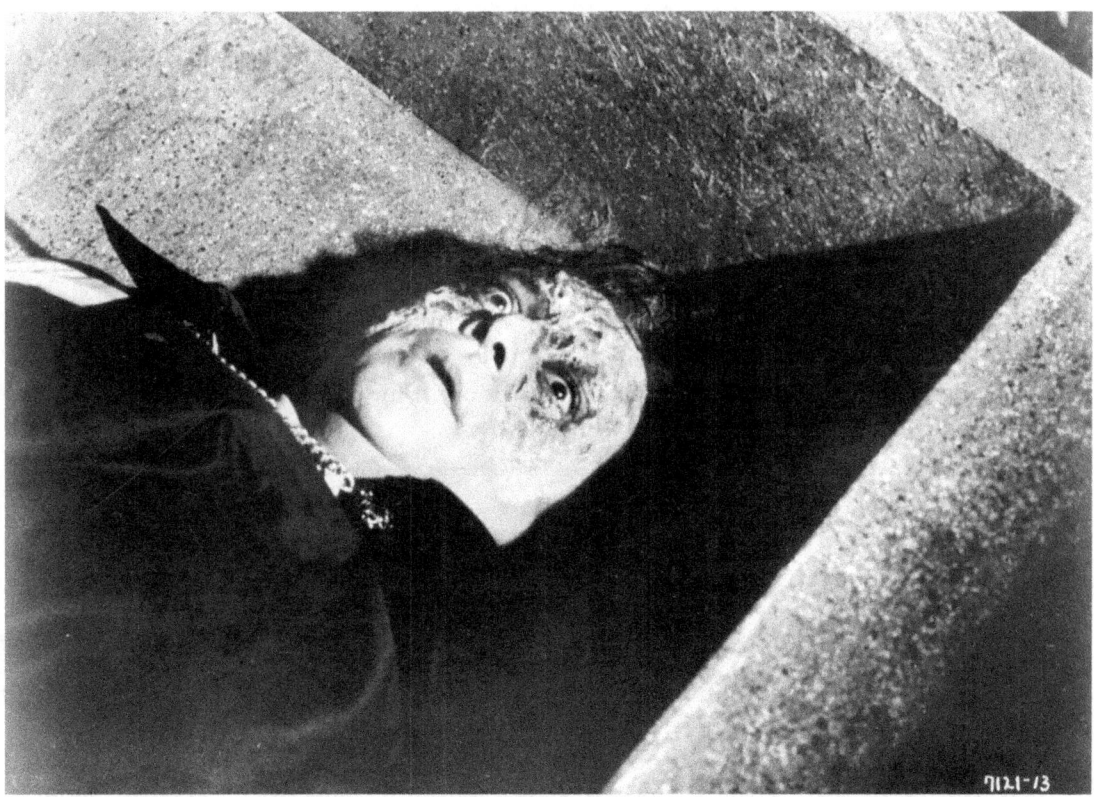

Herbert Lom was a disfigured maniac in the 1971 version of Poe's *Murders in the Rue Morgue*. The Lom character never appears in the original tale (American-International).

Again, they made some very large changes in Poe's story. Dupin is no longer a little-known amateur sleuth, living the life of an eccentric, night-crawling bachelor. In this version, he's a retired police inspector who was once regarded as the greatest detective in France. He also has a grown daughter named Claire (Rebecca DeMornay), who urges him to come out of retirement to solve a pair of murders in the Rue Morgue.

For a change, there's no mad scientist who keeps a murderous ape. In fact, Epstein's script generally follows Poe with the murders of the two women, the hullabaloo heard by neighbors behind the locked door of the upstairs apartment, the confusion over the language spoken by the killer and the arrest of a man named Le Bon who may have been the last to see the women alive.

But Epstein creates a history of bad vibes between retired Inspector Dupin and the current prefect of police, played by a mustachioed Ian McShane. Dupin is reluctant to get involved because, he says, "The Prefect of Police wants nothing to do with me."

Yet Dupin does get involved and makes an examination of the crime scene, noting the lightning rod someone might have climbed to get into the upstairs apartment and most of the other clues Dupin discovers in the original story. Like Poe's Dupin, he also runs an ad in a boating journal and flushes out the sailor whose ape is responsible for the murders.

During the 1970s and 1980s, producer Robert Halmi's company made some of the best new versions of literary classics ever shown on television. His *Murders in the*

Rue Morgue looks expensive and makes good use of the authentic French locations, although, unaccountably, there are lots of signs in English all over the backgrounds of some scenes.

Unfortunately, though, Scott and DeMornay don't really seem to belong in 19th century France and they give an artificial ring to everything. Even worse, there's a character called Philippe who seems to have no purpose except to bring some romance into Claire's life. He's played by Val Kilmer, then still in his 20s and not yet a leading man. He looks about as comfortable playing a Frenchman as Clint Eastwood would be playing a ballet dancer.

The film's director Jeannot Szwarc had previously done several outlandish films, including *Jaws 2* (1978), *Somewhere in Time* (1980) and *Supergirl* (1982). Altogether, the 1986 *Rue Morgue* is not a very successful effort, but it may be more faithful to Poe, by default, than any of the versions described above.

Edgar Allan Poe
"The Mystery of Marie Roget"

The 1845 short story and the 1942 movie

Edgar Allan Poe, father of the modern detective story, has been ill-used by filmmakers over the years. His first story to feature consulting detective C. Auguste Dupin, *Murders in the Rue Morgue,* was loaded with cinematic fabrications every time it was adapted for the screen. And his second Dupin story, "The Mystery of Marie Roget," was turned upside down and inside out in the most infamous movie version, made by Universal in 1942.

In fairness, one must point out that "Marie Roget" is a terrible story, totally unsuited for dramatization, so I suppose we should not be too surprised that Hollywood went to work on it without any particular reservations.

Poe's original short story was inspired by a real criminal case, the murder of Mary Cecilia Rogers in 19th century New York. But because Poe's Dupin was a Frenchman who lived in Paris, Poe quite naturally shifted the case to Paris in the 1840s.

His story concerns a young Parisian girl named Marie Roget, who works as a sales girl in a popular perfume shop and is well-known to many Parisians because of her great charm and physical beauty. When she disappears, the search makes lots of headlines, but the various theories about what happened to her all come to a sudden end when she reappears and simply explains that she had taken a hasty trip to visit a relative and didn't know anybody was looking for her.

Later, when Marie disappears again, it generates even bigger headlines because her body is found floating in the Seine. She had obviously been abused by someone and most likely was murdered somewhere else, and then her body tossed into the river.

The prefect of police is stumped and many Paris newspapers demand a quick solution to the mystery while others claim she may not really be dead, the body may be that of some other girl and the whole thing may be yet another phony disappearance by Miss Roget. What else can the prefect do but call upon Dupin, who had been so successful

Edward Norris, in cloak, menaces Camille Roget (Nell O'Day) and her grandmother (Maria Ouspenskaya) in Universal's 1942 Poe adaptation *Mystery of Marie Roget* (Screen Gems).

investigating the murders that occurred in the Rue Morgue section of Paris just a few years earlier?

The balance of Poe's story is about how Dupin pulls together all the newspaper articles about her disappearance and uses them to figure out that she was indeed murdered, not by a gang of ruffians as some writers had suggested, but most likely by a seaman she may have been involved with at the time of her first disappearance.

However, nobody is ever convicted of the murder and Dupin never comes up with either a motive or a definitive guilty party. As a story, it's pretty much a half-empty cup that probably satisfies nobody who reads it today.

So why make a movie from this insubstantial tale? Well, consider the fact that by 1942, Poe's name was well-established with movie fans as being associated with horror rather than detective-oriented mystery. Universal had a hit with its 1932 *Murders in the Rue Morgue*, which gave actor Bela Lugosi his juiciest role since he became a movie sensation in Universal's *Dracula* the year before. Universal followed that up by teaming its two biggest horror movie stars, Lugosi and Boris Karloff, in another Poe-inspired movie, *The Black Cat*, in 1934. The following year, they re-teamed Lugosi and Karloff in *The Raven*, which took its title from a Poe poem and part of its plot from Poe's "The Pit and the Pendulum." Universal made another version of *The Black Cat* in 1941, so Poe had certainly become a reliable source for Universal screenwriters. None of these Poe-related movies had much to do with his original stories.

For *Mystery of Marie Roget*, screenwriter Michel Jacoby began mangling the Poe original from the very first frame of film. It begins with a newspaper front page with the headline "Musical Comedy Star Marie Roget Missing!" Right away we know Marie is an actress and not a salesgirl in a perfume shop. The incident involved is distantly related to the Poe story, though, because it represents her first disappearance and her subsequent return just as the Paris gendarmes are going nuts trying to find her.

The prefect of police immediately emerges as a comic buffoon, played that way by pudgy comic actor Lloyd Corrigan, who made a specialty of such roles. And he doesn't need to recruit Dupin to help with the case because Dupin is now a full-time employee of the police, wearing a white lab coat as if he's fresh from the forensic department that probably didn't exist in Paris, circa 1849, the year the movie is set.

What's more, Dupin is now Dr. Paul Dupin instead of C. Auguste Dupin, and he no longer has a sidekick, as he does in Poe's stories, to serve as his Dr. Watson–style narrator and to explain to readers what Dupin is thinking.

Screenwriter Jacoby created a number of characters not in the original story. Gone is the Mother Roget that Maria lived with in the story; in her place is Grandmother Roget, played by the elderly Russian actress Maria Ouspenskaya, and a beautiful sister named Camille, who makes no appearance in the original tale.

Perhaps because the popular *Murders in the Rue Morgue* depended for much of its horror on a murderous ape, Jacoby dreams up a ferocious spotted leopard that Grandma Roget keeps as a house pet. After Marie disappears the first time, the body of a young woman, her face mangled, is found, and at first it is believed to be the body of Marie. Dupin opines that the face looks as if it had been ripped off by a savage animal.

We learn that Camille is about to inherit a fortune left to her by her late grandfather and that a young man named Marcel has asked for her hand in marriage, even though he was really romancing Marie. Obviously Marcel and Marie plan to do Camille in so they can take her fortune. Grandma Roget overhears them discussing the plot and offers Dupin 50,000 francs to accompany Camille to the big party where Marcel plans to kill her, hoping the famous detective will be able to protect her.

But none of this happens the way it was planned and Marie gets killed, her face ripped off and her body dumped in the Seine instead of Camille. This is all dreamed up without Poe's assistance and it's so illogical and absurd that one might have assumed that even the dumb bunny prefect of police could figure that out.

Anyone who cares about Poe is going to recoil from the nonsensical movie. And anyone addicted to Universal's horror movies of the 1930s and 1940s is going to be quite bored since there's nary a single frightening moment in it.

The few character names carried over from the Poe story wind up attached to people who have nothing to do with the characters with those names in the story. The leopard winds up innocent of all crimes and Dupin never cashes his check for 50,000 francs for talking Camille to the party.

In retrospect, *Mystery of Marie Roget* now seems like a film thrown together in order to keep some of the studio's contract players busy during a month or two in 1942.

Maria Montez, who plays Marie Roget, was a hopeless amateur as an actress, but she became a big star in Technicolor fantasies like *Arabian Nights* (1942), *Ali Baba and the Forty Thieves* (1944) and *Sudan* (1945). She died of a heart attack at age 33. Patric Knowles, who played Dupin, was a handsome English-born actor who appeared in such Universal horror pictures as *The Wolf Man* (1941) and *Frankenstein Meets the Wolf Man* (1943).

Nell O'Day, who played Camille Roget, was a leading lady to silent comic Harry

Langdon in the late 1920s. By the '40s she was mostly a "B" movie Western leading lady. Maria Ouspenskaya was a distinguished actress in her native Russia and had important character roles in such big Hollywood films as *Dodsworth* (1936), *Love Affair* (1939) and *The Rains Came* (1939). She is probably best remembered by horror movie fans as the gypsy Maleva in *The Wolf Man* (1941) and *Frankenstein Meets the Wolf Man* (1943).

Ellery Queen
The Chinese Orange Mystery

The 1934 novel and the 1937 movie *The Mandarin Mystery*

Ellery Queen is one of the most enduring fictional detectives in American literary history. He was still underaking new investigations more than 40 years after his debut in the 1929 novel *The Roman Hat Mystery*.

Though a sort of cross between England's mannered Lord Peter Wimsey and America's gentleman sleuth Philo Vance, Ellery still had his unique points. For one thing, he wasn't really a detective, but rather a mystery writer who helped his father, Police Inspector Queen, solve crimes. He didn't need any Dr. Watson to chronicle his adventures because he wrote about them himself in his own popular series of novels.

There was something else unique about the early Ellery Queen novels, including *The Chinese Orange Mystery*: He stopped the story near the conclusion for what he called "the challenge to the reader," a chance for you to sort through all the clues and try to solve the mystery before reading on to the climax.

Ellery Queen was dreamed up by a pair of cousins, Manfred B. Lee and Frederic Dannay. He was the main character in a novel they wrote collaboratively, in hopes of winning a literary contest. They didn't win the prize, but their manuscript was published anyway and was a huge success, launching them on a fabulous career that included books, radio shows, movies, TV shows and their own monthly publication, *Ellery Queen Mystery Magazine*.

In the books, Ellery was a tall, handsome young man, gifted at solving the most puzzling mysteries. If he hadn't been so devoted to his detective work, he might have been mistaken for a rich playboy. Instead, he comes off in the novels as a sophisticated, intelligent fellow without the rough, tough demeanor of his father, a respected career cop who seldom had time for anything but his detective work.

Ellery first appeared on screen in *The Spanish Cape Mystery* (1935), a low-budget Republic film taken from a Queen novel published that same year. Playing Queen was Donald Cook, a young, good-looking "B" movie star of the 1930s. He wasn't exactly a charismatic performer everybody wanted to see as often as possible, so Republic decided to recast the role when filming began on another Queen novel a year later. By some bewildering logic, they now cast small and slight Eddie Quillan, a light comic actor, perhaps hoping to capture the same sort of whimsical feeling of MGM's 1934 *The Thin Man*, a box office winner that already had spawned a series. Unfortunately, Quillan was no William Powell, and didn't get a series.

The Queen novel Republic adapted this time was *The Chinese Orange Mystery*, a clever "locked room" puzzler set in the world of international stamp collecting. Three screenwriters worked on the adaptation: John Francis Larkin, Gertrude Orr and Rex Taylor. Orr had just written a comedy for the silly Olsen & Johnson team while Rex Taylor's most recent film script was for the miserable Poverty Row production *The Shadow Strikes*, the first feature film about radio's famous crime-fighter.

The writers altered almost everything about the book, including the title, which became *The Mandarin Mystery*. They took great liberties with the characters, including Ellery himself, and even picked a different murderer from among the suspects.

In the novel, an unidentified man is murdered and his body left in the waiting room of book publisher Donald Kirk, a renowned collector of rare postage stamps. The most bizarre aspect of the case is that the man's clothes had all been taken off, then put back on the body backwards.

Not much is made of the important "backwards" clues of the original mystery and there is no Donald Kirk in the movie. Much of his function as a character is taken over by Dr. Alexander Kirk (George Irving), who's Donald's father in the book and has other things to do.

Among the suspects in the novel are Jo Temple, a pretty writer who has attracted Donald Kirk's attention; Irene Llewes, a fortune hunter with designs on Kirk; Marcella, Kirk's troubled sister; Osborne, Kirk's personal assistant; Miss Diversey, the secretary Osborne has romantic notions about; Macgowan, Marcella's intended husband, and Hubbell, the butler. Most of the action in the book takes place at the Chancellor, a luxury residence hotel where both Kirks have their lodgings and the business office for their company, the Mandarin Press.

The movie changes Marcella into *Martha* Kirk and transforms slinky Irene Llewes (that's "Sewell" spelled backward) into Irene Kirk, who's now a Kirk sister not in the book. There is a "Donald" in the movie: Donald Trent (George Walcott), who seems to take the place of the novel's Macgowan character. A prissy hotel manager named Mellish is added, apparently so that Hollywood's definitive "prissy" actor, Franklin Pangborn, could supply comedy relief.

But the most fundamental changes occur with the Ellery Queen character. The writers, director Ralph Staub and actor Quillan turn him into something of a silly ass, incapable of doing anything very effectively.

At the start of the film, we see a Times Square neon news bulletin alerting the public that the world's most valuable stamp, "The Chinese Mandarin," is arriving on an ocean liner that day in the possession of Jo Temple, who hopes to sell it to Dr. Kirk for $50,000. This is all invented for the movie and doesn't happen in the book.

What also was invented for the movie was a ridiculous love affair for Ellery, who's smitten by Miss Temple and meets her at the dock with a bouquet of flowers. She's played by Charlotte Henry, a pert 23-year-old blonde who's best remembered for playing the title role in Paramount's 1933 *Alice in Wonderland*. She certainly looks as if she could do a lot better than a twerp like this movie's Ellery. She also seems quite unimpressed by him once she learns he's the same Ellery Queen who writes "those detective stories."

Acting like a high school boy on his first date, Ellery puffs up with pride and asks if she's read his books. She confesses she did actually read *one* of them. When he asks if she found it interesting, she cools his ardor a bit by replying, "Not very."

The effort to make *The Mandarin Mystery* into a sophisticated comedy begins to flop as soon as Eddie Quillan shows up. He never had an ounce of romance in him and he's seriously miscast. You don't believe for a moment that Miss Temple would ever waste a minute with this little squirt. (Quillan, who never married, lived most of his adult life with his mother and sisters. He does much better with women in this movie than he ever did in real life.)

Despite the obvious lack of chemistry between the leads, the movie still forces a romance to develop between Ellery and Jo, which is what happens in the book between Jo and Donald Kirk.

Inspector Queen (Wade Boteler) and son Ellery don't seem to fit together very neatly either. In fact, the elder Queen often looks as if he'd like to run DNA tests on Ellery to make sure some mistake wasn't made in the delivery room. At one point, when the inspector seems about to tell Ellery to put his theories where the sun don't shine, Ellery petulantly tells him, "Oh, Dad, play ball with me and I'll bring you a pennant!"

The Mandarin Mystery didn't please anyone much, so Quillan followed Donald Cook into cinema history as a one-shot Ellery Queen and no further films were made until 1940 when Columbia Pictures launched a new Ellery Queen series with Ralph Bellamy in the title role. Again, too much emphasis was placed on silly comedy and Bellamy left after four films. He was replaced by William Gargan for three more films, none of them worth remembering. Columbia ended its series in 1942.

Because Ellery Queen continued to be one of the most popular mystery characters in books and stories for more than 40 years, there were efforts to dramatize his adventures in other media. Radio's *The Adventures of Ellery Queen* debuted on CBS in 1939 and continued off and on through 1948, switching to NBC a couple of times and finally ending its run on ABC. Among the actors who played him on radio were Hugh Marlowe, Howard Culver, Larry Dobkin, Carleton Young and Sidney Smith.

In the early days of television, *The Adventures of Ellery Queen* moved to the new medium, first on the DuMont network with Richard Hart as Ellery Queen in 1950 and '51. When 30-year-old Hart died of a sudden heart attack, the program was recast and moved to ABC in the latter part of 1951 for two years there with Lee Bowman in the role. In 1954, former radio actor Hugh Marlowe played Ellery in a syndicated non-network series. In 1958, NBC launched its own series with George Nader as Ellery. Lee Philips took over the role in 1959.

Ellery was off TV from 1959 to 1975 when NBC revived the character for a new series starring Jim Hutton as Ellery and David Wayne as Inspector Queen. John Hillerman, famous in later years for playing Tom Selleck's sidekick Higgins on *Magnum, P.I.*, appeared as Ellery's rival, a radio reporter called Simon Brimmer. The new series lasted only a year, but it did bring back one very nostalgic bit: the "challenge," this time to viewers rather than readers: Ellery would turn to the TV audience and ask, as the climax approached, "Have you figured it out?"

Patrick Quentin
Black Widow

The 1952 novel and the 1954 movie

From the 1930s through the 1950s, European mystery lovers widely hailed Patrick Quentin as one of America's greatest mystery writers. In fact, British mystery novelist

Ginger Rogers talks with detective George Raft in *Black Widow*, **the 1954 movie version of the Patrick Quentin mystery novel (20th Century–Fox).**

Francis Iles called Quentin "No. 1" in that category. And that wasn't a shabby endorsement: Iles was among Britain's very best mystery writers, a pioneer of the "inverted" mystery genre who wrote two novels still acclaimed as masterpieces, *Malice Aforethought,* twice dramatized on *Mystery!,* and *Before the Fact,* which Alfred Hitchcock turned into one of his greatest suspense films, *Suspicion.*

But that loud cheer from Iles has to be one of the mystery world's great in-jokes. You see, Francis Iles was a make-believe person—the pen name of author Anthony Berkeley. What's more, Patrick Quentin never really existed either. He was the pseudonym, at one time or another, of not one, not even two, but actually four different writers: Richard Wilson Webb, Hugh Wheeler, Martha Mott Kelly and Mary Louise White Aswell.

How did that weird mélange of writing talents come about? It began in 1931 when Webb, a British-born pharmacist living in Philadelphia, decided, just for fun, to write a mystery novel called *Cottage Sinister* and took Ms. Kelly as his collaborator. They wanted to use a single pen name rather than write under both their names, so they chose the surname "Patrick" by combining parts of their nicknames—"Patsy" for Kelly and "Rick" for Webb—and just adding the letter "Q" in place of a first name.

Their mutual creation, Q. Patrick, published two mysteries, *Cottage Sinister* in 1931 and *Murder at the Women's City Club* in 1932. Then Kelly got married and gave up her half of the make-believe author. Webb wrote *Murder at the Varsity* (1933) by himself, still using the Q. Patrick pen name, then took Mary Louise White Aswell, an editor at *Harper's Bazaar*, as his new partner and published two more Q. Patrick mysteries with her, *S.S. Nightmare* (1933) and *The Grindle Nightmare* (1935).

Webb found his perfect partner in Hugh Wheeler and in 1936 they wrote *Murder Gone to Earth*, the first of nine Dr. Westlake mysteries, under a new pseudonym, Jonathan Stagge. Bristling with new ideas, that same year they also created the character who would become their most popular "detective," Broadway producer Peter Duluth. On the cover of Duluth's first adventure, *A Puzzle for Fools*, was another new pen name made from the original one: Patrick Quentin.

Peter Duluth really isn't a detective, but in the rich tradition of Agatha Christie's Miss Jane Marple he keeps getting mixed up in crimes that require his clever, facile mind, usually to get himself out of some terrible pickle. As a mystery writer, Webb came from the English tradition of "puzzle" mysteries, which accounts for the use of the word "puzzle" in the titles of so many of the early Peter Duluth mysteries. But once Wheeler came on board, the mysteries began to reflect his deep interest in psychology and police procedure.

The result was a stream of extremely credible mysteries that may have embraced the charming, "cozy" style of Christie and Dorothy Sayers, but also hewed closely to the facts and seldom put Duluth or their other characters into situations that were too fanciful. The Duluth mysteries give us a constant backstage view of the Broadway theater world, but also a comfortable notion of how modern police work functioned from the 1930s through the 1950s.

Black Widow (1952) was the eighth of nine Peter Duluth mysteries and the last one both Webb and Wheeler worked on together. Webb's failing health finally caused him to bow out of the process and Wheeler went on to write many more mysteries as Patrick Quentin, including a final Peter Duluth case.

Black Widow is still a very readable mystery. I read it first in 1954 after seeing the movie released that year. Many fans consider it the peak of the Duluth canon. In the storyline, Duluth's wife Iris, a famous stage and screen actress, leaves their New York apartment for Jamaica to be with her ailing mother for several weeks. Peter stays behind because he's in charge of a current hit Broadway show starring their upstairs neighbor and friend, Charlotte "Lottie" Marin, who's perhaps America's most popular stage star.

Shortly after Iris departs, Peter reluctantly goes alone to a party Lottie has given and meets a plain, rather drab young woman named "Nanny" Ordway, who tells him she wants to be a writer. He's bored with the party and so is she, so he invites her out to dinner and very quickly they become friends. Peter really isn't anxious to two-time his beautiful wife—even though she has cheated on him at least once—but he's drawn to Nanny mostly because she flatters him a great deal and appeals to his "fatherly" side.

Peter's great mistake is offering Nanny the use of his apartment during the day as a place to do her serious writing. It's a large, luxurious Manhattan apartment while her own place is a shabby flat she shares with another girl. The seriousness of his error finally becomes apparent when Iris comes home and together they find Nanny dead, her corpse hanging by the neck in the bathroom, an apparent suicide.

It's a scandalous situation, because everybody believes the girl was used and abused by Peter while his wife was out of town and, when she discovered she was pregnant, she killed herself where he'd find her hanging, her crude, illustrated suicide note nearby.

When the police determine that Nanny was murdered, Peter is in the deepest doo-doo of his long career in mysteries. Police Detective Lt. Timothy Trant, who was a character in his own series of Q. Patrick mysteries, naturally believes Peter is the prime suspect because he has the most obvious motive.

That means there isn't much effort being given to find out who the real killer was and Peter has to conduct his own investigation before he's hauled into court to face a murder charge. Not only is his marriage now on the rocks, but his future starts to look very grim indeed. It's a nifty situation for suspense.

There are several other suspects, including the unknown older man who really fathered Nanny's expected child; the young brother of her roommate, who had proposed marriage to Nanny not long before she died, and an aging, not very successful Broadway actor Nanny apparently lived with for a time before moving in with the other girl. Peter attempts to find the truth from each of these characters.

Black Widow has a rich assortment of characters, which made it an ideal prospect for a feature film. Altogether, three of Patrick Quentin's Peter Duluth mysteries have been turned into movies but, oddly, only the first of them called the main character Peter Duluth: Republic's *Homicide for Three* (1948), based on Quentin's 1944 novel *Puzzle for Puppets*. It starred Warren Douglas as Duluth and Audrey Long as Iris.

Black Widow, which came next in 1954, was one of the very first 20th Century–Fox films to utilize the CinemaScope process. Peter Duluth is renamed Peter Denver and is played by veteran character actor Van Heflin, winner of a Supporting Actor Oscar for MGM's *Johnny Eager* (1942).

The third film, *Strange Awakening* (1958), known as *Female Fiends* in the U.S., was a European feature based on Quentin's 1946 novel *Puzzle for Fiends*. Lex Barker, who had recently played Tarzan in several movies, played a character called Peter Chance.

Of the three films, *Black Widow* is the only one that got major studio treatment. It was written and directed by Nunnally Johnson, one of the best screenwriters in Hollywood history. He began writing for the movies in the early 1930s and among his credits were *The Grapes of Wrath*, *Jesse James*, *The Prisoner of Shark Island*, *Tobacco Road*, *The Pied Piper*, *The Moon Is Down*, *The Keys of the Kingdom*, *Three Came Home*, *Mr. Peabody and the Mermaid*, *The Desert Fox*, *How to Marry a Millionaire*, *Flaming Star* and *The Dirty Dozen*. He directed few films, but two are well-remembered: *The Man in the Gray Flannel Suit* and *The Three Faces of Eve*, for which Joanne Woodward won the Best Actress Oscar in 1958.

Why Johnson decided to change Duluth to Denver is anybody's guess. (He wasn't from either city.) He also made one other serious character switch: He removed Lt. Trant and replaced him with a much older character, Detective Lt. C.A. Bruce, played by veteran screen tough guy George Raft. Top-billed Ginger Rogers played Peter's upstairs neighbor and troublesome star "Lottie" Marin.

In the book, Lottie's husband Brian is a younger American character, but Johnson cast the much older, very British Reginald Gardiner as Brian, perhaps to go better with the aging Ginger Rogers.

The notorious "Nanny" Ordway was played by former child star Peggy Ann Garner and her roommate was played by Fox studio "starlet," Virginia Leith, a Stanley Kubrick discovery. Leith was pushed into several leading roles in the 1950s, but never really became a star.

Gordon Ling, the older actor Nanny lived with earlier, was played by Otto Kruger.

Peter's wife, Iris Denver, was played by former leading lady Gene Tierney, whose career was starting to fade. The young man who hoped to marry Nanny was played by frequent screen "bad guy" Skip Homeier who, like Garner, had been a child star.

Black Widow was included in a 2007 DVD film noir boxed set from 20th Century-Fox, but it's really a stretch to put it in that category of dark, moody suspense films. Director Johnson was not very inventive in "opening up" the story and getting it out of the principal set—the apartment of Peter and Iris. In CinemaScope, the result is a boring series of tableau-style scenes in which several characters are spread out across the living room set as if Johnson were trying to fill up the extra wide space. The script is also very talky, so the film often seems very static. The bright colors also prevent you from thinking of *Black Widow* as a film noir. There's nary a shadow in the whole picture.

But the acting is of a pretty high order. Ginger Rogers chomps down on the grotesque Lottie character with gusto and Heflin was always very good at portraying genuine nice guys trying to get themselves out of trouble by being extra-earnest. Peggy Ann Garner is just right for Nanny; Tierney, Gardiner and Kruger all seem just as their characters should be. However, George Raft seems a bit stiff in his role and you tend to hope he'll punch somebody out or get gut-shot by the killer while flipping a coin. No such luck.

Peter Duluth is a great character, who starts out in the earlier novels as a recovering alcoholic, goes through marital hard times and has an awful lot of ups and downs. He's one of my favorite amateur "detectives" and is definitely due for a revival in the 21st century.

Duluth's co-creator, Richard Webb, did nothing significant in the mystery field after he wrote *Black Widow* with Hugh Wheeler in 1952, but Wheeler went on to make an even bigger mark for himself by writing the "book" (the dramatic storyline) for several Stephen Sondheim musicals, including the composer's mystery-oriented show *Sweeney Todd*. Webb's last pure mystery effort was writing the teleplay (with Leonard Stern) for the 1972 TV movie *The Snoop Sisters* with Helen Hayes and Mildred Natwick playing elderly mystery writers who solve real crimes. It led to a short-lived NBC series of the same name.

The name Patrick Quentin doesn't mean much to today's mystery readers, but it certainly ought to since it represents one of the weirdest combinations of mystery talents in the history of the genre.

Ruth Rendell

A Judgment in Stone

The 1977 novel and the 1995 movie *La Cérémonie*

Ruth Rendell's 1977 novel *A Judgment in Stone* is about the psychological pressures that eventually lead a severely inhibited, socially alienated domestic servant to suddenly erupt in an orgy of violence that turns her into the mass murderer of her aristocratic employers.

It's one of Rendell's darkest novels—had she written it later in her career, it would have been under her pseudonym, Barbara Vine, an identity she created for her occasional excursions into the twisted world of *roman noir*. It's also an incisive study of the pathological turn a person's life can take when living with the shame of illiteracy and trying to conceal it.

Ruth Rendell's English mystery novel *A Judgment in Stone* was turned into the French film *La Cérémonie* by director Claude Chabrol. Isabelle Huppert (left) and Sandrine Bonnaire play the film's conspiring murderesses (New Yorker Films).

It's unlikely that film producers scrambled for the rights to this novel, which has no central character you'd want to encounter, and doesn't exactly have a cheerful ending. But in the mid–1990s, filmmaker Claude Chabrol, often called the French Alfred Hitchcock, tackled an adaptation of the film: *La Cérémonie*.

Chabrol and screenwriter Caroline Eliacheff shifted the story's locale from rural England to rural France, to give the storyline some twists that might appeal to modern moviegoers. The protagonist, household maid Eunice Parchman, gets a new name, Sophie, along with a physical makeover that lowers her age from late forties to mid-twenties and her general build from muscular to sleek. With the attractive Sandrine Bonnaire in the role, it's only Sophie's dull personality and dour outlook that puts us off.

Rendell's story portrays the wealthy Coverdale family as reasonably decent. The father, George, offers to pay for new glasses for the maid when she uses poor vision as her excuse for not being able to drive or read certain notes she's handed. His wife Jacqueline happily drives the maid to town and their teenage daughter Melinda urges the family to treat the maid more as an equal.

Chabrol overhauled the family slightly, giving them all a French surname, eliminating one daughter (Paula) and changing Jacqueline's name to Catherine, perhaps because the actress cast in the role, Jacqueline Bisset, already had that name. But, basically, the movie sets up the family as Rendell did in the book. They represent the French upper class, living in a very large country manor that requires the attention of a very industrious housekeeper, which Sophie turns out to be—at least in all outward respects.

Chabrol made an even more fundamental change designed to increase our interest in the goings-on. In the book, the maid's head is turned by a middle-aged local village woman named Joan, a religious fanatic who's married to a drab shopkeeper whose little store has a post office in it. Joan serves as the postal clerk and uses that role to spy on village people she dislikes, especially the family for which Sophie works. She routinely opens George's mail and then clumsily re-seals it. He notices this and is furious about it.

Chabrol really went to work on the character of Joan, eliminating her husband, toning down her religious fanaticism, changing her name to Jeanne and casting one of France's sexiest and most attractive stars, Isabelle Huppert, in the role. There's also a significant effort to suggest a lesbian relationship between Jeanne and Sophie, though we're never shown anything beyond some light kissing between them. This is a big departure from the book, where Rendell made both women pretty much asexual.

The event that precipitates the violent conclusion of the story is a phone call from Melinda to her boyfriend—Jonathan in the book, Jeremy in the movie—in which she tells him she fears she's pregnant and may need an abortion. The maid overhears this conversation on an extension phone, so when Melinda discovers the maid's illiteracy, the maid threatens to tell Melinda's family about her pregnancy if she outs her as illiterate.

In both the book and film, Melinda comes clean with her family. George, furious that the maid tried to blackmail Melinda, gives the maid a week to pack up and get out. The movie leaves out one element: Melinda discovers that she's *not* pregnant before the showdown with Sophie.

The postal clerk comes to help the maid pack, but starts to destroy the family's personal goods while they're all downstairs watching an opera on TV. Their vengeful activity escalates until they use George's own shotguns to massacre the family.

The movie preserves the book's twist ending: Melinda was tape-recording the opera, so the massacre is on audio tape. The result of all the manipulation of Rendell's story is a pretty effective thriller, although there's still nobody you really care about when the dust settles.

Craig Rice

Home Sweet Homicide

The 1944 novel and the 1946 movie

Craig Rice was such a make-believe person that who can tell what was real and unreal about her weird, amazing life? Take the case of her 1944 novel *Home Sweet Homicide*, which became a bestseller and, two years later, a popular movie.

Rice, whose real name was Georgianna Craig, is often called the queen of the comic mystery, and *Home Sweet Homicide* is the classic example of that genre. It's all about Marian Carstairs, a single mom who writes mystery novels, keeping at it so long each day that her children Dinah, April and Archie are pretty much raising themselves and sort of taking care of her at the same time.

One day the children hear gunshots from the home of their next door neighbor. It turns out the woman who lives there has been murdered. They decide to solve the murder,

Kids play a crucial role in solving a murder in *Home Sweet Homicide*, the 1946 movie version of Craig Rice's novel. Pictured from left are Peggy Ann Garner, Connie Marshall, mother Lynn Bari, and Dean Stockwell, watching as Randolph Scott and James Gleason question a murder suspect (20th Century–Fox).

but to give credit to their mom, figuring it will be great publicity for her new mystery novel.

Now if anyone reading this book tried to sell that premise to a publisher or a Hollywood studio, it's reasonably certain that person would be escorted promptly to the door and given a swift kick in the rump to hasten his or her departure.

But Craig Rice could spin something like that into a wonderfully entertaining story, and she did. You don't question the fact the kids are hiding the dead woman's husband, a prime suspect, in their back yard playhouse. You're too busy laughing at all the stuff those kids get into.

What's really interesting is the fact that Rice told a great deal about her own life story while dishing out this kooky mystery tale. In her dedication to the book, for instance, she wrote that she owed her own three children Nancy, Iris and David for the story idea.

In real life, Rice probably wasn't exactly the *Woman's Home Companion* choice for ideal mom. She was an alcoholic who frequently worked around the clock. She also seemed to do whatever she could to dodge her parental responsibilities. She left two of her children with Nan and Elton Rice, who pretty much raised them. They felt they couldn't also take on the author's young son, so the poor little guy was bounced from one foster home to another for the first ten years of his life, hardly ever seeing his sisters.

The author did reunite her children in the early 1940s while she was living with poet Lawrence Lipton, the first time they'd ever lived under the same roof. That's when she wrote *Home Sweet Homicide*. If they ever had the fun-loving and warm relationship you find between Marian and her kids in the book, it must have been during that time.

Both the book and the 1946 movie suggest that the kids were more adult than their mom. Their primary mission, besides solving the murder, is to bring their mom together in a romantic relationship with the investigating homicide detective, Bill Smith, so they can have a dad who would have something in common with their mystery-writing mom.

Though Rice wrote movies for a living, too—she worked on RKO's *Falcon* detective series—she didn't write the *Home Sweet Homicide* screenplay. That was done by comic writer F. Hugh Herbert, who borrowed heavily from the comic dialogue in the novel. The film follows the book pretty closely. The things omitted, like little Archie's gang of neighborhood brats, seem to have been deleted so the film could focus on the family.

Lynn Bari, who played Marian, was not a conventional beauty and, in some photos, seems to resemble the author quite closely. Detective Smith was played by Randolph Scott in an amusing departure from his usual action roles. Star billing went to teenage Peggy Ann Garner, who plays Marian's oldest daughter Dinah. Garner was very hot in Hollywood then and had already won the juvenile version of an Academy Award. She had been in 20th Century–Fox's *A Tree Grows in Brooklyn* (1945), which propelled her to star status there.

April was played by Connie Marshall, another well-respected juvenile player, and the girls' young brother Archie was played by Dean Stockwell, who went on to be a Disney regular and eventually mature into one of Hollywood's finest character actors.

Building up the juvenile cast was just the right thing to do because the adults are really minor figures in *Home Sweet Homicide*. They're also kind of dumb figures, too, if you consider how much wool the kids pull over their eyes as they pursue their "investigation," which includes hiding suspects and either faking or withholding evidence.

What I've concluded about *Home Sweet Homicide* is that it must have been Craig Rice's fantasy notion of what she wished her life had been like with her children. It's brimming with love for the children, who stand out as very special little people to their mom. It's just sad to know that Rice never really had much quality time with her youngsters, then died prematurely, leaving them this happy little novel as perhaps the only legacy of her love.

Dorothy L. Sayers

Busman's Honeymoon

The 1937 novel and the 1940 movie *Haunted Honeymoon*

During her lifetime, Dorothy L. Sayers can't have been too enamored with the notion of seeing her books about gentleman sleuth Lord Peter Wimsey turned into screen entertainment. Consider her history with the movies:

Sayers concocted an original Wimsey story for the movies in the early 1930s. It was filmed by British Gaumont in 1935 as *The Silent Passenger*. It's rumored that the studio

Robert Montgomery (left) and Constance Cummings play Dorothy L. Sayers' Lord Peter Wimsey and wife Harriet Vane in the 1940 *Haunted Honeymoon*, based on the mystery novel *Busman's Honeymoon*. Showing them a cactus plant with special plot implications is Aubrey Mallalieu as the vicar (MGM).

people didn't much care for what she'd written and made wholesale changes. What's more, the actor cast as Lord Peter Wimsey, Peter Haddon, played him as rather an affected twit. Nobody was much interested in seeing him do Wimsey in any more movies.

In the biography *Dorothy L. Sayers: A Careless Rage for Life* (1992), David Coomes reports that she turned down MGM's $10,000 offer for the rights to *Murder Must Advertise* and steadfastly refused to see the studio's movie version of *Busman's Honeymoon*.

Sayers had become one of England's most popular mystery novelists by the mid–1930s, but none of her best Wimsey mysteries were filmed during her lifetime. The books that made her a giant in British mystery circles—*The Unpleasantness at the Bellona Club*, *Murder Must Advertise* and *The Nine Tailors*—weren't filmed until the 1970s when British television began a popular series of adaptations, first with Ian Carmichael as Wimsey, then Edward Petherbridge. Sayers, who died in 1957, never saw those films.

In 1940, Sayers' final Wimsey novel, *Busman's Honeymoon*, was filmed in England by MGM with a mostly English cast, but American Robert Montgomery playing Wimsey and English actress Constance Cummings as his new bride, mystery writer Harriet Vane.

The film was re-titled *Haunted Honeymoon*. It may have been reasonably well received by those mystery fans who hadn't read any of Sayers' mysteries, but it's not remembered fondly by anyone who admired the original Wimsey mysteries.

Sayers' book is an important coda for the Wimsey saga because it begins with his marriage to Harriet Vane and then immediately plunges them into a murder mystery that grips them literally on their wedding night. Sayers carried on the Wimsey saga in some short stories, but never again completed a novel featuring her most famous character. (She left behind an unfinished Wimsey mystery that another writer completed; it's not regarded as a genuine Sayers work.)

Haunted Honeymoon is not a very successful effort on anyone's terms. One can imagine that MGM saw the potential to create another husband-wife detective team like their very successful Nick and Nora Charles *Thin Man* series with William Powell and Myrna Loy. After all, Wimsey is a very clever amateur sleuth and his wife is a bright and audacious mystery writer. One suspects that MGM saw many further cases for this new team.

But the film doesn't work as either a romantic comedy or a suspense-filled mystery. The first problem is that Montgomery seems like a fish out of water in a British murder mystery. Though he had a refined, gentlemanly persona in most of his screen roles, he wasn't British and he makes no effort to do a British accent in *Haunted Honeymoon*. Moreover, he doesn't wear the monocle that was Wimsey's most famous accessory and doesn't go about quoting the great poets as Wimsey does all through the source novel.

In effect, someone watching *Haunted Honeymoon* may wonder how an American wound up as a titled English lord in 1940. One assumes he's supposed to be English, but there's no evidence of it.

Sayers' novel is more about the beginning of the Wimsey marriage than it is about the mystery that arises. On the first night of their honeymoon, they arrive at Talboys, a country estate that Wimsey has bought as a surprise for his new bride, who grew up in the neighborhood and always admired the place. They're disappointed when Noakes, the home's previous owner, isn't there to welcome them and hand over the keys to the manor as he promised. As it turns out, Noakes is there all right, in the cellar, dead after a massive head wound from a blunt instrument.

The rest of the novel involves Wimsey's efforts to figure out why someone would want to kill the chap and which of the many suspects did the deed. The movie scrambles the story around a bit to make it work a lot faster than the meandering way it does on the printed page. For one thing, the movie shows us Mr. Noakes (Roy Emerton) making all kinds of enemies among his servants and neighbors, scattering motives for murder all over the place, before the Wimseys turn up.

Though that might have helped make the movie more involving, we really needed to start liking Peter and Harriet right away—and there's just no romantic chemistry between Montgomery and Cummings.

Though readers of the earlier Wimsey novels will understand that Lord Peter has a very strong bond with his manservant Bunter, who saved his life when they were in World War I together, people who are meeting Wimsey for the first time in the movie will think he's nuts for taking Bunter (Seymour Hicks) with him on his honeymoon.

In the Wimsey mysteries, Bunter serves the traditional sidekick role that Watson fills with Sherlock Holmes, but Bunter doesn't do much of anything in *Haunted Honeymoon*, so some may conclude that Lord Peter might not be capable of fulfilling his marital duties and needed Bunter to come along to help him out.

The film is loaded with some fine British supporting actors, including Robert

Newton as Frank Crutchley, the sinister gardener-handyman; Googie Withers as Polly, Frank's barmaid girlfriend; Joan Kemp-Welch as Aggie Twitterton, the dead man's niece, who wants to marry Frank; James Carney as the local constable who owed the dead man a sum of money, and Leslie Banks as Scotland Yard Inspector Kirk. Nobody of normal intelligence will have any problem figuring out who the killer is before the end of the movie. The way the murder was committed was reasonably clever in the book and the movie sticks pretty closely to the literary setup of the crime. Still, suspense is not built up to any fever pitch.

The screenplay takes some liberties with the Sayers storyline, most notably by adding a silly sequence in which Wimsey's roadster collides with a wagon full of hay. Perhaps it was meant to be a comedy highlight to relieve our suspense, but it's not funny and there was little suspense to relieve.

Busman's Honeymoon doesn't stand tall in the Sayers canon of Lord Peter Wimsey stories, but so far it's been the most often dramatized of all her novels. It first was developed as a stage play by Sayers and playwright Muriel St. Clare. After the MGM movie, it was filmed twice more for British television under the title *Busman's Honeymoon*, first in 1947 with Harold Warrender and then in 1957 with Peter Gray.

After his experience playing one of England's stuffiest detectives, Robert Montgomery wisely turned his attention to more domestic sleuthing and in 1946 was more successfully playing American private eye Philip Marlowe in a rather offbeat movie version of Raymond Chandler's *The Lady in the Lake*.

Maj Sjöwall and Per Wahlöö
The Laughing Policeman

The 1968 novel and the 1973 movie

Maj Sjöwall and Per Wahlöö's ten novels about Swedish police Detective Supt. Martin Beck are now widely viewed as the seminal works that began what is considered the booming literary genre of "Scandinavian noir." Their influence is most vividly felt in the Wallander detective novels of Henning Mankell that followed and the novels about computer hacker Lisbeth Salander from the late Stieg Larson.

All ten Martin Beck novels have been turned into movies in Europe and the characters also were the subject of a Swedish television series. In 1973, 20th Century–Fox producer-director Stuart Rosenberg adapted their 1968 novel *The Laughing Policeman* into an American feature film.

Strange as it may seem, there was no effort to cash in on the popularity of the books or to transfer the successful Martin Beck brand to America the way other filmmakers had done with such popular foreign detectives as Agatha Christie's Hercule Poirot and Miss Jane Marple.

Instead, Martin Beck was eliminated, along with all the characters that made the novels such a welcome addition to the tradition of the modern police procedural school of crime fiction. The Beck character was transformed into a new character called Jake Martin, played by Oscar-winning American actor Walter Matthau, who was then best

Walter Matthau (left) and Bruce Dern play San Francisco police detectives trying to solve a mass murder aboard a local city bus in *The Laughing Policeman*. The original Maj Sjöwall–Per Wahlöö novel took place in Sweden (20th Century-Fox).

known for his dour comic portrayals in movies. And the names of all the novel's other central characters were jettisoned and only traces of the original characters remained.

To more fully "Americanize" the story, it was shifted from Stockholm, Sweden, to San Francisco and laced with all the knee-jerk 1970s idioms of that West Coast city: hippies, gays, lesbians, male and female strippers, cross-dressers, "militant" African-Americans and Hare Krishna street people.

What remained was the basic core situation: Someone armed with a submachine gun boards a municipal bus and kills the driver and all the passengers, including a member of Beck's Swedish homicide squad. Nobody knows the motive or why Detective Inspector Stenstrom was on board the bus, armed with his service handgun.

Beck and his team establish the fact that Stenstrom, though off duty, was privately trying to solve a classic department "cold case" in order to make his reputation golden and rise among his fellow detectives. But the department's investigation is complicated because Stenstrom left no notes about the progress of his probe. Worse yet, the investigation now brings about overwhelming public scrutiny that such a mass murder case would obviously prompt in a nation like Sweden where atrocities of this type just don't happen.

The screenplay by Tom Rickman, one of the most acclaimed movie scenarists of the period, contains only scant references to the original novel while endeavoring instead to develop a tense relationship between Jake Martin and his new partner Leo Larsen (Bruce Dern, then building his sterling reputation as one of Hollywood's best character actors). Beck was a troubled character through most of the ten novels, having marital difficulties and a home life that suffered greatly under the pressures of his work. Rickman made an effort to give Jake Martin a similar set of issues with his wife and children, but not much real character development results.

Though some of the book's supporting police characters seem to surface now and then under new American identities, it seems more as if Rickman tossed several of them into a blender and mixed their traits up a good deal. One example is the black detective played by Louis Gossett, Jr., who seems to carry some traits of a Swedish detective in the novel, but is weighted down with lots of 1970s-style black jive talk.

In the novel, a poignant character is Stenstrom's live-in girlfriend Asa, who is devastated by her lover's brutal murder and seems to be coming apart at the seams as his fellow detectives swarm all over her apartment with questions about why he was riding that bus. In the movie, Asa is turned into Kay (Cathy Lee Crosby), an emotional wreck who resents Jake's questioning. At one point, Jake slaps her several times and orders her to get her act together. It doesn't seem like anything Superintendent Beck would have done in Stockholm—and it doesn't speak well for the Jake character.

Another major story point in the novel that's eliminated in the movie is the fact that the killer shot a key figure in the bus massacre in the face, virtually eliminating his features. Since he carried no identification, his identity remains a mystery through much of the book. This doesn't happen in the movie and, in fact, the movie begins with that character talking on the phone with the presumed killer before the massacre, clearly linking him to the plan to kill Stenstrom and other bus passengers. It erases a certain amount of suspense that otherwise might have developed.

Another wholly unnecessary story change is made when a gunman holding hostages is involved in a shootout with the San Francisco PD. By that time, movie viewers already know that the guy holding hostages has nothing to do with the bus massacre, so it looks as if the whole sequence was tossed into the movie to add gunfire and action because there hadn't been any for an hour or so.

Finally, the filmmakers somehow decided to make the villain a closeted gay man, which does nothing to enrich the storyline and, in retrospect, seems totally absurd and a rather feeble link to the "cold case" that precipitated the bus massacre as a cover for the assassination of a police detective who was digging into the old murder case.

The Martin Beck novels by Sjöwall and Wahlöö, an unmarried couple who lived and worked together until his death in 1975, are still greatly respected not only for their well-researched police procedural storylines, but also for their pro-social approach to many crucial issues in contemporary Swedish life. They didn't need to have this fine novel run through the Hollywood sausage grinder for the sake of making an insignificant American-style feature film.

Mickey Spillane
My Gun Is Quick

The 1950 novel and the 1957 movie

In the early 1950s, no crime-mystery writer was as popular as Mickey Spillane, whose novels about hard-boiled private eye Mike Hammer sold in the tens of millions since his phenomenal debut with *I, the Jury* (1947). His novels, violent and drenched in pulp fiction–style sex, appealed to the largely male readership who were part of the paperback novel revolution of the era.

Hollywood brought *I, the Jury* to the screen in 1953 in a 3-D movie starring Biff Eliot as Hammer. A movie version of Spillane's non–Hammer novel *The Long Wait* followed in 1954 with Anthony Quinn as an amnesiac hero; and then Robert Aldrich's *Kiss Me Deadly* (1955) starred the first really convincing Mike Hammer in the person of Ralph Meeker. In 1957 came the first of three Hammer TV series, the syndicated *Mickey Spillane's Mike Hammer* with Darren McGavin. It ran for 78 episodes over two years. Stacy Keach took on the role in the CBS version of *Mickey Spillane's Mike Hammer* that ran from 1984 to 1987. He returned to the role in *Mike Hammer, Private Eye*, in first-run syndication for 26 episodes in 1997 and '98.

But also in 1957, as big-screen interest in Spillane's hero was waning, United Artists released an independently made version of Spillane's 1950 novel *My Gun Is Quick* featuring little-known actor Robert Bray, a rugged-looking ex–Marine, as Mike Hammer.

One can only assume that the filmmakers were hoping that the loyal Spillane readers would only remember the vivid title of the novel and not much else since they virtually threw out most of the storyline and nearly all the characters and let screenwriters Richard Collins and Richard Powell dream up an entirely new scenario for the pulp fiction sleuth.

Obviously the filmmakers pinned a lot of their expectations for success on Bray, a tall, well-muscled actor, whose most notable screen appearance was as Ranger Corey Stuart on TV's *Lassie* from 1964 to 1969. He looked the part, all right, but his rendering of Hammer lacks the inbred toughness of Meeker's searing *Kiss Me Deadly* performance.

In the novel, Hammer is in a cheap café one rainy night when he meets a hard-up young prostitute he knows only by her nickname, "Red." He takes pity on her and gives her some cash to get some new clothes and pay her fare out of town to a more decent life away from New York City. While with her in the café, Hammer gets into a scuffle with a shady "greaseball" named Feeney Last, who's giving Red a bad time. Red later turns up dead in a hit-and-run accident that Hammer suspects was a murder that may be related to the café thug.

Hammer follows a series of clues that lead him from Red's death into a secret network of criminals involved in the city's flesh-peddling business and into corruption among high-level local politicians and even the police. As usual in the Hammer novels, Mike gets an assist from Homicide Detective Capt. Pat Chambers, his reluctant ally in several murder cases, Pat helps him track down Feeney Last, who's working as a bodyguard for a millionaire. When Hammer confronts the millionaire, the man promptly fires Feeney Last and hires Mike, helping finance Mike's search for Red's full name and background.

Private Eye Mike Hammer (Robert Bray) is worked over by two hooligans in *My Gun Is Quick*, the movie version of Mickey Spillane's novel (United Artists).

Mike has one other clue to follow up: the very unusual ring Red was wearing, which was apparently ripped from her finger at the time of her death.

When the filmmakers got around to adapting Spillane's novel for the screen, they made wholesale changes, most of them rather routine in fashion. For one thing, they moved Mike from New York City to Los Angeles and brought Homicide Capt. Chambers along with him. Obviously it was cheaper to film in L.A. than do any location shooting in Manhattan and environs.

They retained the character of Red and her ring, but instead of linking her to the big city prostitution underworld, they made the ring part of a missing horde of valuable jewels known as "the Venacci diamonds," stolen from their owners by the Nazis in World War II.

The "greaseball" thug Feeney Last is turned into a commonplace creep named "Louie" (Richard Garland) who works as a servant in the home of glamorous and wealthy Nancy (Whitney Blake), who's anxious to find the jewels and is happy to romance Mike while using him to track down the loot.

Also involved in the race to find the jewels is Col. Holloway (Donald Randolph) and a gang of French treasure hunters, who beat Mike up whenever they see him. One of these Euro-thugs is a one-armed man with a hook he wants to sink into Mike at the earliest opportunity. None of these sinister characters appears in Spillane's book.

The only familiar characters in the movie are loyal Hammer secretary Velda (Pamela

Duncan), Pat Chambers (Booth Colman) and the red-headed prostitute played by Jan Chaney.

Missing from the story is the dancer-prostitute Lola, who helps Mike follow up clues and endears herself to him so much that he appears ready to marry her and turn her life around if Spillane will only let him. The movie has a similar but far less endearing dancer-hooker named Maria (Genie Coree) who doesn't even do anything to earn any sack time with the sleuth.

Much of the book's mystery surrounds the search for Red's real identity, which turns out to be very meaningful to the resolution of the story. This is such a non-issue in the movie that her surname and real identity pop up automatically and mean nothing to anybody.

There's also another mighty deficit with the movie version, which abandons the thrilling climax of the novel (Mike and the archvillain trapped in a burning building) and settles instead for a pedestrian shootout at a boat harbor. There is no boat harbor in the book.

The problem with the movie is the new storyline, which is totally lacking in original thinking. (One of the screenwriters, Richard Collins, was just coming off the notorious Hollywood blacklist for his leftist leanings, so maybe he was a little out of practice.) But the terribly slack direction by co-producers George A. White and Phil Victor, who directed the movie together though neither man had much directing experience, accounts for the total lack of suspense and cinema savvy.

Since the making of *My Gun Is Quick*, the movies have had scant interest in Spillane's famous hero. *I, the Jury* was remade in 1982 with Armand Assante as an unconvincing Hammer. However, a pretty good version of Spillane's later Hammer novel, *The Girl Hunters*, was made in England in 1963 by a pretty good director, Roy Rowland, with, of all people, Spillane himself playing Mike Hammer. I'd have to say Spillane was a better Mike Hammer than almost everybody else who ever played him on screen, especially Robert Bray.

Josephine Tey
A Shilling for Candles

The 1936 novel and the 1937 movie *Young and Innocent*

When it was announced that England's hottest young movie director, Alfred Hitchcock, was going to film the latest Inspector Alan Grant novel by Josephine Tey, one of England's hottest young mystery writers, one can imagine the excitement it stirred in the mystery world.

Hitchcock already had begun to build what would be a towering international reputation as the Master of Suspense with his films *Blackmail, Murder, The Man Who Knew Too Much* and *The Thirty-Nine Steps*. And the new Alan Grant mystery, *A Shilling for Candles*, seemed ideal for Hitchcock because it was a fast-paced thriller with a chase element reminiscent of Hitch's *The Thirty-Nine Steps*.

But the 1937 film, known in England as *Young and Innocent* and in America as *The Girl Was Young*, was sure to disappoint fans of the popular book. As he did with his version

In this scene from Alfred Hitchcock's 1937 thriller *Young and Innocent*, fugitives Derrick DeMarnay (left) and Nova Pilbeam (far right) visit Nova's unsuspecting aunt (Mary Clare, center) during a festive birthday party for children (Gaumont British Films and Janus TV).

of John Buchan's *Thirty-Nine Steps*, Hitchcock, working with the same screenwriter, Charles Bennett, took liberties with the original story.

For starters, they eliminated her detective, Alan Grant, from the story. Then they changed the occupation and personality of the film's hero, an innocent man accused of murder. Finally, they chose a different murderer. And, for all that, none of Hitchcock's most famous scenes from the movie come from incidents in the book. The original title of the book had to go, too, because all reference to "a shilling for candles" was eliminated from the movie.

How the author reacted to their treatment of her book isn't known, but one can imagine. Anyway, Hitchcock never again adapted a Josephine Tey novel, even though several of her later books seemed right up his alley—especially *Brat Farrar*.

Tey (real name: Elizabeth Mackintosh) was one of the great writers from England's "golden age of mystery." She wrote novels and plays under the pen name Gordon Daviot, but is best remembered for the mystery novels written as Josephine Tey. In 1929, using the Daviot pen name, she introduced Inspector Alan Grant in *The Man in the Queue*. Her first Alan Grant mystery written as Josephine Tey was 1936's *A Shilling for Candles*. She wrote Grant novels over a span of 25 years, including her most famous novel, *The Daughter of Time* (1951), which is almost always listed among the top ten mysteries of all time.

In her original story, popular movie star Christine Clay is found dead, apparently by drowning, near her remote English seaside hideaway. An examination shows she was strangled. The chief suspect is young Robert Tisdall, an unemployed and penniless gentleman who had been befriended by Clay. Things look grim for him when they learn that the actress had bequeathed him a ranch property in America worth quite a sum. Police also found a button from a man's coat with the body—and Tisdall's coat is missing.

There might be other suspects, but Inspector Grant ignores them because the evidence is so solid against Tisdall. Clay's estranged husband and a composer who may have been her lover also are hovering in the background. Grant later learns that the actress despised her brother, who has a criminal record, and cut him out of her estate—except for her insulting and puzzling bequest to him of "a shilling for candles."

With the evidence stacked high against Tisdall, he realizes he's going to be convicted if he doesn't act quickly, so he escapes and becomes a fugitive. Helping him out is Erica Burgoyne, the teenage daughter of the local police constable, who believes he's innocent and incapable of any sort of violence.

The real killer is none of the above. Tey cleverly leads us up several twisty paths, all the while dangling the real culprit before us in a way that doesn't arouse our suspicions. The case is finally solved by Inspector Grant, who comes to realize the fugitive is innocent when additional evidence turns up while Tisdall is still in hiding.

Hitchcock and Bennett decided against using Tey's story. They eliminated the character of the real killer and morphed one of the other suspects into the killer. They also decided it would be much more of a thriller to have Tisdall and Erica team up to try and prove his innocence. Their flight from police is much like the situation dreamed up for *The Thirty-Nine Steps*, in which the hero and heroine are handcuffed together when they first elude their pursuers. (The female character in Hitchcock's *Thirty-Nine Steps* was a Hitchcock invention.)

They also used a gimmick similar to the one used in *Thirty-Nine Steps* to identify the culprit. In *Thirty-Nine Steps*, the villain has a missing finger. In *Young and Innocent*, he has an uncontrollable twitch of his facial muscles. No such thing exists in the novel.

Another "borrowing" from the earlier film is a scene where Erica has to attend a children's birthday party where a game of "Blind Man's Bluff" is going on. Tisdall is dragged into the party, too, and has to make up a new identity on the spot. This is much like the sequence in *Thirty-Nine Steps* where the fugitive hero is mistaken for the speaker at the political rally and has to go to the podium and deliver a speech in order to throw off his pursuers.

Bennett and Hitchcock also must have concluded that they couldn't transform Tisdall into a hero if he remained a rather shopworn and ineffectual member of the upper class. Therefore they make him a screenwriter who had met Christine Clay in America and was befriended by her because she wanted him to write a story for her. That also explains why Tisdall (Derrick de Marney) suddenly becomes a lot more charming and witty than he is in the book.

The Erica character also is much built up for the movie. She's also a little older and more sophisticated than the virtual child of the book. In the movie, she's played by onetime British child star Nova Pilbeam, who had appeared as the kidnapped youngster in Hitchcock's 1934 *Man Who Knew Too Much*.

Two of the movie's biggest scenes are pure Hitchcock and have no counterparts in the book. The first comes when the fugitives drive their car into an abandoned mine to escape pursuing police—and the floor of the mine collapses under the car. Tisdall finally rescues Erica, who's about to sink out of sight, by stretching out his hand until their fingertips touch, then catches her whole hand just as the car slides away beneath her. Hitchcock fans surely will notice the similarity between that moment and the moment in *North by Northwest* when Cary Grant stretches out his hand and saves Eva Marie Saint from sliding down the face of Mount Rushmore.

The other big sequence comes after they've found the man who wound up with Tisdall's missing coat—a drunken china-mender played by Edward Rigby—and he tells them the man who gave him the coat had a horrible twitch. Erica drags the china-mender around with her, looking for a twitching man. They finally find him as the drummer in a dance band, wearing blackface that conceals his real features.

Hitchcock has his camera wander across the crowded dance floor and finally close in on the face of the twitching man. It's a stirring scene that reminds one of the same kind of shot Hitch used in *Notorious* to close in on the key Ingrid Bergman is trying to pass to Cary Grant at a crowded party.

For those who don't care about reading the classic mysteries, but enjoy mystery films, Hitchcock's *Young and Innocent* should be quite entertaining. Though not rated as one of his great films, it has its moments and isn't a waste of anyone's time.

I might carp a bit about the lack of chemistry between the romantic leads, but for me the major drawback is the way the Tisdall character is drawn in the film. He seems too nonchalant about the mess he's in through most of the film—especially for a man who faints dead away when he learns the dead actress has left him 10,000 pounds sterling in her will. The result is a sort of *Thirty-Nine Steps Lite*, brisk and entertaining, but not very credible at any time.

Tey's novel, on the other hand, has a lot going for it and advances the character of Inspector Alan Grant a good deal, showing him capable of making miscalculations of a major kind while pursuing a case, yet still able to buckle down and get to the bottom of things before it's too late.

The book and Hitchcock's film are readily available these days, and checking them out is well worth the effort.

Jim Thompson
Pop. 1280

The 1964 novel and the 1981 movie *Coup de Torchon*

Since the French film critics invented the term film noir to describe the dark, pessimistic mystery movies coming out of Hollywood in the 1940s, it should be no surprise that French filmmakers always have doted on the works of our best noir novelists, including James M. Cain, Cornell Woolrich and Jim Thompson.

It still was a surprise to learn that Bertrand Tavernier's Oscar-nominated 1981 French film *Coup de Torchon* actually was based on Thompson's 1964 pulp fiction novel *Pop. 1280*, especially since Tavernier's film takes place in French Equatorial Africa in 1938 while Thompson's novel is deeply rooted in the racist atmosphere of the Jim Crow American South.

Yet if you first read Thompson's severely pessimistic and darkly comic novel, then see the film, you realize that the two remote worlds are not so far apart after all—and the French and American sensibilities dovetail quite nicely.

Thompson's novel is about Nick Corey, the sheriff of Potts County, a nowhere spot in the rural South long before the coming of civil rights. He's a handsome man, incredibly appealing to the seriously deprived women of the territory, even though he's generally regarded as only a step or two above moron in intellect. He's also lazy, cowardly and lets the high mucky-mucks of his desolate little township push him around something awful.

Nick is married to an abusive slattern named Myra, who keeps her halfwit adult brother around the house and lavishes all her affection on him—perhaps even more so than would be natural, even in the rural South that Tennessee Williams wrote about so often. Nick doesn't much mind his wife's

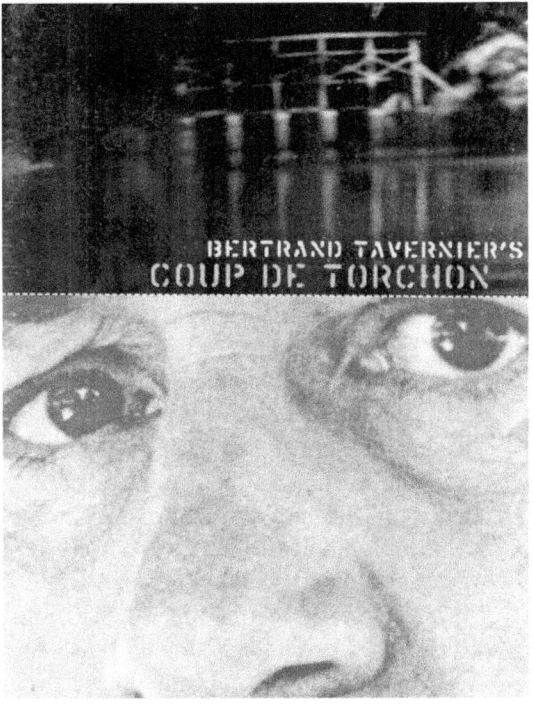

The DVD package cover for *Coup de Torchon*, the 1981 French film version of Jim Thompson's novel *Pop. 1280*. The movie shifted the locale from the American South to French West Africa (Criterion Collection).

coldness because he regularly visits Rose, the much-abused wife of the town's most notorious wife-beating drunkard, and pleasures her no end. At the same time, Nick longs to renew his relationship with the lovely Amy, the woman he was engaged to marry before he got swept off his feet by Myra.

Now most of us surely would advise Nick to divorce Myra, throw Rose's husband in jail and introduce Rose to a divorce lawyer, then either marry Amy or Rose.

But Nick is anything but a man of action when we first meet him. He's so used to looking the other way when laws are broken that the town's two most prominent pimps routinely walk all over him without fear of reprisal. In fact, just about everybody pushes him around except the town's African-Americans, who consider him reasonably fair and not much of a threat.

The turning point in Nick's life comes when he takes the train to the next county to see Ken Lacey, head lawman of a much bigger territory, to seek his advice about how to handle the pimps. Lacey, who has nothing but contempt for Nick, gives him a vivid demonstration of what to do: He and his deputy both kick Nick in the ass. His point: If somebody does something to you, do it back to him twice as hard.

In fact, Ken explains, he would blow the two pimps away and solve the problem pronto.

Nick muddles that one around in his mind a good deal on the way home. He's certainly aware he's the town's laughingstock because Myra constantly reminds him. And he knows he almost never forces his ideas of law and order on anyone. Instead, he usually says, "I won't say you're right, but I won't say you're wrong either" or some variation on that.

So Nick decides it's time to wipe the slate clean. After all, he's up for election again soon and he might not be re-elected if he's still the town fool. He takes Ken's advice and starts by blowing the two pimps away.

Once Nick starts doing things like that, we discover he's a lot craftier than we thought. Next thing we know, he's arranging some nice payback schemes for Ken Lacey, Myra, her halfwit brother and others. And the nice thing is he's such a dissembling goof-off that nobody ever suspects he'd do any of the things he winds up doing.

Thompson's novel is wry, ironic and uncommonly funny, considering the stuff that goes on. Nick Corey is a character you might expect Erskine Caldwell and Raymond Chandler to have dreamed up together one evening over brandies with Alfred Hitchcock.

French filmmaker Tavernier (*The Clockmaker*) read the novel in the late 1960s and loved it, but he couldn't figure out how to translate the Jim Thompson milieu into the culture of France. Then, after maybe five years, he read a book by Celine about French colonial life and suddenly hit upon the idea for the film that became *Coup de Torchon*, which in English means "Clean Slate."

If he set the story in French colonial Africa during the 1930s, he'd have the same cultural remoteness and racial tensions that Thompson found in the American South. Suddenly, the pieces fell together. To write the screenplay he hired Jean Aurenche, who knew French Africa quite well. Together they worked out the translation of all the major Thompson elements into French terms.

In the 1982 film, Nick Corey becomes Lucien Cordier. To play the part, Tavenier departed from Thompson's concept and cast one of France's best character actors, Philippe Noiret, who's overweight, balding and grubby-looking—far from the literary model. But Noiret can play the Thompson brand of fool perfectly because he has the light of shrewdness in his eyes, which is perfect for the role.

The Tavernier-Aurenche script hews pretty closely to the book's outline, although the pending election for sheriff is eliminated and Amy, the ex-fiancée, becomes Anne, the town's new schoolteacher.

Lucien is still picked upon by everybody, starting with his wife, now called Huguette and played by Stephane Audran. Rose was played by Isabelle Huppert, one of France's hottest young stars, and Ken Lacey—now called Marcel Chavasson—is perfectly played by Guy Marchand.

In many ways, the territorial African setting works even better for the story's race issues. The two pimps spend much of their spare time taking target practice on the bloated corpses of blacks, which are being dumped into the river upstream by tribesmen who believe the water will "purify" the bodies during a disease epidemic.

Tavernier says he did everything he could to reproduce Thompson's "dark perception of life," to preserve the story's bleak humor and to retain its "strange, unpleasant violence" while also showing its effects on people. Made on location in Senegal, *Coup de Torchon* was shot with a hand-held Steadicam, which Tavernier decided helped create the "unbalanced" effect he wanted for the imagery.

The result is a very dark but entertaining film that succeeds in rendering the Thompson story as well as it might have been if filmed in a stateside environment—and perhaps even better.

The opening scene, for instance, does not occur in the book: Lucien watches from cover as black children try to build a fire during a solar eclipse on the African plain. Then he helps them get the fire going. In the final scene, Lucien is back watching the children again, but this time he takes his gun out and contemplates killing them before apparently realizing how pessimistic his outlook on life has become.

Thompson's point seems to be Tavernier's as well: Once you clean the slate and become a different person than you were, perhaps you'll gain the respect of everyone but yourself.

Jim Thompson
After Dark, My Sweet

The 1955 novel and the 1990 movie

It's easy to figure out why Jim Thompson's slim novel *After Dark, My Sweet* waited 35 years before someone finally turned it into a motion picture. You can almost hear the studio boss yelling at the guy who first suggested it as a movie, "Are you nuts? The main guy is an escapee from the loony bin and his leading lady is a lush. If that's not bad enough, they kidnap a kid! And damn near everybody gets killed! Who's gonna pay good money to see that?"

Well, as it turned out, not much of anyone. James Foley's 1990 film version of *After Dark, My Sweet* was not exactly a box office bonanza. Still, a lot of critics found things to like about it. And it turned out to be one of the most faithful adaptations of Thompson's dark, twisted noir tales ever put on the screen.

Thompson still remains a cult figure on the American literary scene several decades after he died in almost total obscurity. He had always predicted he wouldn't be famous until maybe 20 years after his death. As a matter of fact, he became a hot property almost exactly on that schedule. Now nearly all his 29 novels—most of them paperback originals from the 1940s and '50s—are back in print and scholars are poring over his unique contribution to the genre of literary noir.

Thompson always had an affinity for film and he ended up writing screenplays for two career-making films by director Stanley Kubrick, *The Killing* and *Paths of Glory*. The French, who first recognized the genre of noir, turned two Thompson books into acclaimed films: Bernard Tavernier's *Coup de Torchon*, based on Thompson's *Pop. 1240*, and Alain Corneau's *Serie Noire*, adapted from Thompson's *A Hell of a Woman*. Burt Kennedy filmed *The Killer Inside Me* in 1976 and Sam Peckinpah made Thompson's *The Getaway* in 1972. Roger Donaldson remade *The Getaway* in 1994. Stephen Frears filmed Thompson's *The Grifters* in 1990, earning rave reviews. For a time, it seemed there was a rush to see who could get Thompson projects on the screen first.

Most of Thompson's stories were about troubled people on the fringes of society who wind up in a crisis of one kind or another. In *After Dark, My Sweet*, ex-prizefighter William "Kid" Collins is haunted by his memories of beating a man to a pulp in the ring. Unable to control his outbursts of extreme violence, he has spent the past several years in a mental hospital. When we first meet him, he has escaped and is going nowhere fast as a drifter in the American southwest.

Jason Patric is a drifter who falls under the spell of sexy Rachel Ward in *After Dark, My Sweet*, based on the darkly sinister Jim Thompson novel (Avenue Entertainment).

In a small town saloon, he's befriended by a good-looking widow, Fay Anderson, who's attracted to his handsome face and trim body. She's a lush, going down the tubes rapidly, but she latches onto Collins—she calls him "Collie" because "you look like one"—and draws him into a plot being devised by her associate, "Uncle Bud" Stoker, to kidnap the little boy of a rich family living nearby and collect a big ransom.

Thompson's lean, grim tale is really about Collins' struggle with his own conscience as he finally realizes he's being set up to steal the boy, then take the fall. He begins to feel protective toward the little boy, who turns out to be afflicted with a severe case of diabetes, and that makes Collins' relations with Uncle Bud and Fay go sour very quickly.

In the film, little-known Jason Patric played Collins. He has remained on the fringes of stardom ever since. (He played Jim Bowie in the 2004 *The Alamo*.) Fay was played by Rachel Ward, whose biggest part was the female lead in the TV miniseries *The Thorn Birds* (1983). Uncle Bud was played by veteran Hollywood bad guy Bruce Dern.

Foley's film follows the original storyline quite closely. Its primary concession to box office concerns was a decision to make Fay less the fall-down drunk she is in the book and not quite so nasty. (She's still nasty enough, though. When Collins tells her he doesn't "get the point," she tells him to feel around on top of his head!) The film also shows us a good deal more bed-bouncing between Collins and Fay than Thompson could get away with in 1955. The finale is shifted to an airport, which makes a bit more sense as the site for a showdown between kidnappers and police.

Without a real hero to root for in Thompson's downbeat novel, the film shoves Collins into a quasi-heroic situation, making him the only one with any obvious moral or ethical values. Given that Collins is an escapee from a nuthouse, Thompson's comment on the general level of American values seems cynical, to say the least.

If the Collins character was just a bit more appealing—and Patric's rather goofy performance more interesting—*After Dark, My Sweet* might have been one of the most successful attempts at bringing Thompson's truly offbeat point of view to the movie screen.

S.S. Van Dine

The Kennel Murder Case

The 1933 novel and the 1933 movie

Whenever mystery movie fans talk about the series of 14 *Philo Vance* mysteries made between 1929 and 1947, there's hardly ever any disagreement about which was the best.

That would be *The Kennel Murder Case*, released by Warner Bros. in 1933. It was directed by Michael Curtiz (*Casablanca, The Adventures of Robin Hood*) and starred the best-ever Philo Vance, wonderful William Powell, in his signature dapper detective role—a whole year before he played Dashiell Hammett's Nick Charles in *The Thin Man*.

Without a doubt, *The Kennel Murder Case* is still entertaining more than 80 years later. It has a complex yet easily followed plot, lots of interesting suspects, a crackling finish and a super cast that included Mary Astor, Ralph Morgan, Eugene Pallette and Jack LaRue. But Powell rules in this film, smoothly solving the mystery with the utmost sophistication, seldom even breaking a sweat.

The movie does, however, abandon many features of the 1933 novel by S.S. Van Dine, the pen name of author Willard Wright. For example, it completely leaves Van Dine himself—Vance calls him "Van"—out of the story. In the Philo Vance mysteries, Van Dine functions as the Dr. Watson figure, accompanying Vance on his cases as a "consulting detective" to the New York Police Department and serving as narrator of the action. Actually, fair-minded critics should face the fact that we really don't miss "Van" in the movie. He's so invisible in the book—he never really does anything but watch what Vance is doing—that we hardly notice when Vance does his own narration every now and then.

In the book, Vance and Van are invited to accompany District Attorney John Markham and Homicide Detective Sgt. Ernest Heath to the home of wealthy art collector Archer Coe, who has committed suicide by gunshot in his bedroom. All the windows and the door are locked from the inside. They see Coe's body through the keyhole in the door, seated in a chair, a gun in one hand, a bullet hole in his forehead.

Vance knew Coe, who shared his enthusiasm for collecting rare ancient Chinese porcelain vases, and rather doubts the man would commit suicide. He talks with some of the other people in Coe's life, and it seems many of them had reason to want him dead. Could he have been murdered?

After the door is broken down, the medical examiner concludes that Coe *was* murdered. He had been struck a heavy blow on the head, then stabbed with a dagger, which caused an internal hemorrhage that killed him. He was shot after he had already died.

Almost immediately, another mystery arises: Where is the dead man's angry brother, Brisbane Coe? He supposedly left on a train journey, but never arrived at his destination. Did he get off the train at the next stop, double back to the house and commit the murder?

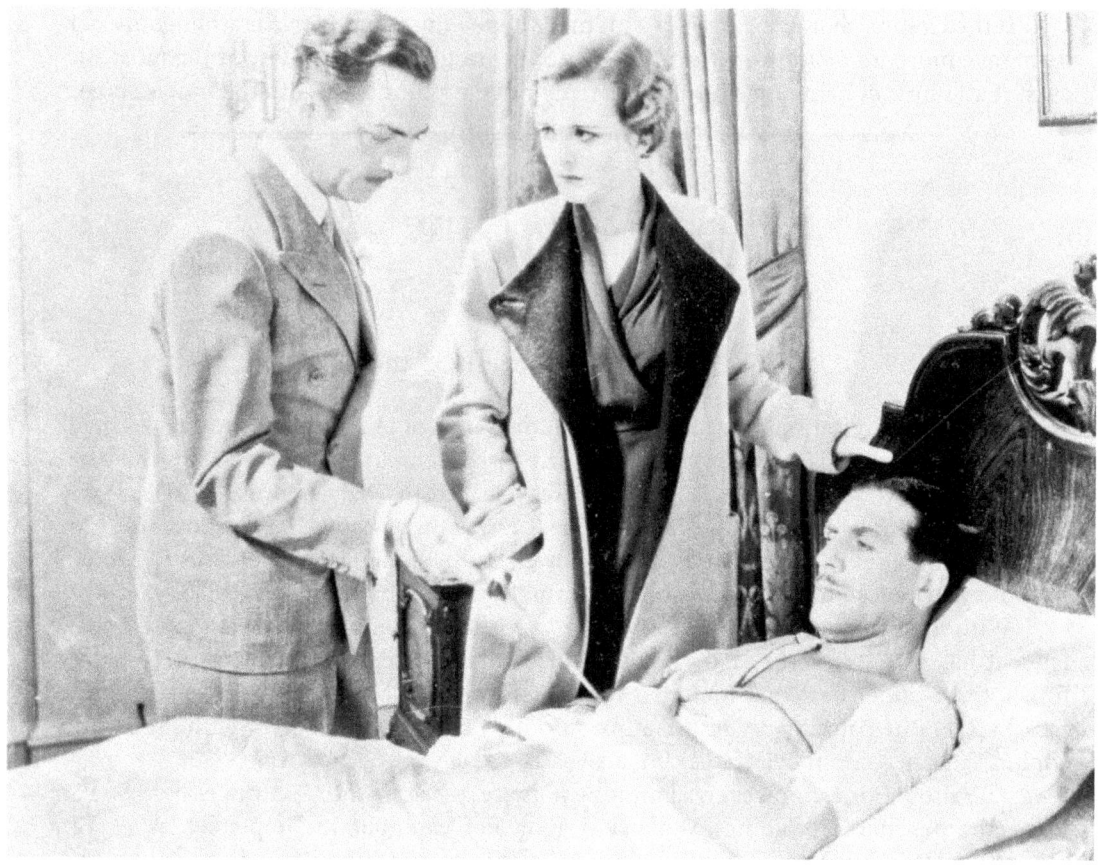

William Powell (left) is detective Philo Vance in the 1933 mystery *The Kennel Murder Case*. With him are leading lady Mary Astor and Paul Cavanagh (Warner Bros).

That's a firm possibility until Brisbane Coe's body is found in a downstairs closet, stabbed with a similar instrument.

Then a most perplexing third mystery turns up: They find a seriously wounded Scottie dog behind a curtain, apparently hit over the head and left for dead. The dog is a proud specimen, a show-quality animal, but the Coes hated dogs and wouldn't have them in the house. Nobody in the house has ever seen the animal. How did it get into the house and why did someone try to kill it?

In the novel, nobody goes near a kennel until the final chapters when Vance believes that the key to solving the murders will be to find out who owns this wounded animal. Vance has a vet patch the animal up and takes it around to various show judges and dog breeders who specialize in Scottish terriers.

In contrast, Curtiz begins the movie at a dog show where Vance is showing his own Scottish terrier in a competition that also includes the Scottie owned by Archer Coe, the dog-hater of the book. Coe's dog is outclassed in the judging by the dog owned by another wealthy man, Sir Thomas MacDonald, a character who doesn't appear in the book. When MacDonald's dog is found beaten to death after the show, MacDonald vows, "I'll kill the man who did this!"

The new opening not only serves to get us into the dog world, somewhat justifying the movie's title, but also sets up a number of possible suspects with strong motives for wanting Archer Coe dead. Besides MacDonald, there's Coe's niece Hilda Lake (Mary Astor), who lives in the Coe house and is unhappy with her uncle because he's stingy with money and opposes her plan to marry and leave his home.

There's also Grassi (Jack LaRue), who had been putting together a huge deal to purchase Coe's Chinese porcelain collection, before Coe reneged. Liang, the family cook, is secretly working with the Chinese government to recover the porcelains in Coe's collection. Raymond Wrede (Ralph Morgan) is just a friend of Coe in the book, but becomes his personal secretary in the movie. Wrede, who is poorly treated by Coe, wants to marry Hilda. The movie even gives the family butler a sinister criminal background that he doesn't have in the book.

All this is very effective for the movie because it arouses suspicions about virtually everybody. The enhanced motives are a worthy addition to a movie that sacrifices lots of boring material in the book that sets Philo Vance up as an expert in Chinese porcelain vases as well as Scottish terriers.

There's another significant change for the movie: The dog that was left for dead in the book is no longer a Scottish terrier, but is now a Doberman that nobody can identify. By switching dogs, the film saves all the time needed in the book for Vance to identify the owner of the Scottie. It also sets up the film's payoff scene where the recovered Doberman is brought into the room where Vance has assembled all the suspects—and immediately attacks the man who hit it with a poker on the night of the murder, the killer of Archer Coe. (In the book, there is a Doberman, but he's not the dog found in the murder house. In a similar scene to the movie's climax, the Dobie rips out the killer's throat, finishing him off, and the police shoot the dog.)

In one of the movie's highlights, Vance figures out how the killer got rid of Coe while leaving him in a locked room. The movie simplifies it grandly, but it's all very understandable and impressive. The explanation of how the wounded dog got into the Coe house is also handled skillfully.

Philo Vance was not a very original detective, but if you (like me) grew up on American sleuths and had never heard of Hercule Poirot or Lord Peter Wimsey, you probably thought he was the epitome of the suave gentleman detective, as I did until I grew up and started reading British mysteries.

Just the same, Powell eschews many of the trademark Philo Vance mannerisms, including his habit of saying, "Dontcha know," "sportin'" instead of "sporting," etc. Still, Powell's Vance was always dressed to the nines—often with calfskin gloves, flower in his lapel, carrying a walking stick.

At the end of the *Kennel Murder Case* novel, Vance adopts the bruised little Scottish terrier. In the movie, he starts out owning one—and that plucky little guy gets a lot of screen time, just as another dog, Nick Charles' Asta, would in Powell's *Thin Man* movies at MGM.

If you've never read the book or seen the movie, please do both. The book is a brisk read and a perfect example of the American pseudo–British detective novel, but the movie is a mystery classic in all senses of the word. There are some beautiful, low-cost copies available on DVD.

S.S. Van Dine
The Gracie Allen Murder Case

The 1938 novel and the 1939 movie

Certainly one of the oddest match-ups in mystery history came in 1938 when best-selling mystery novelist S.S. Van Dine decided to put two of his real-life celebrity friends, comedienne Gracie Allen and her husband, George Burns, into one of his Philo Vance mysteries.

The result was *The Gracie Allen Murder Case*. If the book sounded like a movie deal in the making, that suspicion was confirmed a year later when Paramount released the movie version, starring Warren William as Philo Vance and—what a surprise!—Gracie Allen as herself. The script came first and then the book, which may account for why they're so remarkably different.

In my view, both Philo Vance and Gracie Allen are "acquired tastes" that I've been trying, in vain, to acquire for more than half a century.

After reading quite a few of the original Philo Vance novels and seeing the films made from them, I've concluded that Vance was a pompous ass and more or less the American version of Dorothy L. Sayers' titled English sleuth Lord Peter Wimsey. As for Gracie Allen, her oddball brand of daffiness is best taken in very small quantities. Putting these two characters together may have seemed like an inspired idea in 1938, but it now looks like something Van Dine dreamed up on a dare, possibly after having too many sloe gin fizzes.

Van Dine was a pseudonym used by Willard Wright, an art critic and editor when he wasn't writing mystery novels. He usually appeared in the Philo Vance stories as "Van," the Dr. Watson–like narrator and sidekick to the wealthy and erudite Vance. He's in the book version of *The Gracie Allen Murder Case*, but doesn't show up in the movie.

In fact, the Nat Perrin screenplay is superior to the novel, so it's too bad Van Dine didn't just adapt Perrin's script as a book instead of writing his own much weaker version of the story. For my taste, *The Gracie Allen Murder Case* is by far the worst of the Philo Vance novels and might have been even crummier without Perrin's ideas about what should be going on.

In the novel, Vance meets Gracie Allen by accident and is rather smitten by her. He often refers to her as a "child" and clearly finds her awfully attractive. When we meet her in the book, she's still single and is working at a perfume factory where her boyfriend, George Burns, is an expert "scentologist" who mixes up new perfumes for the company.

If you're familiar with Gracie's comedy, you'll know that she constantly told improbable stories about her brother. Or did she have several brothers? Frankly, I can't remember. In the Van Dine novel, her brother Philip and her mother are major characters. Both are left out of the movie.

In fact, so is George Burns. That may seem quite strange since Burns & Allen were big radio stars in 1939, had made quite a few movies together and always worked as a team. Maybe George read the script and realized his part didn't amount to much, so he opted out. Or, more likely, Gracie wanted to see what she could do on her own. She again flew solo two years later, playing Mrs. North in MGM's movie version of the radio mystery show *Mr. and Mrs. North.*

In the book, George becomes a murder suspect and goes to jail. In the movie, this happens to a young man named Bill Brown, who fills in for the Burns character but never gets very romantic with Gracie. (His on-screen romantic object is played by Ellen Drew.)

In the book, an escaped convict wants to kill New York District Attorney John F-X Markham, who sent him to prison. The convict is connected to a crime ring in which nightclub owner Dan Mirche is a key figure. Several murders take place and Gracie helps Philo Vance solve them, usually quite by accident. In one case, a cigarette butt

The poster for *The Gracie Allen Murder Case*, the unusual Philo Vance mystery movie featuring the famous radio comedy star playing herself (Universal).

is thrown from a passing car and burns a hole in her new dress. She saves the butt and it turns out to be laced with poison. Later, it plays a key role in Vance's solution of the crimes that complicate the mystery.

The movie retains that plotline, but scrambles it up quite a bit, having the dress-burning accident happen at a family picnic sponsored by the perfume company run by a relative of Gracie's. Perrin's script also kills off one character, sexy dancer Dixie Del Marr, who's alive and kicking when the book ends.

One great improvement the movie makes over the book comes in the comic banter assigned to Gracie. Van Dine couldn't write comedy lines very well because her routines in the book aren't at all funny and just underscore the dumbness of the Gracie character.

Perrin does a much better job with Gracie's lines, especially in one scene where Vance comes up with a major clue and Gracie tells him he has "the nose of a greyhound." Warren William, who's playing Vance, had a fairly prominent nose and he seems somewhat taken aback by her "compliment" until she adds, "But don't worry. The rest of your face is pretty."

William, who had played Philo Vance in *The Dragon Murder Case* (1934), seems old and burned-out in *The Gracie Allen Murder Case*, even though he was only 44 when he made it. Gracie, who was 37, looked about the way she always looked. Maybe William looked burned-out after too much exposure to Gracie's daffiness She really needed George Burns to keep her properly stifled and William's Philo Vance isn't up to the job.

If I've left the impression that Perrin's lines for Gracie were always on target, I should correct that by pointing out an example where he missed pretty badly. In that sequence,

Vance reminds Gracie, "We're here for clues," and she tells him she has a lot of them. Naturally he asks her "Where?" and Gracie blithely answers, "In my clues closet." Ouch!

The movie succumbs to one temptation it should have resisted: A climactic screwball slapstick sequence with Gracie riding on the back of a motorcycle driven by a cop through heavy Manhattan traffic, desperately trying to get to Vance in time to stop him from smoking a poisoned cigarette.

I guess I'm suggesting you skip reading the book because it's a turkey by any standard. Watch the movie if you like, but only if you're seriously addicted to Gracie Allen's humor.

Ethel Lina White
Some Must Watch

The 1933 novel and the 1946 and 1975 movies *The Spiral Staircase*

Ethel Lina White was one of the U.K.'s great innovators in the genre of the mystery thriller, but her novels are little read today except for those that were turned into famous movies, such as Alfred Hitchcock's *The Lady Vanishes* (from her 1936 novel *The Wheel Spins*) and *The Spiral Staircase* (based on her novel *Some Must Watch*).

A classic "woman in jeopardy" thriller, *Some Must Watch* (1933) takes place almost entirely in the country home of the Warren family in the English countryside. Helen, the heroine, is a new maidservant described by White as a petite redhead, "small and pale as a slip of crescent moon." She is intimidated by nearly everyone in this peculiar household, most especially Lady Warren, an ornery invalid who may have a loaded pistol hidden somewhere in her room.

Like most English domestics in the early years of the 20th century, Helen is not expected to show much backbone when dealing with her employers, who tend to order her around quite freely. Consequently, she's most definitely not someone you would expect to bravely stand up to a demented strangler who's preying upon young women in the region surrounding the Warren estate.

But here's something important to note right away about the Helen of White's original novel: She is *not* a mute, as she is in all the movie versions of White's story.

One can argue about the addition of such a gimmick to a novel that's quite tense without it, but I'm inclined to believe screenwriter Mel Dinelli and director Robert Siodmak came up with just the right story twist to make us deeply sympathize with Helen even before we know anything about her character. And the fact that she's mute was something that could be heavily promoted to make the public respond to her plight. The appeal is obvious: Your heart automatically goes out to a woman who knows a strangler is coming for her—and she can't even scream for help!

Could *The Spiral Staircase* be just as much a thriller if the filmmakers hadn't made Helen mute? Of course. She is, after all, alone in a creepy house two miles from the nearest town. Even if she could scream, who would hear her? Telephone service could be knocked out by the raging storm outside, so it wouldn't matter if she had the voice of a professional hog-caller!

Dorothy McGuire plays a mute servant checking on the condition of ailing Ethel Barrymore in the 1946 thriller *The Spiral Staircase*. In Ethel Lina White's novel *Some Must Watch*, the servant isn't a mute (ABC and the James Bawden Collection).

Siodmak and Dinelli realized that most ticket-buyers would have a subconscious fear of being unable to speak. By adding that little gimmick, it made everyone in the theater instantly bond with desperate Helen.

White also dreamed up some really creepy characters to keep Helen company in that shadowy Gothic mansion, then added a terrible storm that cuts her off from help and prevents escape.

First there are Lady Warren's stepchildren: Prof. Warren, a widower, and Miss Warren, his unmarried sister, who runs the household. Helen thinks of them as "academic, frigid, and well-bred, but otherwise devoid of the vital human interest." Also living in the house are the professor's son Newton and Newton's wife Simone, a sexy and beautiful vixen who's "an experimentalist with men." At the time, she seems intent upon experimenting with Stephen Rice, who lives at the house as the professor's "resident pupil."

On the household staff are Oates, the handyman, and Mrs. Oates, whose domain is the kitchen—and, it so happens, the wine cellar. (She likes to chug down prodigious amounts of liquor from the basement stock.) The latest addition to the staff is Nurse

Barker, a grim, mean-spirited creature who more resembles a man than a woman. A frequent visitor is Lady Warren's physician Dr. Parry, a young fellow who has taken a fancy to Helen.

In the novel, White finds ways to leave Helen alone and at the mercy of the killer. For example, Lady Warren, who always seems hovering near a fatal attack, is confined to bed. The professor has been drugged with too much sleeping potion. Mr. Oates is locked outside in the raging storm and his wife has passed out, dead drunk. And so on. If you're a strangler, you couldn't have a better setup.

The first film version of *Some Must Watch* was released in 1946 under a new—and much more provocative—title, *The Spiral Staircase*. Though there is a spiral staircase in the novel, it plays no significant role in the events of the storyline. But who's going to quibble. It's definitely a better title for a thriller than *Some Must Watch*.

The film was the first of several under a somewhat unusual collaboration between RKO studios and David O. Selznick, the phenomenally successful independent producer of *Gone with the Wind*, *Rebecca* and some of Hollywood's most important productions of the 1930s and 1940s. Selznick's company, Vanguard Films, owned the rights to the novel and had two of the film's leading actors, Dorothy McGuire and Ethel Barrymore, under personal contract. Selznick also provided the Dinelli screenplay, director Siodmak and producer Dore Schary while RKO supplied all the studio facilities, the rest of the cast and crew and the network for distribution to theaters.

As a result, *The Spiral Staircase* has the lush, big-budget look of all Selznick films and most specifically resembles the classic thriller he made the year before with director Alfred Hitchcock: *Spellbound*. In that film, Gregory Peck played a psychiatrist whose strange behavior was motivated by a long-buried psychological trauma. Hitchcock made significant use of dream sequences to portray the inner torment of Peck.

In *The Spiral Staircase*, Siodmak does the same thing with two leading characters. Helen lost her ability to speak in childhood because of the psychological trauma of watching her parents die in a fire. She dreams she's marrying Dr. Parry (Kent Smith), but can't say "I do" because of her affliction. And Prof. Warren, who's phobic about women with disabilities, dreams of Helen with a blank space where her mouth ought to be.

Roy Webb's haunting musical score makes use of the Theremin, the same eerie electronic musical instrument used to such good effect by Hitchcock in *Spellbound*, for those scenes where we see closeups of the eyeball of the killer, peering at his next victim.

Since the exclusive working partnership between Selznick and Hitchcock had only a short time left to run in 1946, it's easy to imagine the producer was using other directors like Siodmak to make *The Spiral Staircase* and other thrillers in his inventory that Hitchcock wouldn't be able to direct.

Whatever the reason, *The Spiral Staircase* is clearly the most Hitchcockian film Siodmak ever made—and, like Hitchcock, he was not afraid to make fundamental changes in a story to make it more cinematic.

The first big change was a decision to shift the entire locale from England to America's rural New England, circa 1904, no doubt to allow for an almost all–American cast. Then Helen (McGuire) was made a mute. Stephen, the resident pupil, was totally reinvented. In the film, he's not a student but a playboy, the younger son of invalid Mrs. Warren (Barrymore). Simone, his sexy wife, is gone. In her place is a character invented for the movie: Blanche (Rhonda Fleming), the lovely unmarried secretary to the professor (George Brent). Blanche is being romanced by the playboy.

For the movie, even "Otto," the Oates' dog, gets an overhaul and becomes "Carlton," a rather sleepy bulldog who hasn't the energy to protect anyone.

Making Helen a mute gave young McGuire the chance to give a bravura performance, more than matching the forceful presence of that great stage and screen veteran, Ethel Barrymore, as the elderly Mrs. Warren. McGuire's big moment comes when Helen realizes she's alone in the house with the strangler and she must descend the staircase to the phone and try to summon help by shattering the grip of psychological paralysis that has taken away her voice.

Except for the Freudian mumbo-jumbo about Helen's mute condition, the movie ends much the same way: Elderly Mrs. Warren shoots the killer with her pistol and saves Helen from certain death.

The Spiral Staircase was a box office hit and the profits, split 50–50 between RKO and Selznick's company, made everybody happy. At Academy Awards time, Ethel Barrymore was nominated in the Best Supporting Actress category, but lost out to Anne Baxter (*The Razor's Edge*). Robert Siodmak was nominated for Best Director, but for *The Killers*, one of the films that secured his reputation as one of the great film noir directors.

In 1975, Warner Bros. produced a color, widescreen remake of *The Spiral Staircase*, based on Dinelli's 1946 screenplay rather than the original novel. It borrows many things from the 1946 film, even the giant closeups of the killer's eyeball while stalking his victims. Helen (Jacqueline Bisset) is again a mute, traumatized by the fiery deaths of her husband and child (not her parents), which causes her to lose her ability to talk.

Director Peter Collinson and screenwriter Andrew Meredith made lots of other key changes, including updating it to contemporary times—the 1970s. Helen is no longer anybody's servant. Instead, she's a widow who goes to the remote country estate of her own family. The professor is turned into Helen's Uncle Sherman (Christopher Plummer), who runs a "psychological institute." Blanche, his secretary, is a much more salacious lady than Rhonda Fleming's Blanche in the 1946 film. She's played with aggressive sexuality by Gayle Hunnicutt. "Steven" (John Philip Law) is an unmarried playboy, who's having it on with Blanche. Elaine Stritch is the hard-edged nurse to Helen's invalid but well-armed grandmother (Mildred Dunnock), who fills the place of Lady Warren–Mrs. Warren in the book and earlier film.

Made in England, the 1975 film generates almost no suspense and somehow the bright colors and modern settings make it hard to believe much of anything in the shadowy storyline.

At least two television versions of *The Spiral Staircase* have been filmed to date. The first was made by NBC in 1961 with Hayley Mills, Elizabeth Montgomery, Eddie Albert and Gig Young. In 2000, a new version was done by Fox Family Channel, a cable network, with Nicollette Sheridan as Helen.

As it stands today, the other film versions are barely remembered, but the 1946 *Spiral Staircase* is regarded as one of Hollywood's enduring thrillers, even with all the liberties it took with the original novel.

Cornell Woolrich
Black Alibi

The 1942 novel and the 1943 movie *The Leopard Man*

In 1942, RKO persuaded writer and former studio publicist Val Lewton to head a new production unit set up to produce low-budget horror films. RKO hoped to rake in the sort of profits that rival Universal Pictures had enjoyed for a decade with its steady lineup of monster movies. Though not all the films were profitable, Lewton produced nine films between 1942 and 1946 that today are regarded as masterpieces of understated horror.

One of them, made in 1943, Lewton's second year running the horror unit, was *The Leopard Man*, an adaptation of Cornell Woolrich's 1942 novel *Black Alibi*. Though Ardel Wray's screenplay departed significantly from the original story, the film is an offbeat thriller with several bloodcurdling sequences taken almost directly from the novel.

Woolrich's reputation was based largely on his series of *Black* novels of the early 1940s. (They all have the word *Black* in their titles.) In the 1960s, French New Wave film critics proclaimed Woolrich the father of the literary style they called *roman noir* because of his books' dark themes and atmosphere of paranoia. The French critics dubbed the films made from such stories films noir because of the grim, shadowy style filmmakers used when adapting such stories to the screen.

That style never was more evident than in *Black Alibi*, the story of a trained jaguar that's spooked during a nightclub performance in one of the largest cities in South America and runs off into the night, terrorizing the public for days.

In the most harrowing section of *Black Alibi*, imaginative teenager Teresa Delgado is sent off after dark to run an errand for her mother. Teresa is afraid to go because she has heard the jaguar is on the loose, but her mother insists and even locks the door behind her. Teresa dreads the dark route she must take beneath a railroad trestle, along an aqueduct and down shadowy streets. As she returns from the store, she senses the escaped beast is near, stalking her. She runs for her life and pounds on the door of her house. But her mother, certain that Teresa's imagination has taken command of her senses, wastes precious time unlocking the door while her daughter screams for help. Before the mother gets it unlocked, she sees a puddle of Teresa's blood seep under the door.

In the capable hands of director Jacques Tourneur, that sequence becomes a masterpiece of visual terror in *The Leopard Man*, an unforgettable sequence that ranks among the most terrifying in movie history.

Black Alibi and *The Leopard Man* are classic examples of the work of both author Woolrich and producer Lewton because they place the reader-moviegoer in a world governed by superstition, an environment where evil men and women can have their way because they do their wicked deeds in the shadows where few are willing to shine any light.

Though *Black Alibi* is still a chilling story to read, the film is even scarier because the gloomy style of director Tourneur so enhances the terror hinted at in Woolrich's novel. The changes made in the original by the filmmakers are plentiful, but they don't

Pursuers Richard Martin (left) and Dennis O'Keefe, right, apprehend villainous James Bell (center) in the midst of a procession of cult members in *The Leopard Man*, the frightening film made from Cornell Woolrich's novel *Black Alibi* (RKO and National Screen Service).

detract from the purpose of the original: to fill us with a sense of dread that ultimately leaves us truly terrified until the central mystery is finally resolved..

An example of one major change: The setting is shifted from the mythical town of Ciudad Real in South America to a town in New Mexico, a border state where the presence of Latino people and their superstitions is equally valid. The jaguar becomes a leopard, no doubt because there was a black leopard available to rent for the movie—the same one, named "Dynamite," that Lewton and Tourneur used in their first film together, *Cat People*, in 1942.

When Teresa (Margaret Landry) is sent on her late night walk into terror, she's buying cornmeal for her father's dinner, not charcoal for the fire, her mission in the book.

Most importantly, the movie changes the villain who's responsible for the deaths attributed to the escaped animal. In the book it's the local lawman, Robles, who masquerades as the "leopard man" to kill young women, but the movie reduces Robles (Ben Bard) to a minor player and invents a new killer: Dr. Galbraith (James Bell), the curator of a local museum.

Both book and movie have the same hero, publicity man Jerry Manning, who starts the whole thing by acquiring the leopard to get publicity for his client, entertainer Kiki Walker. In the book, Manning gets romantically involved with an American girl, Marjorie King, whose friend Sally is a victim of the leopard. Manning believes a man is the real killer and persuades Marjorie to stay in town to help trap him. Marjorie and Sally aren't in the movie, so Manning (Dennis O'Keefe) winds up romancing his client, Kiki (Jean Brooks), who takes over the function Marjorie served in the book.

Despite its wholesale changes, *The Leopard Man* is a pretty satisfactory adaptation of *Black Alibi*—and a really exciting film to the very end.

Cornell Woolrich
Rear Window

The 1942 novelette, first published as
It Had to Be Murder in *Dime Detective Magazine*,
and the 1954 and 1998 movies *Rear Window*

Of the many movies made from the stories of Cornell Woolrich, one of the founding fathers of the dark literary genre, the most famous is Alfred Hitchcock's 1954 thriller *Rear Window*, a box office champion in its day. It's still widely respected more than half a century later as one of Hitchcock's greatest films.

Hitchcock, true to form, made changes in Woolrich's original tale, adding many characters and incidents to the basic story first published as *It Had to Be Murder* in a pulp detective magazine during World War II. The story is about a man named Hal Jeffries, stuck in his apartment day in and day out, recovering from a broken leg. To relieve the boredom, he watches his neighbors in the apartment house across the courtyard and begins to suspect that one of them, Thorwald, has murdered his wife. His efforts to prove this place him in jeopardy as the man across the way finally realizes someone has been spying on him.

It was a foregone conclusion that something would have to be added to the story if Hitchcock was going to flesh it out to feature length. Hitchcock and screenwriter John Michael Hayes give their hero a slightly different name, L.B. Jeffries, and an occupation he never had in the book, freelance photographer. That gives them a logical reason for Jeffries to have a sophisticated camera with a long telephoto lens to help with his spying.

Woolrich really has only two other characters in his story: Sam, the "day houseman," and "Boyne," a police detective who takes an interest in Jeffries' murder theory. Hitchcock drops Sam and, in his place, adds wisecracking nurse Stella, played by veteran character actress Thelma Ritter.

Hitchcock and Hayes also expanded the story by adding Jeffries' beautiful girlfriend Lisa (Grace Kelly). That turned out to be a most fortuitous move. Kelly, the future Princess Grace of Monaco, was then one of the most sought-after Hollywood leading ladies, and won the Best Actress Academy Award that year for *The Country Girl*.

The Lisa character also gives the audience another source of suspense since she volunteers, over Jeffries' objections, to enter Thorwald's apartment while he's out and search for evidence that his missing wife has been killed. We see her enter the apartment from Jeffries' point of view—and we also see Thorwald return, enter the apartment and catch Lisa in the act. It's a riveting sequence filled with breathtaking suspense.

The movie retains the detective character, now called Doyle. He's played by Wendell

Corey, a leading man of considerable experience. Woolrich's hero is essentially a voyeur and Hitchcock's film builds upon that theme, making all of us in the audience into voyeurs, too, as we look into the private lives of the people in the apartments across the way, just as Jeffries does with his binoculars and camera lens. Hitchcock built the entire facing apartment on a movie soundstage, exactly as it appears in the movie. The people we're watching are really occupying the rooms Jeffries can see from his window.

In the book, Thorwald learns that Jeffries has been spying on him and knows he murdered his wife, so he comes after Jeffries, armed with a pistol, intending to kill him. Jeffries dodges death, but can't escape and is about to be killed by Thorwald when the police arrive and the killer flees.

Hitchcock has Jeffries temporarily confuse Thorwald (Raymond Burr) by blinding him with

James Stewart uses his camera lens to spy on a neighbor in the apartment across the way in Alfred Hitchcock's 1954 thriller *Rear Window* (Paramount).

flashes from his camera, but Thorwald eventually grabs him and throws him out the rear window. Jeffries is hanging there, weighed down by his heavy cast and about to fall to his death when police arrive and shoot Thorwald. In what amounts to an "in joke" for Hollywood insiders, Hitchcock had Burr made up to closely resemble movie producer David O. Selznick, who had Hitchcock under contract for most of the 1940s. Burr was still a few years away from his fame as TV's *Perry Mason*.

Though Hitchcock's *Rear Window* differs significantly from Woolrich's original story, the basic suspense framework remains the same and the film's popularity increased the demand for Woolrich's stories by other filmmakers.

Attempts to remake Hitchcock films have generally been disastrous, but *Rear Window* was re-done as an ABC made-for-television movie in 1998 by director Jeff Bleckner—and the result was quite satisfactory. One of the reasons was that the story was carefully re-tailored to serve as a starring vehicle for actor Christopher Reeve, who in real-life was paralyzed from the neck down after a horseback riding accident.

Reeve, the star of four hugely popular *Superman* movies before his accident, had become the nation's leading spokesman on behalf of spinal injury paralysis victims, leading campaigns to finance research into new experiments to help heal paralysis victims. He also was an outspoken advocate of spinal injury victims returning to work—and had done so himself as an actor and even as a director.

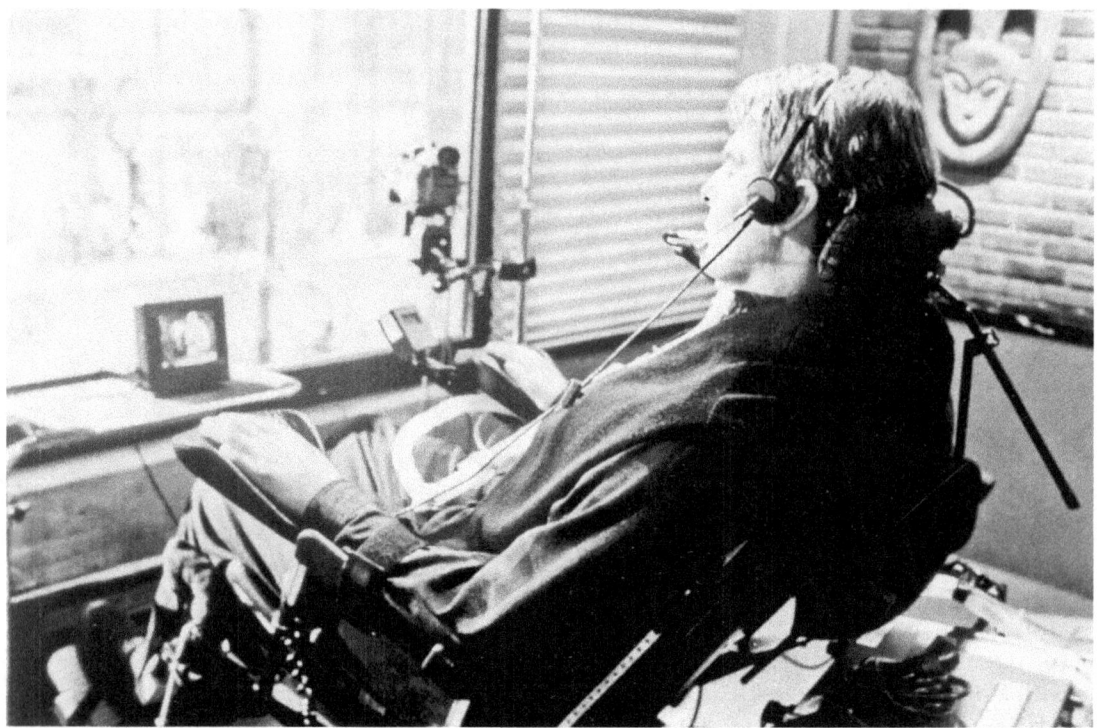

Christopher Reeve, who was paralyzed from the neck down in real life, plays the curious patient who discovers a murder in the apartment across the way in the 1998 TV remake of Alfred Hitchcock's *Rear Window* (ABC).

In the TV *Rear Window,* Jeffries becomes Jason Kemp, an architect who survives an auto accident that leaves him paralyzed. A successful man, he has the funds to set himself up in a luxury three-level apartment equipped with the latest technological marvels to enable him to participate more fully in life.

Jason begins to suspect that Julian Thorpe (Ritchie Coster), the sculptor who lives in an apartment across from his rear window, has murdered his wife. He enlists the help of his rehab assistant, Antonio (Ruben Santiago-Hudson), to set up a video camera system that will allow him to see what's going on in the Thorpe apartment.

Like the Hitchcock *Rear Window,* the TV version has Thorpe invade Jason's apartment and try to kill him by slitting the oxygen line he thinks Jason needs to survive. But Jason has learned to breathe on his own and is able to hang on long enough to be rescued by Detective Moore (Robert Forster) and Antonio.

Though there's a similar love interest between Jason and co-worker Claudia (Daryl Hannah), she doesn't have the crucial things to do that the Lisa character had in the Hitchcock film.

The TV *Rear Window* is quite suspenseful, but it's also especially absorbing because we know that Reeve, who's quite good in the role, is not just acting but is really in the precarious situation Jason is in for the movie. Reeve died from heart failure in 2004, a complication of his paralysis. The remake of *Rear Window* stands as a permanent testament to his talent and his tenacity.

Cornell Woolrich
The Black Path of Fear

The 1944 novel and the 1946 movie *The Chase*

In 1959, when I was a student at UCLA, I enrolled in a course in film direction taught by the legendary filmmaker Arthur Ripley, a dour old veteran who had been the editor on Erich von Stroheim's *Foolish Wives* (1922), a comedy writer for Mack Sennett and the director of W.C. Fields' famous short subjects *The Pharmacist* and *The Barber Shop*. The year before I took his class, he had directed his last movie, Robert Mitchum's *Thunder Road*.

For all his achievements, I wanted to take Ripley's class mainly because I was a big fan of the only film noir he ever directed, a 1946 thriller called *The Chase*, based on Cornell Woolrich's *The Black Path of Fear*, fifth of his six so-called *Black* novels,

One day, to my great pleasure, Ripley decided to screen *The Chase* in class. But not far into the movie, as dozens of students giggled and guffawed at what they were seeing, an enraged Ripley suddenly stopped the screening and told everybody to get the hell out of there. He seemed apoplectic over the reception of his cherished film.

I couldn't blame him. If you're familiar with *The Chase*, you may be wondering what those students could possibly find so funny in such a grim thriller. I figured it out right away: It was Ripley's leading man, Robert Cummings. In 1959, Cummings was best known to young people as the skirt-chasing photographer he was playing on TV's *The Bob Cummings Show*. Though he was uncharacteristically sober-sided in *The Chase*, the kids started to giggle every time he looked at leading lady Michele Morgan, who was playing the troubled wife of racketeer Steve Cochran. The students were positive they knew what Cummings was thinking about doing with the sexy French actress, even when he was probably thinking nothing of the kind. In fact, if Cummings was thinking about anything, it probably was how he was looking in profile.

That problem of *a priori* knowledge about an actor sometimes ruins a classic film for filmgoers of the next generation. Can you believe an actor as a priest, for example, if you know he was busted a few years later for statutory rape? Can you accept Elizabeth Taylor as a poverty-stricken heroine once you've seen her flashing the world's largest diamond in the tabloids? And so on.

Anyway, I believe that's what ruined *The Chase* for so many of my fellow students that day. And that was a special tragedy because Cummings actually was giving a real change-of-pace performance for a light comic actor, probably his best since he played the panicked hero of Alfred Hitchcock's *Saboteur* (1942).

The Chase, an indie released by United Artists, was not a big box office performer and its subsequent video fate has been especially sad. It fell into the public domain quite early and has been sent to market in some hideously bad, grainy, chopped-up, bargain bin versions by all kinds of low-end distributors.

Yet *The Chase* has a very good reputation among devotees of *noir* filmmaking and is well worth watching today for its many attractions, providing you can find a decent copy.

Woolrich's novel asks the reader to swallow some fairly good-sized plot improbabilities,

Robert Cummings is living it up with another man's wife (Michele Morgan) in the 1946 thriller *The Chase*, based on Cornell Woolrich's novel *The Black Path of Fear* (United Artists).

so it wasn't going to be an easy one to adapt for the screen. Protagonist Bill "Scotty" Scott, an unemployed and desperate ex-serviceman, finds a wallet on the street in Miami. It's loaded with cash, so he takes a few bucks to buy himself a meal he badly needs, then returns the billfold to its rightful owner, Ed Roman, whose name and address are on several documents in the wallet. As a reward, "Scotty" is offered a job as the man's chauffeur—even though it means firing the present chauffeur.

It's obvious that Roman was impressed by Scotty's honesty in returning the wallet with most of the money intact. Later, you wonder why Roman should care about somebody's honesty. He's a despicable character—a specialist in criminal activities. He's also a control freak who abuses women, deals in drugs and thinks nothing of ordering people murdered.

The premise of the book is that Scotty falls in love with Roman's beautiful wife, who's anxious to get away from her domineering and cruel husband. Together they flee to Havana. The angry Roman wants vengeance, so he hires people to track the wife down and kill her.

All that is told in flashback later in the book, which opens with Mrs. Roman being stabbed to death in a crowded Havana nightclub and Scotty being charged with her murder. The murder weapon is a knife similar to one Scotty had purchased earlier in the day from a Chinese merchant. He insists it's not the same knife, but he can't find his own and the merchant says the murder weapon is the one Scotty purchased.

Realizing he's been framed, Scotty escapes from the police and decides to track down a nightclub photographer who may have snapped a picture of him and Mrs. Roman just before she was stabbed. He hopes the picture may show the killer, who must have been standing next to Mrs. Roman when he struck her. Scotty is helped by a strange Cuban woman named Midnight, who hides him during the police manhunt because she hates cops.

Both Scotty and the photographer are captured by Roman's Havana associates, but Midnight leads the authorities to the place where they're being held and they're rescued. The photo does prove Scotty's innocence and the novel ends after he goes back to Miami and kills Roman.

When Ripley began to put the screen version together, he was fortunate to be able to work with one of Hollywood's most promising young screenwriters, Philip Yordan, who had just penned *Dillinger* (1945), a classic crime film, and would go on to write such classics as *Detective Story, Johnny Guitar, El Cid, 55 Days at Peking* and Humphrey Bogart's final film, *The Harder They Fall*.

Yordan made some major changes to Woolrich's story. For one thing, he gave Scotty a new first name, Chuck. But by far the most crucial change was his decision to make Scotty (Cummings) a shell-shocked war veteran. But we don't know this until the picture is more than half over. That's when Scotty, still a fugitive, goes to see his former military physician, Comdr. Davidson (Jack Holt), who tells him he's still suffering from anxiety neurosis and has been imagining things.

This is when we realize what Yordan has done: He has tricked us into thinking the murder of Lorna Roman (Michele Morgan) really happened. Turns out it was all in Scotty's head. In retrospect, you can imagine what Ripley and Yordan were thinking: Do we want to kill off the leading lady in the first reel, then have no romantic interest for Scotty through the rest of the picture?

The result: The plot rolls back to the night Scotty and Lorna were rushing to catch the boat to Cuba, while her husband (Steve Cochran) and his chief thug "Gino" (Peter Lorre) are rushing to stop them. By making that huge change in Woolrich's concept, Yordan had to make lots more. The character of Midnight (Yolanda Lacca) is reduced to little more than a walk-on because most of the action involving her isn't needed. The photographer is found dead instead of taken prisoner because the climax of the story now takes place in Florida, not in Cuba.

Yordan also made some changes that seem rather frivolous. For instance, he changes Chin, the Chinese knife dealer, into a woman called Madame Chin, who's played by a non–Asian actress, Nina Koshetz. He also overhauls the character of Giordano, Roman's sidekick, and changes his name to Gino, even though Hungarian actor Peter Lorre didn't look Italian. He adds two characters who aren't in the book: "Johnson" (Lloyd Corrigan), a potential customer of Roman, who gets murdered when he doesn't go along with Roman's terms; and "Fats," another business associate who seems to be there only for the purpose of telling Roman that he saw his chauffeur buying two tickets on the boat to Havana. "Fats" is played by Don Wilson, for years the announcer for Jack Benny's radio show.

By far the best of Yordan's other changes is his brilliant notion of having a second set of controls for Roman's car. The first time they come into play is when Scotty is taking

Roman and Gino for a ride and Roman decides to race a speeding railroad train to a crossing. He starts using his own gas pedal, forcing Scotty to steer the car at speeds approaching 100 miles per hour. When it's clear he's going to lose the race with the speeding train, Roman brakes and brings the car to a screeching halt just inches from the train.

This gives the film its explosive climax when Roman is rushing to stop his wife and Scotty from sailing to Havana. Gino is now driving, but Roman is putting his special pedal to the metal as another train races them to the crossing. The result is a grinding crash that lets the fates decide who's going to get the girl, the abusive Steve Cochran or the earnest Bob Cummings.

Fans of Cummings rate his performance in *The Chase* right up there with his very best dramatic turns—the leading role in Warner Bros. *Kings Row* (1942), the lover of Grace Kelly in Hitchcock's *Dial M for Murder* (1954) and his Emmy-winning performance as a juror in TV's original *12 Angry Men* (1955).

Arthur Ripley's directing career was pretty close to being over when he finished *The Chase*. He worked uncredited as a director on the disastrous *Siren of Atlantis* in 1948, did an episode of Henry Fonda's TV series *The Star and the Story* in 1955, then finished up his career with the moonshine action picture *Thunder Road*, which has since become a cult favorite.

He spent his last years as an academic and was instrumental in setting up UCLA's successful film program. I don't remember him ever talking about *The Chase* at length in our class. Though he was only 64 when he died in 1961, he seemed much older. His bearing in class was that of an irascible character who didn't like his time wasted, so I never bothered to approach him with any questions about any of his films. You can imagine how many times I've regretted that.

Ripley's reputation has suffered some hard hits over the years. Frank Capra, who worked with him in his early years, was especially hard on Ripley and didn't hold him in high regard. But looking at *The Chase* today, you can't fail to recognize that he was an extremely resourceful director, especially when working on a small budget, and somehow turned out one of the enduring noir classics.

Cornell Woolrich

I Married a Dead Man

The 1948 novel by William Irish (Cornell Woolrich),
the 1950 movie *No Man of Her Own*, the 1983 movie
I Married a Shadow and the 1996 movie *Mrs. Winterbourne*

The French still call him "the father of *noir*": Cornell Woolrich. Or, if you prefer, William Irish, or George Hopley. He remains a tragic figure in the history of American literature—a promising young writer who reminded many of F. Scott Fitzgerald when he first attracted attention during the Great Depression of the 1930s.

But Woolrich turned out to be a magnet for dark shadows. They gathered about him the way birds fluttered around St. Francis. They turned his world dark and gloomy and left little room for even the occasional ray of light to shine through. His only marriage

Barbara Stanwyck clings to John Lund as they confront villainous Lyle Bettger in *No Man of Her Own* (1950), the first movie version of Cornell Woolrich's novel *I Married a Dead Man* (Paramount Pictures).

lasted but weeks and his flirtations with a career as a Hollywood screenwriter were equally brief and unsatisfying. He spent most of his life back home with his divorced mother and became an alcoholic, homosexual recluse. He ended his days in pain and suffering delusions, one leg amputated due to gangrene, his dreams twisted into melancholy nightmares.

But while he was drinking himself to death, Woolrich created a long series of dark masterpieces, published under one or another of his various literary identities, and he ultimately changed the world of mystery into one that now includes paranoia and horror along with the nerve-bending suspense. It's what the French call *noir*.

If you don't know his novels and stories, you'll surely know some of the films made from them: Alfred Hitchcock's *Rear Window*, François Truffaut's *The Bride Wore Black*, Jacques Tourneur's *The Leopard Man*, John Farrow's *Night Has a Thousand Eyes*, Harold Clurman's *Deadline at Dawn*, Robert Siodmak's *Phantom Lady*, Roy William Neill's *Black Angel* and many more.

One novel stands out because its plot is so original, its leading character so quintessentially Woolrich-ian and its title so startling: *I Married a Dead Man*, published in 1948 under his pen name William Irish.

The story is deceptively simple: In New York City, an unmarried and friendless young woman, Helen, falls in love with an urban lout in the years after World War II. He gets her pregnant, then rejects her and his unborn child once he has had his fill of her. Locking her out of his flat, he gives her a $5 bill and a one-way train ticket to San Francisco.

Broken-hearted and desperate, she boards the crowded train and is taken under the wing of Patrice, a happy newlywed who's also expecting a baby. Patrice met and married Hugh in Europe and they're taking the train to Hugh's bucolic hometown. Patrice will be meeting his parents for the first time. They've never even seen a photograph of her.

It has all the makings of a warm, romantic postwar melodrama about the recovery of a shattered young woman with the help of two young strangers. But Woolrich couldn't let such a rosy situation go on for long. Instead, he puts them in a terrible train wreck that kills the nice young couple and leaves Helen in a coma, not even aware that she's given birth to her baby prematurely as a result of the trauma.

When she wakes, she's stunned to discover everybody thinks Helen is dead and that she's Patrice. The reason: Patrice had asked Helen to put on her wedding ring for safekeeping while she washed her hands just before the train wreck. When they take Helen from the wreckage, she's wearing the ring and is about to have her baby. Everybody knew Patrice was expecting, but nobody knew anything about Helen, including her name.

Woolrich feasted on such situations. Helen now finds herself doted upon by Hugh's parents. They want her to live with them, to take the place of the son they've lost. They want to give Hugh's baby son the grand life his father had planned for him. Should Helen tell them the truth, then go back on the street with her bawling baby, homeless, unloved and facing a life of poverty? Or should she play the role they so eagerly want her to play?

Woolrich loved giving his characters such heart-rending moral dilemmas, forcing them to choose between right and wrong. And once they've chosen wrong, he labored to make it seem right after all. In this case, he has Helen become the sort of woman Patrice so obviously was. Then he has her fall in love with Hugh's brother Bill, so she can live out the rest of her days without revealing her dreadful secret.

Then Woolrich pulled the rug out from under them both by having Helen's former lover turn up, scenting a big payoff. He threatens to spoil everything for her by claiming his baby son.

I Married a Dead Man figured to become a class-A "woman's picture" from the moment it appeared in print. Paramount snapped up the rights and assigned it to house director Mitchell Leisen, whose penchant for similar material had produced some classic pictures, among them *Remember the Night, Hold Back the Dawn, Hands Across the Table* and that unforgettable tearjerker *To Each His Own* with Olivia de Havilland emoting for her first of two Best Actress Oscars.

To play Helen, Leisen chose the queen of screen heartbreak, Barbara Stanwyck, who had been plucking America's heartstrings ever since *Stella Dallas* more than a decade earlier. To play her new love, brother Bill, he cast young John Lund, who had played de Havilland's grown-up illegitimate son in *To Each His Own*. And to mess things up well for them both, he cast craggy, villainous Lyle Bettger as the baby's real father, a blackmailer *asking* to be murdered by someone. Two years later, Bettger grew even more villainous as the sadistic elephant trainer in Cecil B. DeMille's *The Greatest Show on Earth*.

Everybody agreed they couldn't go with Woolrich's original title because *I Married a Dead Man* might make people think it was a horror picture like *I Walked with a Zombie*.

So they took their title from the 1932 Clark Gable–Carole Lombard comedy *No Man of Her Own*.

Released in 1950, *No Man of Her Own* is viewed by some critics as late 1940s romantic twaddle. But it was a highly successful "woman's picture" and Leisen gave it a clear overlay of noir sensibility that makes it a joy to discover today. Stanwyck wrings every drop of moisture out of her lines; the picture's dark, moody look in the early New York City scenes is classic noir. When Helen-Patrice begins new life in suburban Caulfield, the look of the picture brightens. Then when "Patrice" starts getting anonymous letters from her former lover, the shadows creep back in. The film ends in grand noir fashion.

More than half a century later, *No Man of Her Own* remains the most faithful of the films made from Woolrich's story.

After the French New Wave directors discovered noir and began making their own dark films as homages to the American films of the postwar era, it was only a matter of time until some French filmmaker unearthed *No Man of Her Own* or the original Woolrich novel and think about another version.

That finally happened some 30 years after the 1950 film. Director Robin Davis saw the appeal in updating the storyline and moving it to France. In 1983, his film was released as *J'ai Epouse Une Ombre* (*I Married a Shadow*), but it is known on home video in America under the original Woolrich title *I Married a Dead Man*.

Davis eschewed the trappings of noir, filming his story mostly in bright sunlight and, in fact, in mostly beautiful locations in rural France. Helen (now Helene) is played by Nathalie Baye, one of France's hottest young stars. She's literally dumped by her callous lover—shoved out the door of his car onto the road, immense belly and all—and boards the train, as desperate as Stanwyck was in 1950, though not facing anywhere near the "disgrace" in sin-forgiving France that Helen would have faced in postwar America.

It's interesting to see how the Woolrich tale operates when the story is turned inside out. In the original, newlywed Patrice is an American girl who had been living in Europe and is now coming home. In the 1983 film, Patrice is a French girl coming home from a stay in late 1970s America, "where women don't take any guff." Helene is befriended by Patrice in much the same manner as before, but now the story works a little harder to make the confusion of identities after the train wreck more credible.

For instance, Helene's dress is soaked when a drink spills on her during the train ride. Patrice takes her to the railway cabin she shares with her husband and has her put on one of her clean dresses—as well as the wedding ring. So, when the crash comes, Helene is now found in Patrice's private cabin, wearing her clothes *and* her ring. The confusion over who survived the crash now makes more sense.

Helene is mistaken for Patrice in the hospital and, though she argues with the nurses and doctors about the mistaken identity, they assume she's still in shock. She's "adopted" by the dead husband's parents, who turn out to be millionaires owning a vast vineyard and winery in prime wine country. (They're much richer than the American family was in *No Man of Her Own*.)

The handsome brother this time is called Pierre. He's soon attracted to the lovely widow of his dead brother and, because this is a French picture, Helene and Pierre soon go swimming so that Nathalie Baye may take off her top and show Pierre her breasts. He seems quite appreciative.

The ex-boyfriend surfaces, threatening the happiness of Helene and Pierre. This time he doesn't just threaten, but actually goes to Helene's mother-in-law and tells her the truth about Helene and the baby—something that doesn't happen in the Woolrich novel. The mother-in-law, who has a weak heart, suffers an attack.

The climax of the French film is new. In *No Man of Her Own*, Helen goes to the blackmailer's apartment and shoots him, unaware that somebody has already killed him. Brother-in-law Bill helps her hide the body and they both end up wondering which of them was the real killer. In the French film, Helene arranges a meeting with the blackmailer in the woods and stabs him in the gut, killing him. Pierre helps her hide the body.

In 1996, a third film was made from Woolrich's story—a bizarre one, given the somber tone of the original material. In the black comedy *Mrs. Winterbourne*, Oscar-winner Shirley MacLaine plays the mother-in-law and gets star billing over actress-talk show host Ricki Lake, who plays the central role.

Helen is now Connie Doyle, a rather schlubby girl who gets dumped by the boyfriend after she becomes pregnant and he finds a new girl. The familiar train wreck takes place, but this time the family that adopts are the Winterbournes. If the family prospered into the millionaire stage between 1950 and 1983, they've morphed into billionaires by 1996. Their home in a Boston suburb is a mansion that looks like an urban city library.

As directed by onetime comic actor Richard Benjamin, *Mrs. Winterbourne* is broadly played. Slimmed down, but still slightly chubby Ricki Lake, the original star of John Waters' 1988 "fat girl" musical *Hairspray*, creates a character who seems a little low in brain wattage and decidedly of low-class origin. Her slangy lines often make her sound like a female Bowery Boy.

Meanwhile, MacLaine plays the mother-in-law as a very sophisticated, high-class lady from Old Money. In one of the movie's brighter moments, it turns out that she once was a chorus girl and really comes from the same gum-snapping blue collar background as Connie Doyle. We discover this when they unexpectedly join in a duet rendition of "Sunny Side of the Street" at a fancy garden party! This makes little sense, but it's fun.

The dead husband now has a twin brother named Bill, which permits actor Brandon Fraser to play both parts. It takes him a considerable amount of time to warm up to his sister-in-law, but romance eventually flowers. A gay chauffeur, Paco (Miguel Sandoval), helps Bill and Connie along the way. (No such character exists in the Woolrich story.)

The biggest twist comes at the opening of the movie, the church wedding of Bill and Connie. The police arrive to arrest them for the murder of the blackmailer; the elder Mrs. Winterbourne (MacLaine) tells the cops she's the one they want. This sets up the flashback structure of the whole story, going back to Connie's pregnancy and rejection by her former lover. There's yet another surprise when the flashbacks end: Mama isn't the killer either and a very minor character in the story winds up doing the time.

Mrs. Winterbourne, which was not a box office success, has drained off all the original Woolrich flavor and layers of meaning. It just retains the plot, which seems rather fragile and absurd when the suspense, menace and philosophical points are traded off for feeble comedy.

The book is still a good read, although the opening chapter is clumsy and puzzling because it refers to lots of action that takes place all in the elaborate flashback structure Woolrich concocted. Once you're beyond Chapter 1, though, it's a typically fast and fascinating Woolrich thriller.

Mitchell Leisen's 1950 film is still the best screen version. After you've watched it, the intriguing French version is well worth seeing. As for *Mrs. Winterbourne*, don't go there.

Bibliography

In addition to the many novels and short stories cited in the text, the following works were especially helpful in the writing and researching of this book.

Ashley, Mike (Editor). *The Mammoth Encyclopedia of Modern Crime Fiction* (2002). Carroll & Graf.

Behlmer, Rudy (Editor). *Memo from David O. Selznick* (1972). Viking.

Bruccoli, Matthew J., and Richard Layman. *Hardboiled Mystery Writers* (1989). Carroll & Graf.

Bunson, Matthew. *The Complete Christie* (2000). Pocket Books.

Christie, Agatha. *Agatha Christie: An Autobiography* (1977). William Collins & Sons.

Clarens, Carlos. *Crime Movies* (1980). Norton.

Collins, Max Allan. *The History of Mystery* (2001). Collectors Press.

Coomes, David. *Dorothy L. Sayers: A Careless Rage for Life* (1992). Lion Publishing.

DeAndrea, William L. *Encyclopedia Mysteriosa* (1994). Prentice Hall/Macmillan.

Dimmitt, Richard Bertrand. *A Title Guide to the Talkies* (1965). Scarecrow Press.

DuBose, Martha Hailey. *Women of Mystery* (2000). Thomas Dunne Books.

Friedman, Mickey (Editor). *The Crown Crime Companion* (1995). Crown.

Haining, Peter. *The Classic Era of Crime Fiction* (2002). Chicago Review Press.

Haining, Peter (Editor). *The Mammoth Book of Movie Detectives & Screen Crimes* (1998). Carroll & Graf.

Huang, Jim. *100 Favorite Mysteries of the Century* (2000). Crum Creek Press.

Hughes, Dorothy. *Erle Stanley Gardner: The Case of the Real Perry Mason* (1978). William Morrow.

Huston, John. *An Open Book* (1980). Knopf.

Jakubowski, Maxim (Editor). *100 Great Detectives* (1991). Carroll & Graf.

Layman, Richard, with Julie M. Rivett (Editors). *Selected Letters of Dashiell Hammett* (2001). Counterpoint.

Leitch, Thomas. *The Encyclopedia of Alfred Hitchcock* (2002). Checkmark Books.

MacShane, Frank. *The Life of Raymond Chandler* (1976). Dutton.

Maltin, Leonard. *Classic Movie Guide* (2005, 2010). Plume.

Maltin, Leonard. *Leonard Maltin's Movie Encyclopedia* (1994). Dutton.

Marill, Alvin H. *Movies Made for Television* (1987). Baseline.

McGilligan, Patrick. *Alfred Hitchcock: A Life in Darkness and Light* (2003). Harper Collins.

Murphy, Bruce F. *The Encyclopedia of Murder and Mystery* (1999). Palgrave.

Nevins, Francis M., Jr. *Cornell Woolrich: First You Dream, Then You Die* (1988). The Mysterious Press.

Nolan, William F. *Hammett: A Life at the Edge* (1983). Congdon & Weed.

Osborne, Charles. *The Life and Crimes of Agatha Christie* (1982). St. Martin's.

Panek, LeRoy Lad. *The Origins of the American Detective Story* (2006). McFarland.

Pearsall, Jay. *Mystery & Crime* (1995). Fireside.

Polito, Robert. *Savage Art: A Biography of Jim Thompson* (1995). Vintage Books.

Rehak, Melanie. *Girl Sleuth: Nancy Drew and the Women Who Created Her* (2005). Harcourt.

Renzi, Thomas C. *Cornell Woolrich from Pulp Noir to Film Noir* (2006). McFarland.

Riley, Dick, and Pam McAllister. *The New Bedside, Bathtub and Armchair Companion to Agatha Christie* (1991). Ungar Publishing.

Symons, Julian. *Bloody Murder* (1972). Penguin.

Wilson, Andrew. *Beautiful Shadow: A Life of Patricia Highsmith* (2003). Bloomsbury.

Winn, Dilys. *Murder Ink: The Mystery Reader's Companion* (1977). Workman Publishing.

Index

Abbott, John 53–54
Acuff, Eddie 74
The Adventures of Ellery Queen 165
The Adventures of Robin Hood 59
The Adventures of Sherlock Holmes 58
After Dark, My Sweet 187–189
After the Funeral 4
After the Thin Man 92
Age-Old Friends 137
Aherne, Brian 65
The Alamo (2004) 188
Albert, Eddie 197
Aldrich, Robert 179
Alias Smith and Jones 49
Ali Baba and the Forty Thieves 162
Alice in Wonderland (1933) 164
All in the Family (TV) 137
All That Money Can Buy 83
Allen, Gracie 192–194
Allen, Tanya 151
Allingham, Margery 4, 11
Alton, John 148
The Amazing Colossal Man 83
American Graffiti 39
Ames, Leon 155–156
Anderson, Dame Judith 65, 67
Andrews, Dana 32–33, 157
Another Thin Man 92
Anthiel, George 95
Antony, Scott 69
Arabian Nights 162
Archer, Lew 4, 8, 44, 128–132, 149
Archer, Miles 129
Archinbaud, George 148
Arden, Eve 148
Arlen, Alice 6 110–111
Arlen, Michael 3
Armstrong, Charlotte 11–18
Armstrong, Robert 147
As I Lay Dying 36
Ashby, Hal 18, 20

Ashcroft, Dame Peggy 26
Aslanian, Jean-Jacques 75
The Asphalt Jungle 2, 27–30
Assante, Armand 181
Asta 90, 92
Astaire, Fred 65
Astor, Mary 85, 89, 189–191
Aswell, Mary Louise White 166–167
Atwill, Lionel 59
Audran, Stephane 186
Aurenche, Jean 186
The Avengers 71
Aznavour, Charles 75–76

Bacall, Lauren 35–36, 75, 112, 131
Badel, Alan 54
The Badlanders 27
Baker, Chet 106
Baker, Roy Ward 18
Baker, Tom 61
Ball, John 18
Ball of Fire 119
Ballard, Shirley 137
Balsam, Martin 126, 128
La Bamba 107
Bancroft, Anne 16
Bang the Drum Slowly 137
Banks, Leslie 176
The Barber Shop 203
Bard, Ben 199
Bari, Lynn 172–173
Barker, Lex 168
Barnes, George 68
Barrie, Wendy 60
Barrymore, Ethel 59–60, 194–196
Barrymore, John 59–60, 87
Barrymore, Lionel 59–60
Bauer, Charita 49
Baxendale, Helen 6
Baxter, Anne 194
Baye, Nathalie 209
Beach, Adam 109
Beals, Jennifer 144

Beaton, Jesse 144
Beautiful Shadow 101
Beck, Thomas 134
Before the Fact 113, 166
Behlmer, Rudy 66
Bell, James 199
Bellamy, Ralph 165
Belle of the Yukon 118
Benedek, Laslo 30
Benjamin, Richard 210
Bennett, Charles 24, 182–183
Beresford, Tuppence, and Tommy 90, 92
Bergen, Polly 125–126
Bergman, Ingrid 81, 184
Bergren, Eric 108
Berke, William 135
Berkeley, Anthony 166
Bernstein, Elmer 126
Bettger, Lyle 207–208
The Big Heat 30
The Big Sleep 34–39, 130–131, 149
Biggers, Earl Derr 21–23, 133
Birt, Daniel 12
Bishop, William 80
Bissell, Whit 101
Bisset, Jacqueline 102, 170, 197
Black Alibi 198–200
Black Angel 207
The Black Camel 21–23
The Black Cat (1934) 161
The Black Cat (1941) 161
The Black Path of Fear 203–206
Black Widow (1954) 165–168
The Blackboard Jungle 136
Blanchett, Cate 103, 106
Bleckner, Jeff 201
Blees, Robert 31
Blood Sport 70–72
Blood Work 62–63
The Bob Cummings Show (TV) 203
The Bobbsey Twins 116
Bochner, Lloyd 71
Bogart, Humphrey 7, 27, 35–38, 42, 75, 85, 112–113

213

Index

Bogeaus, Benedict 30
Bonnaire, Sandrine 170–171
Boone, Richard 39
Boteler, Wade 165
Bowen, T.R. 47
Bowman, Lee 95, 165
Boyer, Charles 81
Brackett, Leigh 36
Bradlee, Ben 158
Brahm, John 82
Brat Farrar 182
Bray, Robert 179–181
Brent, George 196
Brett, Jeremy 58, 61
The Bride Wore Black 207
Broderick, Helen 148
Bronson, Charles 38
Brooks, Avery 149–150, 152
Brooks, Jean 200
Bruce, Mona 47
Bruce, Nigel 58, 59
Brute Force 30
Brydon, Rob 47
Brynner, Yul 139
Buchan, John 2, 23, 61
Buono, Victor 83
Burke, Paul 102
Burnett, W.R. 2, 27–30, 77, 79
Burns, George 192–193
Burr, Raymond 72, 74, 201
Busman's Honeymoon 173–176

Cabaret 132
Cagney, James 80, 84, 147
Cain, James M. 4, 29–31, 184
Cairo 27
Caldwell, Erskine 186
Calhern, Louis 29
Callow, Simon 54
Campion, Albert 4, 11
Cape Fear 123–128
Capone, Al 27
Capra, Frank 206
Carella, Steve 4
Carey, Phil 102
Carmichael, Ian 174
Carney, James 176
Carpenter, Jennifer 122
Carradine, John 60
Carradine, Keith 122
Carroll, Leo G. 97
Carroll, Madeleine 24
The Case of the Dangerous Dowager 74
The Case of the Howling Dog 72
The Case of the Velvet Claws 72–74
The Case of the Weird Sisters 11–12
Caspary, Vera 32–34
Cat People 199
Cates, Joseph 48
Caulfield, Joan 14

Cavanagh, Paul 190
Celi, Adolfo 158
La Cérémonie 169–171
Ceremony 149–152
Chabrol, Claude 170-
Chan, Charlie 21–23, 58, 132–133
Chandler, Raymond 1, 3–4, 7, 34–42, 88, 98, 129, 142–143, 149, 176, 186
Chaney, Jan 181
Chaney, Lon 155
Charles, Nick 73, 90–92, 175, 189
Charles, Nora 90–92, 175
Charteris, Lesley 95
The Chase (1946) 203
Chase, Barrie 126–127
Cheadle, Don 144–145
Chee, Jim 106–111
Child, Lee 42–44
The Children's Hour 116
The Chinese Orange Mystery 163–165
Christie, Agatha 4–5, 44–48, 90, 92, 145, 153, 167, 176
The Circular Staircase 48
Citizen Kane 83
Clare, Mary 182
Clark, Candy 39
Clark, Carol Higgins 50
Clark, Carolyn Ann 49
Clark, Mary Higgins 3, 11, 48–50
Clarke, Mae 147
Clément, René 103, 105–106
Cleveland, David 70–72
The Clockmaker 186
Close, Glenn 137
Clurman, Harold 207
Cochran, Steve 203–206
The Cocoanuts 156
Colgate, William 151
Collins, Joan 39
Collins, Richard 179, 181
Collins, Wilkie 50–54
Collinson, Peter 197
Colman, Booth 181
Colman, Ronald 65, 95
Columbier, Michael 108
Columbo 114
Come to Grief 70
Conan Doyle, Arthur 54–61, 153
Confidential Agent 37
Connelly, Michael 61–63
The Continental Op 8, 84, 90
Cook, Donald 148, 163, 165
Cook, Elisha, Jr. 18, 38, 88–89
Cook, Peter 61
Cool Breeze 27
Coomes, David 174
Cooper, Gary 119
Cooper, Wyllis 134

Cop Hater 135–137
Corcoran, Donna 15, 18
Coree, Genie 181
Corey, Wendell 200–201
Cormack, Lynne 151
Corneau, Alain 187
Cornwell, Patricia 135
Corrigan, Lloyd 162, 205
Cortez, Ricardo 2, 74, 85
Coster, Ritchie 202
Cottage Sinister 166
The Country Girl 200
Coup de Torchon 184–187
The Covered Wagon 52
Coward, Noel 47
Cox, Anthony Berkeley 114
Coyote Waits 109
The Cradle Will Fall 48–50
Craig, Georgianna 171
Crawford, Broderick 148
Cregar, Laird 32, 79, 81–84
Crime and Punishment 95
Crimes at the Dark House 52
Crosby, Cathy Lee 178
Cruise, Tom 42–44
Cruze, James 52
Culver, Howard 165
Cummings, Constance 174
Cummings, Robert 203–206
Cunningham, Sean 3
The Curse of Frankenstein 60
Curtiz, Michael 13, 189–190
Cushing, Peter 60

Dahl, Arlene 31
The Dain Curse 8
Dalgleish, Adam 5
Damon, Matt 103, 105–106
A Damsel in Distress 65
Dances with Wolves 111
Dangerous 88
Dangerous Female 86
Daniels, Bebe 86
Dannay, Frederic 163
Dark Passage 42, 75
The Dark Wind 106–109
Darkly Dreaming Dexter 120–123
Darnell, Linda 81–83
Darwell, Jane 67
Dassin, Jules 30, 135
The Daughter of Time 182
Daves, Delmer 42, 75
David, Joanna 47
The Da Vinci Code 9
Daviot, Gordon 182
Davis, Bette 86–87
Davis, Robin 209
Davis, Stringer 45–46
Davre, Serge 76
Dead Cert 68–69
Deadline at Dawn 207
The Deaf Man 138–140

Index

Death of an Expert Witness 5
DeCorsia, Ted 31
DeHavilland, Olivia 208
DeJesus, Wanda 62
Delon, Alain 103
Del Ruth, Roy 85, 158
DeMarnay, Derrick 182–183
DeMille, Cecil B. 208
Demme, Jonathan 144
DeMornay, Rebecca 159
Dench, Judi 69
Denham, Maurice 47
DeNiro, Robert 126–127
Dern, Bruce 177–178, 188
Devil in a Blue Dress 142–145
DeWinter, Max 8
Dexter 120–123
Dexter, Colin 5
Dial M for Murder 206
Dickens, Charles 50
Dieterle, William 86
Dillinger (1945) 205
Dinelli, Mel 93, 194–196
Dobkin, Larry 165
Doctor Who 61
Dodd, Claire 73–74
La Dolce Vita 106
Donat, Robert 65, 24
Don't Bother to Knock 15, 18
Dorothy L. Sayers: A Careless Rage for Life 174
Double Indemnity 29
Douglas, Illeana 126
Douglas, Warren 168
Down There 74–77
Dracula (1931) 22–23, 88, 155
Dragnet 135, 149
The Dragon Murder Case 193
Dragonwyck 83
Drake, Paul 74
Drew, Ellen 193
Drew, Nancy 116–117
The Drowning Pool 44, 132
Dryhurst, Edward 52
Dubois, Marie 76
Duff, Prof. Macdougall 11
Duluth, Peter 166–169
DuMaurier, Daphne 2, 8, 63–68
DuMaurier, George 63
Duncan, Pamela 181
Dunn, Carolyn 71
Dunnock, Mildred 197
Dupin, Auguste 4–5, 153–154, 158,
Duvall, Robert 44
Dwan, Allan 30
Dynasty 39
Dyne, Michael 82

Eastwood, Clint 61, 160
87th Precinct 4, 135, 138–140
Eilers, Sally 22
Eisenhower, Pres. Dwight D. 42

Eliacheff, Caroline 170
Eliot, Biff 179
Ellery Queen Mystery Magazine 163
Ellis, Edward 91
Emerson, Roy 175
Emery, John 53
Epstein, David 158–159
Everhard, Nancy 80
Everhart, Angie 50
The Executioners 123–127
Eyre, Chris 111

Fairstein, Linda 72
The Falcon Takes Over 1, 3
The Fallen Sparrow 112
The Fantasticks 137
Farentino, James 49
Farewell My Lovely (book) 1, 3, 35
Farewell My Lovely (1975) 38
Farrow, John 207
Father Knows Best 95
Father of the Bride (TV) 156
Faulkner, William 35
Feldman, Charles 37
Female Fiends 168
Ferris, Pam 47
Field, Virginia 124
Fields, Gracie 45
Fields, W.C. 87, 203
"The Final Problem" 56
A Fine Romance (TV) 69
Fitzgerald, Barry 32
Fitzgerald, F. Scott 206
Fitzgerald, Tara 54
The Flame Trees of Thika 18
Flashdance 144
Fleming, Rhonda 31, 196–197
Flora, Fletcher 148
Florey, Robert 54–55, 156
Flynn, Errol 59
Foley, James 187–188
Fonda, Henry 206
Fonda, Peter 111
Fontaine, Joan 8, 65–68, 114
Foolish Wives 203
Ford, John 67–68
Foreign Correspondent 114
Forester, C.S. 93
Forrest, Steve 157
Forster, Robert 202
Forty Naughty Girls 148
42nd Street 67
The 400 Blows 75
4:50 from Paddington 44–48
Foster, Norman 134
Fox, Bernard 61
Fox, Sidney 154–156
Francis, Arlene 156
Francis, Dick 68–72
Frankenstein (1931) 155
Frankenstein Meets the Wolf Man 162

Franklin, Carl 142, 144
Frears, Stephen 187
Frewer, Matt 61
Friday the 13th 3
From Here to Eternity 18
Frye, Dwight 23, 88
Fu Manchu 21
The Fugitive (TV) 43
Furthman, Jules 38
Fuzz 138–140
Fywell, Tim 54

Gardenia, Vincent 137
Gardiner, Reginald 168
Gardner, Erle Stanley 72–74, 87
Garfield, John 4, 112
Gargan, William 165
Garland, Richard 180
Garner, Peggy Ann 168–169, 172–173
Garnett, Tay 4
Gaslight 81
Gemora, Charles 157
George, Elizabeth 7–8
The Getaway 187
Gillespie, Bill 18–19
Gilmour, Alexa 151
The Girl Hunters 181
The Girl Was Young 181
Gleason, James 146–148, 172
Glory 144
Glover, John 69
Godard, Jean-Luc 75
The Godfather 27, 106
Godfrey, Peter 53
The Godwulf Manuscript 149
Goldbeck, Willis 148
Goldman, William 128, 131–132
Gomez, Henry 151
Gone with the Wind 63–64, 148, 196
Goodbye, Mr. Chips (1939) 26
Goodfellas 126
Goodis, David 74–77
Goodrich, Frances 91
Goodwin, Archie 45
Goodwin, Ron 47
Goodyear Television Playhouse 45
Gossett, Louis, Jr. 178
The Gracie Allen Murder Case 192–194
Grafton, Sue 5
Grahame, Gloria 113
Granger, Farley 100–101
Granger, Stewart 61
Granny Get Your Gun 74
Grant, Beth 110
Grant, Cary 114–115, 184
Grant, Lee 19
Granville, Bonita 116
The Grapes of Wrath 67
Graves, Caroline Elizabeth 52

Graves, Peter 129
Gray, Cordelia 6
Gray, Peter 176
The Great Lie 89
The Greatest Show on Earth 208
Greene, Graham 77–80, 111
Greene, Richard 59, 60
Greenmantle 26
Greenstreet, Sydney 32, 51, 53–54, 83, 85, 89
Gregory, James 148
Griffin, Merv 157
Griffith, Hugh 12
The Grifters 187
The Grindle Nightmare 167
Grisham, John 72
The G-String Murders 118–120
Guernica 100
The Guiding Light 48–49
A Gun for Sale 77–80
The Guns of Navarone 124

Hackett, Albert 91
Haddon, Peter 174
Hagen, Jean 29
Hairspray 210
Hall, Conrad 132
Hall, Michael C. 120–123
Halley, Sid 70
Halmi, Robert 159
Hamilton, Patrick 80–84
Hammer, Mike 179–181
Hammett, Dashiell 2, 8, 35, 73, 84–92, 149, 158, 189
Hangover Square 32, 80–84
Hanks, Tom 8–9
Hannah, Daryl 202
Hannay, Richard 25
Hannibal (TV) 123
Harden, Marcia Gay 152
The Hardy Boys 116
Harper 4, 128–132
Harper's Bazaar 167
Harris, Julie 131
Harris, Thomas 123
Harrison, Joan 64, 115
Hart, Ian 61
Hart, Richard 165
Hart to Hart (TV) 92
Hastings, Capt. 5
Hats Off 30
Haunted Honeymoon 173–176
Hawk 149, 152
Hawks, Howard 35
Hayden, Sterling 28–29
Hayes, Helen 169
Hayes, John Michael 200
Hayward, Louis 94–95
Heflin, Van 168
A Hell of a Woman 187
Hellman, Lillian 89, 91, 116
Hemingway, Ernest 36
Henry, Charlotte 164

Herbert, A.P. 93–96, 114
Herbert, F. Hugh 173
Hermann, Bernard 83, 125–126, 128
Hessler, Gordon 158
Hicks, Seymour 175
Hickson, Joan 46–48
The Hidden Staircase 116–117
High and Low 4, 140–142
High Sierra 27, 77
Highsmith, Patricia 1, 4, 96–106, 111–112
Hilary, Jennifer 54
Hildegarde Withers Makes the Scene 148
Hillerman, John 165
Hillerman, Tony 6, 106–111
Hitchcock, Alfred 8, 12–13, 83–84, 125, 170, 186, 194, 196; *Rear Window* 200–202, 207; *Rebecca* 63–68; *Strangers on a Train* 1–2, 4, 96–102, 111; *Suspicion* 114–115, 166; *Thirty-Nine Steps* 23–27, 61; *Young and Innocent* 181–184
Hitchcock, Patricia 99
Holden, Amanda 47
Holmes, Ben 61
Holmes, Brown 86
Holmes, Sherlock 43, 54–61, 85, 131, 135, 153, 175
Holt, Jack 205
Hombre 129
Home Sweet Homicide 118, 171–173
Homeier, Skip 169
Homicide for Three 168
Hopley, George 206
Horovitch, David 47
The Horror of Dracula 60
The Hound of the Baskervilles 56–61
The House by the River 93–96, 114
House of Usher 158
House of Wax 83, 157
The House Without a Key 132
Hovick, Louise 118
Hovick, Rose 118
Hud 129
Hughes, Dorothy B. 111–113
Hunnicutt, Gayle 197
Hunter, Evan 136, 138, 140
Huppert, Isabelle 170–171, 186
Huston, John 17, 27–30, 35, 88, 155
Hutton, Jim 165
Hutton, Lauren 49–50
Hyer, Martha 102

I Am a Camera 132
I Married a Dead Man 206–210
I Married a Shadow 206–210

I, the Jury 179
Iles, Francis 93, 113, 166
In a Lonely Place 111–113
In the Frame 70
In the Heat of the Night 18–21
In the Presence of the Enemy 8
Inferno 18
The Investigation 4
Irish, William 206–207
Irving, George 164
"It Had to Be Murder" 200
Ivers, Robert 80

Jack Reacher 42–44
Jack Reacher: Never Go Back 44
Jack the Ripper 82–83, 123
Jacoby, Michel 161
Jaeckel, Richard 149
Jaffe, Sam 28
The Jagged Edge 137
Jamaica Inn 63
James, P.D. 5–6
Jaws 2 160
Jewel in the Crown 26
Jewison, Norman 18, 20
Jimenez, Neal 108
Johnny Eager 168
Johnson, Georgann 80
Johnson, Noble 154
Johnson, Nunnally 168
Jones, James 18
Jones, Jennifer 100
A Judgment in Stone 169–171
Jungle Jim 135

Kagawa, Kyoko 141–142
Kanayan, Richard 75
Kane, Henry 137
Kansas City Confidential 30
Karloff, Boris 161
Karlson, Phil 30
Kashimo 21
Kazan, Elia 30
Keach, Stacy 179
Keene, Carolyn 116–117
Keith, Brian 129
Kelly, Grace 200, 206
Kelly, Martha Mott 166
Kemp-Welch, Joan 176
Kennedy, Arthur 47
Kennedy, Burt 187
The Kennel Murder Case 92, 189–191
The Killer Inside Me 187
The Killing 18, 187
Kilmer, Val 160
Kimble, Richard 43
King, Erik 122
King, Rob 50
King Kong 147–148
King's Ransom 4, 140–142
Kings Row 206
Kinnell, Murray 134

Kirk, Phyllis 89
Kiss Me Deadly 179
Kiss of Death 17
Kitty Foyle 67, 115
Knight's Gambit 36
Knowles, Patric 162
Kojak 4, 126
Koshetz, Nina 205
Kruger, Otto 168
Kruschen, Jack 126
Kubrick, Stanley 168, 187
Kurosawa, Akira 4, 140–142

La Bamba 107
La Dolce Vita 106
L.A. Law (TV) 137
Lacca, Yolanda 205
Ladd, Alan 77–80
The Lady in the Lake 40–42, 176
Lady of Burlesque 118–120
The Lady Vanishes 194
Laforet, Marie 104
Lake, Ricki 210
Lake, Veronica 77–80
Lamberts, Keith 71
Landi, Marla 61
Landry, Margaret 199
Lang, Fritz 30, 93–94
Langan, Glenn 82
Langden, Robert 9
Langdon, Harry 162–163
Lange, Jessica 127
Larkin, John Francis 164
Larson, Stieg 176
LaRue, Jack 189, 191
Lassie 118, 179
Last Laugh, Mr. Moto 135
The Laughing Policeman 176–178
Laura 32–34
Law, John Philip 197
Law, Jude 103, 105–106
Law and Order (TV) 137
Law and Order: Special Victims Unit 50
Lawford, Peter 89
Leaphorn, Lt. Joe 6, 106–111
Lecter, Hannibal 123
Lee, Christopher 60
Lee, Gypsy Rose 118–120
Lee, Manfred B. 163
Lee, Pinky 120
Lehne, Fredric 80
Leigh, Janet 131
Leigh, Vivien 65
Leisen, Mitchell 208, 210
Leith, Virginia 168
The Leopard Man 198–200, 207
Leroux, Gaston 158
LeRoy, Mervyn 27
Lewis, Dawn 110
Lewis, Juliette 127
Lewis, Sgt. 5

Lewton, Val 198–199
Liberace 155
Life with Father (TV) 156
Lindsay, Jeff 120–123
Lipton, Lawrence 173
Litel, John 117
Little Caesar 27, 77, 84
The Lodger 32, 81–83
Loggia, Robert 136–137
Lom, Herbert 158–159
Lombino, Salvatore 136, 138, 140
The Lone Ranger 118
Lone Wolf 87
Long, Audrey 168
The Long Wait 179
Lorre, Peter 85, 89, 133–134, 205
The Lost Missile 136
The Love Boat 152
Lovejoy 70
Love's Lovely Counterfeit 29–31
Lowry, Morton 60
Loy, Myrna 90, 92, 175
Lucas, George 39
Lugosi, Bela 22–23, 88, 154–155, 161
Lund, John 207–208
Lydecker, Waldo 32
Lyndon, Barre 82
Lynley, Carol 101
Lynley, Thomas 7

MacDonald, John D. 123–127
MacDonald, Ross 4, 44, 128–132, 149
MacFadden, Hamilton 23
Mackintosh, Elizabeth 182
MacLaine, Shirley 210
Macnee, Patrick 71
Macy, William H. 50
The Mad Magician 83
Maddow, Ben 28
Madonna 151
The Magnificent Seven 140
Magnum P.I. 165
Mahmud-Bey, Sheik 152
Make Room for Daddy 29
Malden, Karl 157
Malice Aforethought 93, 113, 166
Mallalieu, Aubrey 174
Malone, Dorothy 38
The Maltese Falcon (book) 84
The Maltese Falcon (1931) 2, 18, 158
The Maltese Falcon (1941) 35
Maltin, Leonard 33
Maltz, Albert 78
The Man in the Queue 182
The Man Who Knew too Much (1934) 12, 183
The Mandarin Mystery 163–165
Mandel, Johnny 132
Manilow, Barry 151
Mankell, Henning 176

Mantegna, Joe 7, 152
Mappin, Jefferson 151
Marchand, Guy 186
Markham, Monte 72
Marlowe, Faye 82
Marlowe, Hugh 165
Marlowe, Philip 1, 7, 34–42, 88, 130, 149, 176
Marple, Miss Jane 4, 44–48, 145–146, 167, 176
Marquand, John P. 132–135
Marriott, Sylvia 52
Marshall, Connie 172–173
Martin, Lori 12, 126
Martin, Richard 199
Martini, Steve 72
The Marx Brothers 156
The Mask of Fu Manchu 92
Mason, Perry 72–74, 87, 201
Masterpiece Theatre 1, 18, 26
Matthau, Walter 176–178
Max Headroom 61
McBain, Ed 4, 135–142
McEwan, Geraldine 47
McGavin, Darren 179
McGee, Travis 123
McGuire, Dorothy 195–196
McQuarrie, Christopher 43
McShane, Ian 7–72, 159
Meager, Jill 47
Medford, Harold 157
Medina, Patricia 157
Meeker, Ralph 179
Memo from David O. Selznick 66
Merkel, Una 88
Mifune, Toshiro 141
Miles, Sarah 39
Millais, John Everett 52
Millar, Margaret 130
Millar, Ross 130
Millhone, Kinsey 5
Mills, Hayley 126, 197
Mills, John 39
A Mind to Murder 5
Minghella, Anthony 103–106
Minnelli, Liza 132
The Miracle Worker 17
Mischief 15, 18
The Misfits 17
Mr. and Mrs. North 92, 193
Mr. Ed 156
Mitchum, Robert 38–39, 124–128
Mohr, Gerald 119
Monroe, Marilyn 15, 28
Montez, Maria 162
Montgomery, Elizabeth 197
Montgomery, Robert 40–42, 112, 174–176
Moonstruck 137
Moore, Dudley 61
Moorehead, Agnes 53

Morell, Andre 60
Morgan, Dexter 120–123
Morgan, Michele 203–205
Morgan, Ralph 189, 191
Moriarty, Prof. 56
Morris, Errol 107, 109
Morse, Inspector 5
Mosley, Walter 142–145
Moto, Mr. (I.A.) 58, 132–135
Moussey, Marcel 75
The Moving Target 4, 128–132
Moxey, John Llewellyn 50
Mrs. Winterbourne 206, 210
The Mugger 136
The Mummy (1959) 60
The Mummy's Hand 60
Murder at the Gallop 4
Murder at the Vicarage 145
Murder at the Women's City Club 167
Murder Gone to Earth 167
A Murder Is Announced 45
Murder Must Advertise 174
Murder on a Bridal Path 148
Murder on a Honeymoon 148
Murder on the Blackboard 148
Murder, She Said 44–47
Murders in the Rue Morgue 4–5, 153–161
Murders in the Zoo 59
Murphy, Ben 49
Murray, Jaime 123
My Friend Irma 87
"My Funny Valentine" 106
My Gun Is Quick 179–181
Mystery! 2, 6, 54, 107, 109, 111, 166
The Mystery of Marie Roget 155
The Mystery of the Wax Museum 59, 157

Nader, George 165
The Naked City 30, 135
Nancy Drew (movie) 118
Nancy Drew and the Hidden Staircase 116
The Nancy Drew Mysteries (TV) 118
Napier, Alan 82
Nash, Hamilton 8
Natwick, Mildred 169
Neill, Roy William 207
The New Perry Mason (TV) 72
Newman, Paul 4, 44, 128–132
Newton, Robert 175–176
Niagara 17
Nichols, Dave 151
Night Has a Thousand Eyes 207
Night Must Fall 42
The Night of the Hunter 126
A Night to Remember 18
S.S. Nightmare 167
The Nine Tailors 174

No Good from a Corpse 36
No Hero 132, 134
No Man of Her Own (1950) 206–209
Noiret, Philippe 186
Nolte, Nick 127
Norris, Edward 161
North, Michael 14
North by Northwest 25, 184
Notorious 184

Oaksey, John 69
O'Connor, Carroll 21
O'Day, Nell 161–162
Odds Against 70
O'Keefe, Dennis 199–200
O'Keefe, Michael 119
Oland, Warner 22–23
Old Ironsides 52
Oliver, Edna May 146–148
Olivier, Laurence 8, 65–68
O'Loughlin, Gerald 137
On the Waterfront 30
Once You Kiss a Stranger 96, 101
Once You Meet a Stranger... 4, 96, 102
One False Move 144
One Shot 42
Orbach, Jerry 137
The Organization 21
Ormonde, Czenzi 98
Orr, Gertrude 164
Orth, Frank 117
Ossessione 4
O'Sullivan, Maureen 92
Ouspenskaya, Maria 161–163
Owen, Reginald 54–56

Pallette, Eugene 189
Palmer, Stuart 145–148
Paltrow, Gwyneth 103–105
Pangborn, Franklin 164
Parker, Eleanor 53
Parker, Ellen 136–137
Parker, Joan 150
Parker, Robert B. 1, 6, 149–152
Parry, Harvey 134
Partners in Crime (TV) 90
A Passage to India 26
Paths of Glory 187
Patric, Jason 188
Patrick, Q. 166
Payment Deferred 93
Payment in Blood 7
Payne, Andrew 71
Payne, John 30–31
Peck, Gregory 124, 128, 196
Peckinpah, Sam 187
Pendleton, Nat 92
The Penguin Pool Murder 145–148
The People vs. Withers and Malone 148

Perchance to Dream 149
Perrin, Nat 192
Petherbridge, Edward 174
Petrie, Hay 53
Phantom Lady 207
Phantom of the Opera 155, 158
Phantom of the Rue Morgue 157
The Pharmacist 203
Philips, Lee 165
Phillips, Lou Diamond 106–107, 109
Picasso, Pablo 100
Pilbeam, Nova 12, 182–183
"The Pit and the Pendulum" 161
Pitts, Zasu 148, 260
Plein Soleil 103
The Plot Thickens 148
Plummer, Christopher 197
Poe, Edgar Allan 4–5, 153–163
Poirot, Hercule 4–5, 153, 176
Poitier, Sidney 18–20
Pollock 152
Ponazecki, Joe 49
Poodle Springs 149
Pop. 1280 184–187
Post, William, Jr. 22
The Postman Always Rings Twice 4, 29
Powell, Dick 30
Powell, Richard 179
Powell, William 73, 90, 92, 163, 175, 189–191
Preminger, Otto 32–33
Preston, Robert 79
Price, Vincent 83, 158
The Price of Justice 4
The Prisoner of Second Avenue 137
Promised Land 150
Psycho 23
The Public Enemy 84–85, 147–148
"Purloined Letter" 155
Purple Noon 103, 106
Puzo, Mario 27
Puzzle for Fiends 168
A Puzzle for Fools 167
Puzzle for Puppets 168

Queen, Ellery 148, 163–165
Quentin, Patrick 165–169
Quick, Diana 54
Quillan, Eddie 163–165
Quinn, Anthony 179
Quirk, Lt. Martin 149

The Racing Game 70
Raft, George 88, 166, 168–169
Rains, Claude 13–14
Raksin, David 34
Randolph, Donald 180
Raphaelson, Samson 115
Rathbone, Basil 58–59

Index

The Raven (1935) 161
Ray, Nicholas 111–113
Reacher, Jack 42–44
Rear Window 200–202, 207
Rebecca 2, 18, 65–68, 114, 196
Red Dragon 123
Redford, Robert 106–107, 109
Reed, Donna 18
Reed, Oliver 39
Reed, Tom 72, 155
Reeve, Christopher 201–202
Remar, James 121
Remy, Albert 75
Rendell, Ruth 169–171
The Restless Gun 31
The Return of Mr. Moto 135
Revier, Dorothy 22
Reville, Alma 115
Reynolds, Burt 138–139, 149
Rice, Craig 118, 148, 171–173
Richards, Dick 38
Richardson, Ian 54
Richardson, Tony 68
Rickman, Tom 178
Ride the Pink Horse 112
Rigby, Edward 184
The Right Stuff 107
Rinehart, Mary Roberts 48
Ripley, Arthur 203–206
Ripley, Tom 103–106, 111–112
Ripley Under Ground 104
Ritter, Thelma 200
Roach, Bert 155
Robards, Jason 158
Robinson, Edward G. 27, 84
Robson, May 74
Rodriguez, Paul 62
Rogers, Ginger 67, 115, 166, 168–169
Rogers, Mary Cecilia 160
Roman, Ruth 97, 101
The Roman Hat Mystery 163
The Rookies (TV) 137
Rosenberg, Stuart 176
Rota, Nino 106
Roussel, Elvera 49
Rowland, Roy 181
Roxburgh, Richard 61
Rudd, Martha 52
Ruman, Sig 134
Russell, Ken 69
Russell, Theresa 102
Rutherford, Margaret 4, 45–48
Ryan, Robert 18

Saboteur 25, 203
The Saint 95
Saint, Eva Marie 184
St. Clair, Muriel 176
St. Elsewhere 144
The Saint in New York 63
Sanctuary 36
Sanders, George 83

Sandoval, Miguel 210
Santiago-Hudson, Ruben 202
Satan Met a Lady 86–88
Savage Messiah 69
Savalas, Telly 4, 126
Sayers, Dorothy L. 167, 173–176
Schary, Dore 196
Scorsese, Martin 126–127
Scott, George C. 158
Scott, Randolph 119, 172–173
Seagrove, Jenny 54
The Secret Adversary 90
The Secret of the Old Clock 116
Selleck, Tom 7, 165
Selznick, David O. 2, 8, 65–68, 100, 114, 196, 201
Selznick, Myron 63
Sennett, Mack 158, 203
Serie Noire 187
The Seven Samurai 140
Shadow of the Thin Man 92
The Shadow Strikes 164
Shakespeare in Love 69
Shatner, William 61
Sheridan, Nicollette 197
Sherlock Holmes and the Secret Weapon 59
Sherwood, Robert E. 64
A Shilling for Candles 181–184
Shoot the Piano Player 74–77
Shore, Dinah 119
Short Cut to Hell 80
The Silence of the Lambs 123
The Silent Passenger 173
Silliphant, Stirling 18, 20–21
Silva, Henry 135
Silverman, Susan 149
Simon, Neil 137
Simon, Peter 49
Sinatra, Frank 18
Singin' in the Rain 29
Siodmak, Robert 94, 194–196, 207
Siren of Atlantis 206
The Sitter 18
Sitting Pretty 33
Sjöwall, Maj 176–178
Skerritt, Tom 139
Skinwalkers 107, 109
Skipworth, Alison 87
Slaughter, Tod 52–53
Slay-Ride 70–71
Slightly Scarlet 29–31
Small Vices 152
Smight, Jack 131
Smith, Alexis 51, 53
Smith, Kent 196
Smith, Sidney 165
The Snoop Sisters 169
Solt, Andrew 112
Some Must Watch 94, 194–197
Somewhere in Time 160
The Son of Frankenstein 59

Song of the Thin Man 92
The Sound and the Fury 36
Spade, Sam 2, 35, 84–90
The Spanish Cape Mystery 163
Sparr, Robert 101
Spellbound 196
Spenser 149–150
Spenser: For Hire 6–7, 149
Spielberg, Steven 126
Spillane, Mickey 179–181
The Spiral Staircase 94, 194–197
S.S. Nightmare 167
Stanwyck, Barbara 119–120, 207–208
The Star and the Story (TV) 206
Star Trek 61
Star Trek: Deep Space 9 152
Staub, Ralph 164
Steed, John 71
Steele, Bob 38
Steiger, Rod 18–19
Steinbeck, John 67
Steiner, Max 38, 53, 148
Stella Dallas (1937) 208
Stevens, Ruby 119
Stewart, James 39, 201
Stock, Barbara 149
Stockwell, Dean 172–173
Stone, Jesse 7
Stopover Tokyo 135
Stout, Rex 45
Strange Awakening 168
A Stranger Is Watching 3
Strangers on a Train 1, 4, 96–105, 111
Strangers When We Meet 136
Stratemeyer, Edward 116
Street, Della 74
A Streetcar Named Desire 157
Strick, Wesley 126
Stritch, Elaine 197
Stromberg, Hunt 119
Studi, Wes 109
Sudan 162
Supergirl 160
Superman 201
Suspicion 67, 113–115, 166
S.W.A.T. (TV) 157
Sweet, Blanche 52
Swift, Tom 116
Szwarc, Jeannot 160

The Talented Mr. Ripley 96, 103–106, 112
Taradash, Daniel 16, 18
Tarneverro 22
Tarzan 92, 168
Tavernier, Bertrand 184–187
Taxi Driver 126
Taylor, Elizabeth 203
Taylor, Rex 164
Tey, Josephine 181–184
These Three 116

Index

They Call Me MISTER Tibbs 21
They Shoot Horses, Don't They? 54
A Thief of Time 6, 108–111
Thin Air 152
Think Fast, Mr. Moto 132
The Thin Man 73, 89–92, 119, 163
The Thin Man Goes Home 92
The Thirty-Nine Steps 2, 23–27, 61, 183–184
This Gun for Hire 77–80
This Is Cinerama 42
Thomas, Danny 29
Thomas, Dylan 12
Thomas, Frankie 117
Thomas, Nina 69
Thompson, J. Lee 124–126
Thompson, Jim 74, 184–189
The Thorn Birds 188
Thunder Road 206
Tibbs, Virgil 18–19
Tierney, Gene 32–33, 169
Tiffin, Pamela 131–132
Tiger in the Smoke 4, 11
Time to Be in Earnest 6
Tingwell, Charles 47
To Each His Own 208
To Have and Have Not 36
Toler, Sidney 23
Topper Returns 158
Torrens, Pip 47
Totter, Audrey 13, 41
Tourneur, Jacques 198–199, 207
Tousey, Sheila 6, 110
Trilby 63
Truffaut, François 74–77, 207
Turner, Lana 4
Turow, Scott 72
Tuttle, Frank 80
12 Angry Men (TV) 206
Twice Shy 70

Uhnak, Dorothy 4
Under Orders 70
The Unpleasantness at the Bellona Club 174
An Unsuitable Job for a Woman 6
The Unsuspected 13–14
Urich, Robert 7, 149–150, 152

Valens, Ritchie 107
The Vampire Bat 59
Vance, Philo 85, 87, 163, 189–194
Van Dine, S.S. 85, 189–194
Van Dyke, W.S. 91
Vane, Harriet 174–176
Van Every, Dale 155
Varconi, Victor 22
Ver Dorn, Jerry 49
A Very Missing Person 148
Vickers, Martha 38
Victor, Phil 181
Vidocq, François Eugene 153, 158
Vine, Barbara 169
The V.I.P.s 47
Visconti, Luchino 4
Von Stroheim, Erich 203

Waddell, Justine 54
Wagner, Robert 78, 131
Wahlöö, Per 176–178
Walcott, George 164
Walker, Robert 97, 100–101
Walsh, Raoul 27
Ward, Fred 107, 109
Ward, Rachel 188
Warner, Jack 37
Warrender, Harold 176
Washington, Denzel 143–145
Waters, John 210
Watson, Dr. John 5, 56, 153, 162–163, 175, 192
Waycoff, Leon 156
Wayne, David 165
Webb, Clifton 32–33
Webb, Jack 135
Webb, James R. 125, 157
Webb, Richard Wilson 166, 169
Webb, Roy 196
Weissmuller, Johnny 135
Welch, Raquel 138
Welles, Orson 83
Wellman, William 85, 120
Welsh, Kenneth 61, 71
Weston, Jack 138–139
Wexler, Haskell 20
What Ever Happened to Baby Jane? 83, 87
What Mrs. McGillicuddy Saw 44
What's My Line? 156

The Wheel Spins 194
Wheeler, Hugh 166–167, 169
Whip Hand 70
White, Ethel Lina 94, 194–197
White, George A. 181
Whitmore, James 28
Wicking, Christopher 158
Widmark, Richard 15
Wilby, James 54
Wilcox, Herbert 52
The Wild One 30
William, Warren 72–74, 86, 192–193
Williams, Barbara 151
Williams, JoBeth 123
Williams, Michael 69
Wilson, Andrew 101
Wilson, Clarence H. 146–147
Wilson, Don 205
Wilson, Marie 87
Wimsey, Lord Peter 85, 163, 173–176
Winchell, Walter 118
The Winds of War 39
Winner, Michael 38
Winters, Shelley 131
Wirt, Mildred 116
Withers, Googie 176
Withers, Hildegarde 145–148
The Wolf Man 162
Wolfe, Nero 45
The Woman in White 50–54
A Woman of Substance 54
Woods, Donald 74
Woodward, Joanne 168
Woolrich, Cornell 74, 184, 198–210
Wrather, Jack 118
Wray, Ardell 198
Wright, Willard 192
Written on the Wind 38
Wyatt, Jane 95
Wyler, William 116

Yared, Gabriel 106
Yordan, Philip 205
Young, Carleton 165
Young, Gig 53–54, 197
Young, Robert 23, 95
Young and Innocent 12, 181–184

Zanuck, Darryl F. 33